HOW RELIGION WORKS

HOW RELIGION WORKS

Towards a New Cognitive Science of Religion

BY

ILKKA PYYSIÄINEN

BRILL
LEIDEN · BOSTON
2003

This book is printed on acid-free paper.

Library of Congress Cataloging-in-Publication Data

Pyysiäinen, Ilkka.
  How religion works : towards a new cognitive science of religion / by Ilkka Pyysiäinen
    p. cm.
  Includes bibliographical references (p.) and index.
  ISBN 90-04-13273-2 (pbk. : alk. paper)
    1. Psychology, Religious. I. Title.

BL53. P98 2003
200'.1'9–dc21   2003052462

ISBN   90 04 13273 2

PRINTED IN THE NETHERLANDS

CONTENTS

PREFACE

I have to admit it that the title of this book may sound provocative; this is deliberately so. I want to make a strong claim that the mechanisms underlying religious thought and behavior are something that can be naturally explained, just like any other cultural and cognitive phenomena. I am also perfectly aware that many scholars studying religion want to argue that such explanations always fail because they cannot reach the essence of religion, which is ultimately a mystery, or that such explanations, although possible as such, yet are trivial because they reach only the surface level of religion, not "anything that is of interest" (Levine 1998: 42). In this latter type of view, all that is really important in religion – whatever that may be – is something that can only be reached by emphatic participation or by appreciative interpretive methods. (See McCutcheon 1997a&b.)

I disagree, of course. If what is known to us as 'religion' really conceals some inscrutable mystery, then it would be in vain to seek knowledge about that aspect of religion by any method, at least in a scientific context. A mystery is a mystery. If, on the other hand, we consider that it is important to study how people communicate *about* the idea of something being a mystery, there is no a priori reason why this should be beyond the reach of scientific methods. After all, we are dealing here with human thought and behavior. I also subscribe in principle to the idea of conceptual integration, i.e. the view that the various disciplines within the behavioral and social sciences should make themselves mutually consistent, and consistent also with what is known in the natural sciences. This view entails that there is a universal human nature, which, however, exists primarily at the level of evolved psychological mechanisms and not at the level of cultural behaviors. (Cosmides, Tooby, and Barkow 1995; Tooby and Cosmides 1995.)

Secondly, those who say that an explanatory approach focusing on generalities of thought and action misses an important aspect of religion may well be right, but scholars should not be alarmed by this. Every explanation misses something which is in some way important for many people, and a "(l)ack of humanistic 'significance' or interest is often the price to pay for causal relevance" (Boyer 1994b: 295). No scientific explanation covers every aspect of the phenomenon explained. The range of phenomena that goes by the general name of 'religion' is so varied that it may be unreasonable to expect any theory to account for them all. That would be – to borrow an illustration from Pascal Boyer (1994b: 32) – like trying to construct a theory of all white objects. This would be absurd, because we cannot put forward any meaningful hypothesis about all white objects. It is much more in line with the principles of science to formulate as clearly as possible what particular feature is to be explained, and to ignore the rest. Such broadly delineated classes of phenomena as 'religion' cannot be features to be explained, and therefore we cannot have a theory *of* religion, although we can have theories *about* religion (as Endel Tulving says about theories concerning memory; see Gazzaniga 1997: 92). Failing to take into account some aspect of religion is not a disadvantage for a theory, but an advantage. (Boyer 1994b: 20-21, 31-32, 295.)

If, however, the claim is that explanatory theories ignore precisely *the* important aspect of religion, we can only ask: important for whom, and in what sense? It certainly is not a valid scientific criticism to say for example that cognitive explanations of how ritual structures are mentally represented are not useful or even applicable because they do not say anything about the meaning and function of rituals (Levine 1998: 30, 35, 47). These surely are not the only things we can expect a theory to explain, and the usefulness of for instance Lawson and McCauley's (1990) theory must be evaluated against the background of the questions it is meant to answer. They are not related to the meaning and function of rituals, but to the *implicit* knowledge about both ritual structures and the relevant conceptual backgrounds, which cannot be elicited by direct questions or by studying theological conceptual schemes. We therefore have to employ methods which allow us to elicit information about the tacit cognitive processes at work in actual ritual behavior. (See Boyer 1994b: 185-223.)

From the fact that people ascribe various kinds of meanings to rituals, it does not follow that the question of the mental representation of ritual episodes is unimportant and uninteresting. This question has to be evaluated in terms of what answering it contributes to our understanding of human thought and of ritual as a cultural phenomenon. Whether this is a less important task is a metascientific question, and one which is not easily answered.

Favoring an interpretive approach to religion thus does not *in itself* constitute a valid criticism of the premises of the explanatory approach. Or, the other way around: favoring an explanatory strategy in comparative religion does not *in itself* imply that the interpretive approach is futile. Although I shall be striving throughout the book to show how cognitive scientific considerations can help us better understand and also explain (see von Wright 1975; Lawson and McCauley 1990: 14-31) religious phenomena, this does not necessarily mean that interpretive approaches are totally wrongheaded or futile. All I wish to achieve is to show in what ways cognitive scientific considerations can contribute to the study of religion, so that we can better understand and explain religion as a human activity.

As to the structure of the book: in the Introduction I deal with the category of 'religion;' my purpose is to show that while religion does not form a clear-cut category, there are cross-culturally recurrent patterns of ideas and behaviors that can be termed 'religious' and that can be accounted for by referring to certain cognitive universals. Chapter 2 deals with the widespread idea of "gods," or "supernatural beings," as the defining characteristic of religion. I suggest that cognitive theories of the representation of agency and of counter-intuitiveness can help to make this idea much more precise and useful in empirical research. I also suggest possible kinds of operational, testable empirical hypotheses concerning agency as an element in religion. The idea of counter-intuitiveness, as it is here presented, is also important in all considerations that follow in later chapters.

Chapters 3 and 4 contain critical evaluations of the influential ideas of Clifford Geertz and Émile Durkheim. I have chosen to present a detailed criticism of the foundations on which their views of religion rest, because these views have been so influential in the anthropologically oriented study of religion and of "symbolism" (e.g. Douglas 1984; 1970; Levine 1998). My aim is to bring to the fore the central weaknesses of these views and to show how cognitive theory can help to solve their inherent problems. I try to show for example that the notion of a 'cultural system' cannot help us to understand how religious ideas are actually acquired, represented and transmitted. Such notions are more or less arbitrary abstractions postulated by the scholar, and are not represented as such by the individuals whom the scholar studies. Thus their explanatory power with regard to religious behavior is rather limited (Boyer 1994b). Moreover, if religion is a distinct (although open) category, we need some means of distinguishing it from other cultural or social systems, such as sports or art. I suggest that the idea of counter-intuitiveness provides a partial solution to this problem, and in Chapter 7 I present empirical data to support this view. With regard to Durkheim, I try to show that, although religion has important social functions, these functions cannot be the cause of religion. In giving social functions too central a place, the Durkheimian approach fails to deal with what is specific about religion, i.e. counter-intuitive representations. It is this counter-intuitiveness that makes the social functions of religion possible, not the social functions that explain the existence of such beliefs. The counter-intuitive cannot be reduced to the social. Moreover, although both Geertz and Durkheim want to avoid psychological arguments, I show that their respective theories remain inadequate without explicit psychological arguments. Finally some empirical hypotheses concerning the social functions of religion are outlined for future research.

Chapters 5 and 6 are more constructive in their approach. In Chapter 5, I show that counter-intuitive religious representations tend to provoke strong emotional reactions, which in turn enhance the recall of religious ideas – thus contributing to their becoming widely diffused in a population. Emotions, discussed in the light of the theories of Antonio Damasio and Joseph LeDoux, also play a crucial role in what is usually known as "religious belief." I show that the religiousness of representations cannot be understood without taking into account this specific attitude. This chapter too concludes with suggestions for empirical hypotheses concerning the role played in religion by emotions.

Chapter 6 deals with views of religion as worldview in general and as ethics in particular. I argue that we cannot meaningfully equate 'religion' and 'worldview,' or reduce religion to ethics alone (or vice versa, ethics to religion). Religious representations exist simply because they are possible, and people have religious representations because other people have had them before (Boyer 1994b: ix). Whatever explanatory functions they may have are purely *ad hoc* and unsystematic in nature. The nature of the empirical hypotheses required to test this assumption in a detailed manner is then briefly discussed.

Chapter 7, which concludes the book, presents the results of empirical studies of counter-intuitiveness as a characteristic of religion, as well as theoretical considerations about religion as a distinct cognitive phenomenon. On this basis, a new program for comparative religion is then outlined. Each chapter also includes a short summary; an easy way to read this book is first to read the summaries and only then peruse the detailed argumentation in the respective chapters, when one already has a general idea of what the main thesis in each chapter is.

I want to express my gratitude to those friends and colleagues who
have in so many ways helped me in the course of this study: Veikko
Anttonen, Justin Barrett, Pascal Boyer, Stewart Guthrie, Timo
Honkela, Kimmo Ketola, Tom Lawson, Marjaana Lindeman, Bob
McCauley, Jarkko and Markku Pyysiäinen, Jorun Ruykåsa, Pertti
Saariluoma, Tom Sjöblom, Kari Vesala, Harvey Whitehouse and
Don Wiebe. I also thank Ellen Valle for helping me to express myself
better in English. Thanks also to Sari and Miihkali for forbearance!

I also acknowledge the support of the Academy of Finland that has
made this study possible (project 42719).

Ilkka Pyysiäinen

CHAPTER ONE

INTRODUCTION: COGNITIVE APPROACH TO RELIGION

The Category of 'Religion'

There is no scientific theory of religion as a whole. Besides theories about individual religious phenomena, we only have a number of competing definitions of the word 'religion' and its reference in reality. In practice, scholars employ folk theories of religion, based on the prototype effect of the Judeo-Christian tradition, and which may or may not include transcendent assumptions about the *sui generis* nature of religion. (See Guthrie 1980; 1993: 5-17; Lawson and McCauley 1990: 33-41; Boyer 1993a: 4-18; Saler 2000; McCutcheon 1997a.) Thus 'religion' is not a scientific, explanatory category, but merely a heuristic device, used by scholars to lump together phenomena that seem to have some kind of family-resemblance and that remind him or her of similar phenomena within the Judeo-Christian-Islamic traditions.

In this way, the category of 'religion' is an academic construct, as such authors as Jonathan Smith (1982: xi), Veikko Anttonen (1996: 36-39) and Russell McCutcheon (1997a: viii) have argued. This, however, does not mean that, by having created the category of 'religion,' scholars have also *invented* religion as a phenomenon (Wiebe 1994: 838; 1999a: 295 n.6; 1999b: 267-268 n.6; Jensen 1993: 129). Religious beliefs, behaviors, etc. do have a real existence, independent of the academy, and are understood by believers as a distinct domain. But it is the scholar who by his or her comparative efforts conceptualizes this intuitive distinctiveness as 'religiousness.' To the extent that the scholar is guided by the specific tradition(s) with which he or she is most familiar, those traditions exercise a prototype effect on the way the scholar recognizes something as an instance of religion.

As a universal category, religion also is a construct with no clear boundaries. To quote Boyer (1996b: 201), religion is an "impure subject" (in a chemical rather than a moral sense). Religious representations, considered in isolation, are not a unique type of mental representation, and 'religion' does not refer to objects with distinctive causal properties. It is a more or less arbitrary process whereby certain counter-intuitive representations become selected for a use such

that they are regarded as instances of religion. Thus, as long as there
is no general theory of religion, not much is explained merely by taking some representation to be an instance of religion. (See Guthrie
1980: 181; Boyer 1996b: 206-208, 212; Krymkowski and Martin
1998; Horton 1993: 19-49.) A general theory of religion would
require that there actually exists a separate class of religious phenomena that can be explained by a set of distinct laws. This is not the case
if religious representations are actually produced by cognitive mechanisms that also produce non-religious representations. Timothy
Fitzgerald (1997: 93) goes so far as to say that 'religion' as a category
identifies nothing distinctive and clarifies nothing. It is merely a
"mystification generated by its disguised ideological function," and
ought to dissolve without remainder into ideology or culture.
(Fitzgerald 1997: 91-93; 1996.)

I agree with Fitzgerald that religion should be studied as part of
human culture, not as something *sui generis*. But this does not mean
that we can only study different values and symbols in different cultural contexts. As Boyer (1994b) has so minutely argued, there are quite
obviously recurrent patterns of religious phenomena across cultures,
and it is these patterns that form the object of the study of religion.
One does not have to commit himself or herself to any truly universal-
ist claims about the substance of religion to recognize this. There may
be no such thing as religion as a clearly demarcated category, but this
does not imply that there are no such cross-culturally recurrent patterns that are explained under the notion of the 'religious.' (See Spiro
1968: 86-88. Also Sperber 1995: x, 147.)

It may be true that scholars here are leaning on a folk theory of religion, based on the Judeo-Christian and Islamic traditions as the most
prototypical religions. This, however, should be merely a starting-
point, a way of detecting and identifying patterns to be studied. (Saler
2000: xii-xiv, 208-212.) Ultimately the scholar cannot be satisfied
merely with the observation that all religions seem to resemble
Judaism and Christianity in some respects, our task being to explain
why this is so. This means exploring the factors that underlie the
acquisition, representation and transmission of religious ideas and of
religious behaviors, especially the microprocesses of cognition. When
we realize that the similarities observed between phenomena within
the Judeo-Christian and other traditions are due to certain underlying
factors, it is no longer necessary to let the research be guided by the
prototype. The Judeo-Christian tradition is not the ultimate measure

of religion; it is merely the most familiar case of religion for most Western scholars.[1]

The use of the term 'prototype' is largely based on the work on categorization done by Eleanor Rosch and her colleagues. They have substituted the prototype approach to categorization for the old idea that it is on the basis of sufficient and necessary features that we decide to which category or class an object belongs. For them, membership in a category is not a simple yes or no question, categories not having any clear boundaries. An animal for example can be classified as more or less of a bird, a robin being very close to the prototype but an ostrich much less so. As a concrete image of an average member of the category, the robin is the most cognitively economical code for the category of birds. Thus people do not recognize different kinds of objects merely by classifying them under some particular concept, but by comparing them to prototypes serving as concrete exemplars for things of the relevant category. Such prototypicality means three things: firstly, a prototypical member of a class is recognized as belonging to that particular class more quickly than others; secondly, when asked to name members of a given class, people mention the most prototypical member first; and thirdly, children learn first to recognize the most prototypical member of a class. (Rosch 1975; Rosch 1978; Rosch and Mervis 1975. See Boyer 1994b: 61-63.)

It is easy to see that, for western scholars, the JudeoChristian tradition may well be a prototype of religion in this sense. It is important to realize, however, that this only tells us about how people recognize something as religious. It does not tell us what makes the category of 'religion' coherent. These are two different questions. The category of odd numbers, for instance, can be clearly defined with reference to sufficient and necessary conditions by saying that it consists of numbers that are not multiples of 2. Yet people tend to judge certain numbers as more prototypically odd than others, as shown by Sharon Armstrong and her colleagues. (See Osherson and Smith 1981; Armstrong, Gleitman and Gleitman 1983; Honkela 2000: 354-355.)

The so-called "theory theory," emerging from research on chil-

---

1   According to Spiro (1968: 91), a definition of religion must satisfy the criteria both of cross-cultural applicability and of intra-cultural intuitivity. Although it is true that we have to start with an intra-cultural intuition and that theories about religion should be cross-culturally applicable, a *definition* of religion is less important than Spiro thinks. It is the theories that are more important. (See Boyer 1994b: 33-34.) Nor do I concur with Spiro's functionalism (see Guthrie 1980: 183 n.6).

dren's thinking about natural kinds and of mental states (see Perner 1993: 240-241; Gopnik and Wellman 1996; Atran 1998: 599; Gopnik, Meltzoff, and Kuhl 2001: 155-162),[2] has been developed as an answer to the question of what holds categories together. Gregory Murphy and Douglas Medin (1985), and Lance Rips (1995), among others, hold that conceptual coherence is based on so-called naïve theories about the world; that people categorize things on the basis of "minitheories" or "microtheories," consisting of three elements: 1) an idea of what makes an instance a member of the category; 2) some specification of the default properties that such an instance possesses; and 3) some account of the relation between a) and b). In other words, categories are not based on a simple similarity between their members, but on an intuitive and implicit theory according to which observed regularities are systematized. We have to have some theory of what similarities are relevant for instance in categorizing cars as cars. (See also Boyer 1994b: 62-68.)

Although the scientific study of religion starts from such naïve theories, it cannot remain satisfied with them. However, as we have seen, it is doubtful whether a scientific category of religion can be constructed, because the category includes so many different kinds of phenomena that the cohesiveness of the category cannot be accounted for by any one theory. In such a case, 'religion' would merely serve as a heuristic tool whereby we identify phenomena that resemble each other in various ways but are accounted for by differing theories.

Such a resemblance may be referred to as a "family resemblance," in the sense that the various religions or religious phenomena resemble each other as the members of a family resemble each other[3]. This simile of Wittgenstein's can easily be misleading, however. Although the point of the simile is that religions resemble each other in many ways, without any one feature being common to all religions, the simile may all too easily lead us to think that religions are in fact like a family.

---

2   The expression 'theory of mind' was originally used in research on the way chimpanzees impute mental states to others (see Perner 1993: 240).
3   In 1988, I used Wittgenstein's similes of family resemblance and of a continuous rope in which no one fiber goes from one end to the other, to illustrate the fact that a given religion's history involves both continuity and change (Pyysiäinen 1988: 88, 98-99.). I've also argued that the various religions likewise do not necessarily have any one thing in common (Pyysiäinen 1992: 166). The most thorough treatment of this idea is of course Saler (2000 [1993]).

This, however, turns the argument upside down, as it implicitly suggests that we are able to name the members of the "family" of religions. But this is precisely something the argument is meant to deny! 'The religious' is a web of similarities the total extent of which we do not know, and of whose exact contents we have no exhaustive list. It is quite easy to say that the Johnsons, for example, consist of mom, dad, and a son and a daughter, all of whom resemble each other in various respects, but not that the family of religions consists of the religions 1, 2, ... and n. It is useless, then, to worry about how to distinguish the family of religions from other families, as this was never the point in the first place. (See Comstock 1984; Saler 2000; Boyer 1994b: 5; Fitzgerald 1996; Geertz 1997.) Thus it is possible to study the various recurrent similarities that go under the general name of 'religion,' without committing oneself to any a priori assumptions about the cohesiveness of the category of religion. Religion is a graded category and can be approached in the light of the prototype theory (Saler 2000: xiii, 197-226).

The Cognitive Approach

In this book, I evaluate from a cognitive perspective the various ways of conceptualizing and explaining/interpreting religion. The so-called "cognitive revolution," that can ultimately be traced to Alan Turing's vision of computing machinery and its realization in the computer, was made possible by new developments in various fields of science from the 1940's onwards. Advances in psychology, linguistics, and information theory led to the emergence of what Norbert Wiener baptized as "cybernetics," and within which the following concrete results were obtained during the period from 1943 to 1953 (Varela, Rosch, and Thompson 1996: 38; Gardner 1987: 17-19):

- The use of mathematical logic to understand the operation of the nervous system
- The invention of information-processing machines
- The development of systems theory
- The development of information theory as a statistical theory of signal and communication channels
- The appearance of the first examples of self-organizing systems

Of particular importance was the fact that the development of the digital computer provided scientists with a new model for the scientific study of the human mind, whose workings could now be modeled by computers. This soon led to the idea that human cognitive activity was merely the digital computation of material symbols in the brain, a view that has come to be known as "functionalism."

For the functionalist, the human mind is exactly like a computer program, and cognition thus consists of computations on the syntactical relations between mental representations. These processes are carried out in a postulated "language of thought" (Fodor 1975: 55-97, 199-200; 1998) which is supposedly innate in all humans. All mental contents are the product of these syntactic operations, which could just as well emerge from something else than the brain. The brain as the "hardware" is not essential; the cognitive "program" could just as well be represented by a few empty beer cans, serving as tokens for a specific syntactical relation. The functional relations are the same in calculating that $2+2=4$ and in picking up two plus two beer cans and putting them together. What is essential is not the medium but the functional relations. Furthermore, as these relations are unconscious, human cognition can be explained without the notion of consciousness and without any appeal to "how it all feels." Emotions too thus fall outside the scope of cognitive science. (See Varela, Rosch, and Thompson 1996: 6-8, 37-57; Searle 1995: 6-7, 40-46, 197-212, 249, 253; Le Doux 1998: 24-29, 34-40; Chalmers 1997.)

Another paradigm is connectionism, which maintains that human experience is an emergent property of the neural organization of the brain, and that therefore it is best explained with reference to global states in the brain. Meaning is a function of these global states, without needing to be symbolically represented, mental abilities being based on a large number of distributed neural computations. These brain-states emerge as the result of interaction with the environment, and learning is based on the formation and strengthening of connections between neural units. It is not the individual neurons that are responsible for conscious mental activity, but the connections between neurons. According to the so-called principle of Hebbian plasticity, "cells that fire together wire together." (Churchland 1995; Varela, Rosch, and Thompson 1996: 85-103; LeDoux 1998: 214-219; Elman et al. 1998: 47-106; Mcleod, Plunkett, and Rolls 1998: 1-50, 268-277, 314-330.)

Functionalism and connectionism might be somehow reconciled; in principle there is no reason why connectionist models could not be modular for example (Elman et al. 1998: 392). The well-known functionalist Dan Dennett (1993; 1997a) even describes himself as being "in agreement with the Churchlands [who are connectionists] about everything except minor details, mainly of emphasis and method" (Gazzaniga 1997: 191). Dennett says that he is agnostic about how deep into the particular details of neurophysiology one will have to go to build models of the mind. He also says that folk psychology has such conceptual and predictive power that it will never be discarded, despite what the Churchlands say (Gazzaniga 1997: 191-192. Cf. Churchland 1995: 264-269; McCauley 1996.) Varela, Rosch, and Thompson (1996: 100-103) in turn say that the symbols of the functionalists can be regarded as higher-level descriptions of properties that are ultimately embedded in an underlying neural system.

On the other hand, it may well be that we have to postulate the existence of a third level, between conscious rule interpretation and non-conscious neural processing: the level of subjective phenomenology. In this view, as put forward by Antti Revonsuo, consciousness is a special level of organization, a "virtual reality" that emerges from neurobiology, to which it is supervenient in like manner as biological phenomena to chemical phenomena. This level of reality, however, should be studied empirically (as in Damasio 1999), not by the methods of Husserlian phenomenology. (Revonsuo 1995: 31, 35-37, 51-53, 117. See Bechtel 1994. Cf. Varela 1996.) The classification of the contents of dreams (Revonsuo 1995: 105-120, 147-159) is one interesting example of such empirical research. I believe that Boyer's idea of intuitive ontologies, discussed below, could well contribute to this kind of research.

The cognitive approach has provided the sciences studying the human mind and human behavior with a new way of conceptualizing thinking and perception, which entered ethnography and anthropology in the 1950's. Cognitive anthropologists, however, have not been particularly interested in religious traditions, and have preferred to focus on various kinds of folk taxonomies, in particular on kinship terminology. (See D'Andrade 1995; Bloch 1989.) Only quite recently has the cognitive approach entered comparative religion, especially through the works of Boyer (1993a&b; 1994a&b; 1996; 1998; 2000; 2001), Stewart Guthrie (1980; 1993; 1996), E. Thomas Lawson and Robert N. McCauley (1990), Dan Sperber (1975; 1994; 1996b), and Harvey Whitehouse (1995; 2000).

Like Dennett, the cognitivists studying religion remain by and large undecided how deep on the level of the brain it is necessary to go in order to develop explanations of religious thought and behavior. Lawson and McCauley (1990) and Boyer (1994b) for instance have not directly dealt with questions of neurophysiology, but have focused their research on cognitive processes at a more abstract level. Lawson and McCauley have presented a theory of the representation of ritual structures, and Boyer has showed in detail how cognitive constraints can explain the cross-cultural recurrence of certain religious patterns. These constraints relate to the so-called intuitive ontologies, the violations of which make religious representations possible. On the whole the contribution of cognitive science to the study of religion is in that it provides a framework for empirical study of how religious concepts are acquired, represented and transmitted. I shall also argue that neurophysiology, which is sometimes excluded from cognitive science(s), provides important insights to religious belief.

CHAPTER TWO

GOD AND TRANSCENDENCE

'God' as an Emic Concept

The concept of 'god' is the cornerstone of the Judeo-Christian-Islamic prototype of religion. According to this view, religion is above all belief in god; various traditions can be judged as religious to the extent that they seem to contain representations of beings that can be interpreted as gods. As William Paden (1994: 121) puts it: "Gods are a central, unavoidable subject matter for the study of religious life." Notwithstanding Paden's warning that Western theistic premises are here misleading, the legitimacy of the use of the concept of 'god(s)' has usually been taken as self-evident. Historians of religion have published hundreds of books about the "gods" of such and such peoples and cultures, without much discussion concerning the way they use this concept. In such studies, 'god' is employed as a basic unit of analysis, as though it were a scientific, explanatory concept. (See Pyysiäinen and Ketola 1999.) We thus have such books as *The Gods of Northern Buddhism* (Getty 1962), *The Goddesses and Gods of Old Europe* (Gimbutas 1982) or *The Gods of the Celts* (Green 1997).

Although the concept of 'god' has thus been quite liberally generalized, it is important to realize that this concept has its historical roots in the traditions of the particular and historically related religions of Judaism, Christianity and Islam. It is not my purpose here to engage in any detailed historical consideration of these religions (see Armstrong 1994; Pyysiäinen 1997); rather, I offer a theoretical discussion of the concepts of 'god' and 'transcendence' and of the idea of god as a personal being, i.e. as an agent.

The idea of some kind of invisible, "transcendent," reality behind the visible one is old and widespread. Shamanistic cultures, for example, are based on the idea that the shaman is responsible for the relationships between his or her society and various kinds of supernatural beings, the shaman's soul being able to visit the "nether" and "upper" worlds (Hamayon 1990: esp. 738-739). Similarly, during the Assyrian-Babylonian period in Mesopotamia it was believed that the visible reality was closely tied to an invisible reality inhabited by gods (see Jacobsen 1976). In native American religions there is the belief in a mysterious, invisible power, inherent in all beings; this power is personified in the Witshi Ma'nitou of the Algonquin and the Wakan Tanka of the Sioux; the Orenda of the Iroquois is an impersonal force only. (Hultkrantz 1980: 11-14, 22-23, 45, 124.)

In the Western tradition, Plato is the true "father of otherworldliness," as Arthur Lovejoy once put it. Plato postulated the existence of the Completely Other, which is called "Being" in the *Phaedo*, "the Good" in the *Republic*, "Beauty" in the *Symposium* and *Phaedrus*, and "the One" in the *Philebus*. This completely self-sufficient otherworldly reality is the ontological ground of the sensible world. In Neoplatonism, Plato's ideas concerning this transcendent reality were combined with Aristotle's idea of natural hierarchies, and the notion of a "ladder of nature" (*scala naturae*) was developed. The transcendent Absolute was at the top, and all other types of beings at graduated levels below it. The ladder thus provided humans with ascending steps to the divine reality. (Lovejoy 1964: 39-50, 58-63, 89-90; Wolfson 1965: 32-42; Louth 1985: 1-3; Kenney 1991: xvii, 3-10, 38-42.)

It was the (Neo)platonic idea of god as the Absolute that Philo Judeus (c. 20 BC – 50 AD) and such Fathers of the Church as Clement of Alexandria (d. c. 215) took as the paradigm according to which they started to systematize Judaic mythology into theology. Clement for example saw the Platonic cosmogony as being parallel to Genesis, and substituted the Judeo-Christian representation of god for Plato's Demiurge. In accordance with Plato's *Timaeus*, Clement explained that god had created the world out of unformed preexisting matter, not out of nothing. It was only later that the idea of creation out of nothing became the dogma, and that by the same token an ontological gap between the realms of the human and the divine was established. There was no natural ladder from the sphere of humanity to the reality of god. (See Chadwick 1966: 46-47; Pyysiäinen 1998: 165-167; Wiebe 1991: 176-199.)

The concept of 'transcendence' was in due course established in the theological vocabulary by St. Thomas Aquinas in the 13th century. In his conception of god, he follows the traditions of Philo, the Neoplatonists and Pseudo-Dionysius in thinking that we can only know that god exists, not his essence. His description of god therefore consists mainly of negations, saying what god is not; this gradual elimination of predicates supposedly finally leads us to distinguish god from all other beings as the Ultimate Reality. Yet Thomas emphasizes that denying attributes of god does not mean that He lacks them, but that

He exceeds them. God also has such positive predicates as 'good' and 'wise,' which, however, merely describe him in so far as our intellect can know him, and thus represent him only imperfectly. (Copleston 1950: 347-362; Pyysiäinen 1999b.) According to Thomas: (*Summa Theologiæ* I Q III art. 1-8):

1) God does not have a body (*Deum non esse corpus*)
2) God is not a composition of matter (*materiam*) and form (*forma*)
3) God is one with his essence (*essentia*) and nature (*natura*)
4) God is not only his essence but also his existence
5) God is not in any genus as a species (*Deus non est in genere sicut species*) or as a cause (*sicut principium*)
6) There can be no "accidents", or properties (*accidens*) in God
7) God is totally one (*Deum omnino esse simplicem*)
8) God cannot be combined with anything

This of course is not the concept of 'god' the great majority of believers employ in actual religious reasoning. Many scholars of religion have for long been aware of the distinction between the official doctrine and popular religion of the majority (e.g. Pataï 1954; Geertz 1960: 4-7, 121-130, 227-238; Spiro 1972: 4-5), but only recently Justin Barrett and Frank Keil (Barrett and Keil 1996; Barrett 1998; 1999) have experimentally shown that such highly abstract conceptions of god as the Thomist one are not the ones people make use of when they reason about god's doings in an everyday context. Such a conception does not have the necessary inferential potential; it is difficult to infer anything concrete from a highly abstract and counterintuitive representation (see Boyer 1994b: 114, 120-121.)

Moreover, there is no reason to suppose that people simply internalize a "cultural model" or "worldview" (Boyer 1994b; 1999: 70; see below, Chapters 3 and 6), and therefore claims that such and such people believe in such and such a "god" are always selective abstractions made by the scholar. They may give a general, descriptive outline of a particular "religion," but more precise accounts and especially explanations must be based on the study of people's actual representations. The concept of 'god' is mentally represented in individual minds, and the actual content of these representations may vary enormously in different cultural contexts – even if scholars, guided by the Judeo-Christian prototype, refer to all of them as 'god-beliefs.'

Superhuman Beings, Religion and Science

Anthropologists have usually been more careful to avoid "ethnocentrism" and have used the so-called "emic"[4] terms, i.e. the terms used by the people they have studied. At the "etic" level, they have used such expressions as 'superhuman beings,' 'superhuman agents,' 'supernatural beings,' or 'extra-human entities' (Spiro 1968: 91-98; Lawson and McCauley 1990: 61, 82, 89, 112, 124, 165; Boyer 1993a: 4; 1994b: 32, 36, 37, 42, 290.) In the following, I shall deal with the ideas of 'supernaturalness' and 'superhumanity,' leaving anthropological interpretations of religion to be discussed in later chapters.

The use of the concepts of 'supernatural' or 'superhuman' reflects a view of religion that has two defining characteristics: 1) religion involves belief in something that transcends the known reality; and 2) this something is represented in the form of personal beings transcending the sphere of humanity. Gods are "points at which humans relate to 'the other,'" as Paden puts it. According to him, the word 'god' refers to "any superior being that humans religiously engage." (Paden 1994: 121-122. Also Guthrie 1980: 182.) This view, however, involves serious difficulties. While the notions of 'transcendence,' 'supernatural,' and 'superhuman' seem so obviously to belong to religion, they are, as we shall soon see, also highly problematic.

There are basically two alternative ways of understanding 'transcendence' and 'superhumanity:' either we accept that there is an objective and universal way of defining what is natural and what belongs to humanity, and judge everything else as supernatural and superhuman; or we argue that 'supernatural' and 'superhuman' must always be understood in relation to what the particular people in question regard as natural and human.

In the first case, we would be obliged to opt for a science-inspired naturalism (e.g. Nielsen 1997) or even for a scientific realism that takes science as the measure of what is real, and by the same token defines everything transcending scientific explanation as non-existent and illusory (see Sellars 1963; Tuomela 1985). Thus the supernatural would simply be something non-existent, and analogously the super-

---

4   The terms 'emic' and 'etic' refer to the respective perspectives of the people studied and of the scholar, i.e. the particular and the general levels. The terms were first used by Kenneth Pike (1967), who adopted them as abbreviations from the concepts of 'phonemic' and 'phonetic.'

human would be something that is thought to be somehow humanlike but which nonetheless does not exist.

It is obvious, however, that mere falsehood cannot be enough for a belief to be categorized as religious. No one claims that every false belief concerning reality is a religious belief. (See Sperber 1995: 3-4.) Again, 'superhumanity' is a problematic concept in this respect, since it is unclear what exactly is meant by it. Are gods really *any* superior beings? Superior in what sense? While it is true that many animals and also machines, especially computers, are superhuman in the sense that they can perform all kinds of feats we humans cannot, we do not usually consider them gods. (See Pyysiäinen and Ketola 1999.) Finally, if we argue with Paden (1994: 122) that only superior beings that we engage *religiously* count as gods, we are defining gods in terms of religion and therefore cannot define religion in terms gods.

Thus there has to be some specific sense in which we speak of superhuman beings as the defining characteristic of religion, although this has not been clearly spelled out. Falsehood as determined by scientific analysis can – theoretically speaking – be at most a necessary, but not a sufficient, criterion of religion. There need to be some additional criteria, according to which we use the notions of 'supernatural' and 'superhuman' to characterize religion.

It should also be pointed out that defining religion in contrast to the scientific conception of reality makes the religiousness of a belief or a tradition dependent on scientific progress. We therefore have to ask: how, in that case, is it possible for people to recognize the objects of religious belief as religious objects, if they have no knowledge of science? Although not all people(s) have an explicit category of religion, they are nevertheless able to recognize certain things and phenomena as belonging to a distinct category, set apart from ordinary things and requiring specific attention (see also Boyer 1994b: 94; Atran 1996: 236). Were that not the case, there could not be any specific type of behavior, such as is found in religious rituals, and thus nothing to be categorized as religious by the scholar. But if such recognition depends on the fact the beliefs in question are not true from the scientific point of view, then only people with an explicit scientific picture of the world could have religion (in the form of violations against that picture). And this clearly is not the case.

Thus the alternative – defining 'supernatural' and 'superhuman' in relation to what is natural and human for the people in question – seems a better choice. However, two problems emerge in this case as

well. First, if there are too many differing ways of understanding 'natural' and 'human,' there cannot be a cross-cultural category of religion, much less a universal one, based on the concept of the 'supernat-
ural/superhuman.' Second, what people say they regard as natural in
some sense can be different from what they take to be natural in
another sense, in their daily life (see Barrett and Keil 1996; Barrett
1998). People may say for instance that it is natural for them that a
god exists, although in reality they consider it most unnatural that
there should be a personal being who does not have a body (see Boyer
1994b: 116-124; Atran 1996: 234-243). As Boyer (1996a: 629) says,
intuitively unnatural things can be considered to be definitely real.
They are counter-intuitive with respect to people's intuitions about
their subject matter, although peoples' reflective reasons for accepting
them may still seem intuitively compelling (Sperber 1994: 62). As I
shall argue in due course, it is this counter-intuitiveness of "superhuman beings" that distinguishes them from human beings. What is
common between humans and superhumans is that both are *agents*
(see Lawson 1999; Lawson 2001). In the next section, I explain what I
mean by 'agency,' and then move on to a discussion of the concept of
'counter-intuitiveness' as an alternative to 'superhuman.'

Intentional Agents

The specific mechanical property of agents is that they are self-propelled, as though they had some kind of internal source of energy or
force. Second, they have such actional properties as acting teleologi-
cally in pursuit of goals, and also of reacting and interacting. Third,
they possess cognitive capacities: they perceive, think, know, remember and are conscious. They are also able to recognize other agents for
what they are. It is especially important that this ability to attribute
mental states to others is an independent capacity, not a matter of
general intelligence. (Leslie 1994; 1996.)
   Alan Leslie's theory of agency is based on the so-called modular
view of human cognition (to be discussed in more detail in the last
chapter). A cognitive module is a "specialized, encapsulated mental
organ that has evolved to handle specific information types of particular relevance to the species." It independently processes inputs per-
taining to specific cognitive domains, such as living kinds, physical
objects, and people. These domains consist of sets of entities that have

been evolutionarily selected to trigger the proper module. (Elman et al. 1998: 35-42; Atran 1990; 1996; Sperber 1994: 39-46.) Leslie's "theory of mind module," for example, has been located to the frontal lobes of the brain (McNamara 2001. See p. 129 below).

However, agency can also be explained within the "theory theory." Annette Karmiloff-Smith (1992: 117-138) for example suggests that the ability to correctly attribute mental states to other humans, i.e. to treat them as agents, is not based on a genetically specified, encapsulated cognitive module, although it may well involve *some* genetically specified predispositions, such as attentional bias toward human faces and human speech. It has for example been shown that newborn infants preferentially attend to face-like arrangement of elements and thus have to possess some innately specified structural information about human faces. Likewise, neonates attend preferentially to human speech over other auditory input. The child's theory of agency is then formed out of these basic attentional biases. (See Gopnik and Wellman 1996: 280-288; Perner 1993; Elman et al. 1998.)

The word 'theory' is here used in the sense of an implicit naïve theory, as in folk biology or naïve physics, and will be discussed in more detail in the last chapter. According to such scholars as for example Susan Carey, rather than innate modules we are dealing with domain-general theory-building capabilities and the related intuitive theories (Carey 1996a: 268-276; Carey 1996b). Alison Gopnik and Henry Wellman (1996) refer to the theory view of cognition simply as "theory theory," in accordance with the theories of Murphy and Medin (1985) and Rips (1995). Gopnik and Wellman (1996: 264-267) admit that even in infancy children have some vague notions of internal psychological states in others, but consider that an important change from one mentalistic psychological theory to another occurs somewhere between 2½ and four years of age. This change is actually a gradual transition, a theory change of sorts, toward a "representational model of mind" at the age of five at the latest.

Josef Perner (1993) is one of the first to have adopted the view that we employ a specific folk theory of mind in our common sense psychology. According to Perner, already very young infants are sensitive to behavioral expressions of mental states, although they are not born with the concept of 'mental state.' During the second year, infants come to understand other people's inner states as mental, and can explain behavior using such mentalistic notions as 'knowledge.' They do not, however, yet have a theory of mind, and do not for instance understand such things as pretence and false representation. It is only at the age of four or five that children develop metarepresentational abilities that allow them to understand that the human mind is representational, i.e. that representation does not simply copy reality but represents it as being of certain kind. Only now can the child be said to have a theory of mind. (See Ch. Seven.)

It is of interest for us that there is now some evidence that, although the Christian god is understood as an agent by the child, god seems to be free of some of the restrictions that normally characterize the representational mind. For example, in the so-called false belief test, children are shown a cracker box containing rocks and are asked what their mother would think is in the box before looking into it. It is only around the age of five that children become capable of understanding that mother would be fooled by the appearance of the box and would mistakenly say "crackers." When asked what god would think is in the box, on the other hand, children at all ages are equally likely to answer "rocks." Thus the belief that god is omniscient continues in the child after the adult is no longer believed to possess this property. (Barrett 2001.) In the last chapter, I shall try to explain this as caused by the retention of what Perner (1993: 73-76, 251-253) calls a "situation theory," which at the age of four is extended by the representational theory.

The theory of agency thus can help us explain what actually is at stake in "anthropomorphism" (cf. Guthrie 1993; 1996. See Lawson 2001). It is not the human-like form that is important, but the fact that gods resemble ourselves in being agents (Boyer 1996c; Barrett 1998; 2001). What has been referred to as "anthropomorphism" results from the fact that our cognitive apparatus, emotions included, leads us to see meaning and goal-directedness in all kinds of events, in life itself, or even in the existence of the world. This is what Boyer, following Boyd and Richerson, has called a "runaway" process, a genetically determined process which is extended beyond its initial domain. Agents being the only sources of meaning, people tend to postulate the existence of superhuman agents to ascribe meaning to life. Thus there are such proofs of god's existence where the observed order in the universe is taken to prove that "there must be an intelligent designer behind all this".[5] (See Pyysiäinen 1999b. Cf. Guthrie 1993;

---

5   Richard Swinburne (1996: 49), for example, says: "If we can explain the many bits of the universe by one simple being which keeps them in existence, we should do so – even if inevitably we cannot explain the existence of that simple being."

1996; Barrett 1998.) Here the genetically determined intuitive psychology is extended to counter-intuitive formations, although this does not necessarily contribute to the survival of the species. (Boyer 1994b: 289-294.)

Daniel Dennett (1987: 15-34, 69-80; 1997: 35-54) describes interpretations of the behavior of entities by treating them as though they were rational agents as the adopting of an "intentional stance," i.e. treating entities as intentional agents in order to predict their actions. The intentional stance adds a new dimension to the physical stance and the design stance. We use the design stance to make predictions about such things as alarm clocks and vending machines. The intentional stance, however, becomes almost obligatory when we need to explain the behavior of more complex artifacts, such as, for instance, chess-playing computers. These are not rational agents, but the intentional stance works perfectly well as an as-if explanation of their behavior.

Can we, then, apply this principle to so-called animism as well? According to Dennett (1997: 43-45), our ancestors actually did attribute intentions and desires to natural phenomena, whereas we have now withdrawn the intentional stance from inanimate nature and only occasionally use it as an "aid to comprehension." However, for us the attribution of desires to natural phenomena is only a manner of speaking. It is only in our "ancestors" that it was a sign of ignorance of the real nature of things.

When exactly those ancestors lived and on what grounds it is said that they were ignorant is not made explicit by Dennett. Yet it could just as well be argued that adopting the intentional stance toward nature was merely a manner of speaking for our ancestors as well. In the absence of writing and the related task-specific cognitive skills (see Rubin 1997: 15, 60-62, 196, 308-318; Pyysiäinen 1999a), as well as of advanced technology, the human and animal worlds, quite concretely understood, were the only sources from which they could derive concepts to explain and predict the behavior of nature. We cannot *a priori* assume their way of speaking to show that they actually believed that rivers and clouds had intentions just like human beings. In fact, such a view would counter our general knowledge of how intuitive physics and biology seem to work in all cultures. As we will later see, such counter-intuitive objects as benevolent rocks or weeping statues for example are always deviant members of the categories to which they belong. Not every rock or every statue is believed to have humanlike intentional properties. (See Boyer 1994a; 1994b: 118; 1996a; Atran 1996: 234-243; Sperber 1996a; Stanovich and West 2000: 664; Pyysiäinen 2001b.)

In the context of religion, the intentional stance thus means that *in some instances* people treat natural phenomena and events as manifesting the intentions of one or more invisible agent(s). It is not simply that people consider every river, rock and plant to behave intentionally, but that certain specific natural phenomena, objects and events can be taken to reveal something about the will and intentions of counter-intuitive agents behind the appearances of things. We can therefore try to specify the category of 'gods' using the notion of agency as a key. Gods are agents like humans, but they have such counter-intuitive properties as not growing old, not needing food, etc. None of these properties as such need to be a universal characteristics of gods; it is only the idea that there is *something* counter-intuitive in gods that serves as a defining characteristic. (See Boyer 1994b: 117-124.) Agency in turn relates counter-intuitive beings to humans, insofar that their behavior can in principle be explained by folk psychology.

The concept of an agent being a micro-theory, it follows that also the concept of a superhuman agent can be understood as being based on a folk theory (Pyysiäinen 1997). In theology, this theory is then theoretically elaborated, much in the same manner as naïve physics is elaborated in science, notwithstanding such differences that constructive theology is not empirical and includes some non-scientific assumptions. The principles of reasoning, however, are the same. (See Pyysiäinen 1999a; Wiebe 1991; Kuhn 1996.)

Now that we have reconceptualized super*humanity* in terms of the idea of agency, it is time to look at the *super*human aspect of gods.

Counter-Intuitiveness of Gods

I suggest substituting the concept of 'counter-intuitiveness' for that of 'superhumanity' as a characterization of 'gods.' In this way we avoid the problems inherent in attempts to define religion in contrast to science. The starting-point is not in what is objectively real, but in what people consider intuitively natural. As there very probably exist universal, intuitive principles according to which people reason in such domains as living kinds, physical objects and people, counter-intuitiveness too must be a universal phenomenon (Boyer 1994b; Atran

1996: 234-243, 249). This in turn makes religion possible as a universal category, without imposing on other cultures and historical periods
standards that cannot by any means have been known to the people in
question. Counter-intuitive representations are unnatural even for the
believers themselves (Boyer 1994b: 3; Atran 1996: 234.)

This idea of counter-intuitiveness partly derives from Scott Atran's
(1996) and Dan Sperber's (1994: 62; 1996b: 69-74, 96-97, 119-150)
idea that beliefs can be counter-intuitive with respect to our intuitions
about their subject matter even though our reflective reasons for
accepting them seem intuitively compelling. It is for example counter-
intuitive that solid objects are for the most part mere empty space, and
yet this claim is intuitively compelling when presented by a scientist,
because we have developed strong reflective beliefs about scientific
knowledge.

Boyer (1993b: 128-130; 1994a&b; 1996a,c; 1998; 2000) has made
the concept of 'counter-intuitiveness' into a powerful tool in the study
of religion. To understand this concept, we have to start with what is
meant by intuitive knowledge. We all share certain intuitive knowledge in the sense of tacit knowledge which is used spontaneously in
practical reasoning, without that we necessarily are aware of it. The
existence of this knowledge is based on the fact that the material environment surrounding us is *to some* extent everywhere the same. This,
in turn, has shaped our brains and cognitive machinery to be *to some*
extent similar. The material environment does not have primacy over
our brains, and neither is the reverse the case. Our brains and the
"external" reality have coevolved and thus shaped one another in a
process of interaction (Varela, Rosch, and Thompson 1996; Elman *et
al.* 1998).

In being innate (see p. 207-208), intuitive knowledge forms the bias
which makes it possible for us to acquire new knowledge from our
environment. It also enables us to infer such knowledge which is not
explicit. In for example hearing that some rare species of animals one
has never heard of is carnivorous, one immediately also infers that
these animals are mortal and cannot be made of metal, although one
has not been explicitly given any such information. It is beyond reasonable doubt that all humans have such intuitive knowledge concerning physical objects, natural kinds (plants and animals), and persons. We apply physical explanations to physical objects, living kinds,
and persons alike (you cannot e.g. go through them); we know that
(folk)biological explanations apply to living kinds and persons (e.g.

they have nutritional needs); and we know that intentional explanations apply to animals and persons (they act on the basis of beliefs and desires). (Boyer 1994b; 1998; 2001; Barrett 2000.)

In counter-intuitive representation, the boundaries of these domains are violated. For example, intentions may be unnaturally transferred to solid objects, or physical and biological properties denied to a person. These two ways of producing counter-intuitive ideas are called by Boyer 'transference' and 'violation.' It is important to bear in mind that counter-intuitiveness consists precisely of violations against or transferences across the boundaries between ontological categories. 'Counter-intuitive' is not by definition the same as 'false,' 'ridiculous,' or 'odd.' Counter-intuitiveness also contradicts *intuitive* expectations; it is therefore possible that a believer finds some familiar counter-intuitive representations as being quite natural, because this judgement is made at the level of *explicit* knowledge. In such case, it is, for example, considered quite natural that god exists, although one does not intuitively expect a person to lack a physical body. In other words, a believer in god always intuitively assumes that all other persons, except for god, have bodies. (Boyer 1994b: 91-124; 1996c; 1998: 881; 2000; Sperber 1994: 62; Atran 1996: 234.)

Empirical studies (Barrett and Nyhof 2001; Boyer and Ramble in press) show that optimally counter-intuitive ideas are better recalled than ordinary or overly counter-intuitive ones, and thus are also more effectively distributed. Boyer (1994a: 408; 1994b: 122, 124) says that counter-intuitive representations constitute the category of "religious ideas," and that a concept that confirms only intuitive ontologies is *ipso facto* nonreligious, although counter-intuitiveness as such is not a sufficient criterion for religion.[6] (See also Atran 1996: 234.) There is also no domain specialization in religious thinking, i.e. religion does not form a specific cognitive domain (Boyer 1999: 68; Boyer and Walker 2000: 151-153). I shall return to this in the last chapter. For the moment, I only want to argue that 'counter-intuitiveness' can in principle be clearly defined and used to replace 'superhumanity' as a concept.

---

6   It is interesting that the way intuitive ontologies are violated in dreams seems to be constrained by the rules of semantic association, so that not all forms of bizarreness are equally likely to appear. In Revonsuo's study, incongruous elements in dreams were most commonly present in representations of cognitive capacities, language, and events, while the self and emotions were represented in a much more natural fashion. (Revonsuo 1995: 147-159.)

I reconceptualize superhuman agents as counter-intuitive agents in the sense that in their case we are dealing with agents that typically lack some basic biological and physical properties, such as growth, aging or the need for food, in various combinations, or with physical objects that have psychological properties making them agents. Some representations of counter-intuitive beings are construed by denying them psychological properties, as in the case for instance of zombies. In other words, a representation is counter-intuitive if it combines features that belong to two different cognitive domains, or lacks features that it is intuitively expected to have. However, as the boundaries of these domains have not as yet been unequivocally established, the boundaries of counter-intuitiveness too must remain somewhat open. But the principle according to which counter-intuitiveness is produced is clear. (See Boyer 1994b: 117.)

However, as Boyer remarks, counter-intuitive representations form only one aspect of religious cognition, the other being that counter-intuitive representations are embedded in intuitive ones. If for example the concept of 'god' were merely counter-intuitive, we could draw no inferences about it. It would be simply incomprehensible. In fact, the main substance of religious representations is provided by intuitive assumptions, while the nature of these representations that appeals to the human imagination and demands attention derives from their counter-intuitiveness. In order to become comprehensible, memorable, and widely diffused, religious representations thus must strike a balance between the intuitive and the counter-intuitive. Although the gods, for example, violate intuitive biology and physics, they nevertheless act in accordance with an intuitive belief-desire psychology. (Boyer 1994b: 114, 118-124; 1999; 2000; Boyer and Walker 2000: 152; Atran 1996: 234, 239-241.) It is the intuitive aspects of religious representations that make them understandable and learnable, but it is the counter-intuitive aspect that makes them religious.

In sum, an etic category of 'gods' can only be constructed on the basis of the emic term 'god' by dropping the culture-specific contents of 'god' and keeping only the cross-cultural core which is formed by the combination of the ideas of agency and counter-intuitiveness. In this way we can develop a category of counter-intuitive agents, as a cognitive universal that characterizes religion (see also Spiro 1968: 91-98; Lawson and McCauley 1990: 61, 82, 89, 112, 124, 165). And, as gods have traditionally been identified as belonging to the transcendent realm, it is now by the same token possible to replace the idea of transcendence, or of the supernatural, by the idea of a counter-intuitive level of reality. (Cf. Guthrie 1980: 182.)

This is an important step. In principle, it allows for a much more precise account of how the various ideas of religious "other worlds" are produced, although in practice much more empirical research is needed. It may not always be clear whether some specific representation counts as counter-intuitive or not. The jointly sufficient and singly necessary characteristics of 'counter-intuitiveness' have not been described, the use of the concept being based more on a general theory and a few examples. Moreover, the precise nature of such cognitive domains as folk biology and folk psychology is not agreed upon (see Chapter Seven).

Also, not all counter-intuitiveness can be regarded as religious in nature. Many scientific representations, for example, are counterintuitive, and so are schizophrenic and fictional ones. In the final chapter, I return to the issue of scientific, religious, fictional, and disturbed counter-intuitiveness in the light of my empirical findings. Here I merely point out that some counter-intuitive representations always seem to be selected to form traditions which are taken very seriously by groups of people, and which we therefore usually consider "religious." The role that emotions play in this will be discussed in Chapter Five. What is important is that the considerations here presented allow us to construct hypotheses to be tested in future work. Further studies could test for example whether the presence of impersonal counter-intuitive forces and mechanical counter-intuitive agents activate religious interpretations as readily as the presence of personal counter-intuitive agents, and in what way representations of counterintuitive agents structure religious beliefs. Are religious beliefs for example explained by believers in such a manner that an otherwise endless regression of arguments is prevented by introducing at some point a counter-intuitive agent that is itself not in need of any explanation (cf. Lawson and McCauley 1990)?

Summary

'Religion' as a general comparative category cannot be understood as being based on the concept of 'god(s).' Although this concept has been much used in comparative religion, it remains an unspecified conceptual postulate with an implicit Judeo-Christian bias, the implications of which have not been spelled out. It also cannot be replaced by such alternatives as 'superhuman beings,' 'extra-human entities,' etc., because it is not clear what 'super,' 'extra' and the like are here supposed to refer to. Nor is it clear in what sense these beings are "humanlike" or "anthropomorphic."

I suggest, on the basis of the work of Boyer, that we replace these vague concepts with the concept of 'counter-intuitive agents.' 'Counter-intuitive' means 'violating panhuman intuitive expectations' in a well defined fashion. The existence of such universal tacit expectations has been established in developmental and cognitive psychology as well as in studies on culture and cognition. Counter-intuitiveness has also been shown to enhance the recall of items in experimental conditions. This enhanced recall may explain – *ceteris paribus* – why counter-intuitive representations seem so easily to become widespread in and across cultures.

Agency, for its part, is conceptualized in the light of Leslie's theory of a "theory of mind module." An agent is a self-propelled entity that not only moves but also acts in pursuit of goals and has cognitive capacities. Up to now religions seem to have been dominated by representations of personal counter-intuitive agents, but impersonal counter-intuitive forces (e.g. *karma*) and mechanical counter-intuitive agents (UFO's) are also becoming increasingly popular.

By substituting 'counter-intuitive agents' for 'superhuman beings' etc. we are also able to replace the idea of "transcendence" with that of a counter-intuitive level or aspect of reality. As human knowledge of reality is always insufficient and uncertain, we often have the feeling that there is more to reality than meets the eye. This mysterious something is counter-intuitive by definition, but this does not imply that it cannot be the object of serious belief. Religious beliefs are often as unshakeable as our most natural intuitions (e.g. that external reality exists). How this can be so, will be discussed in Chapter Five.

CHAPTER THREE

RELIGION AND CULTURE

In this chapter I shall examine Clifford Geertz's influential attempt to account for religion without the notions of 'transcendence' and 'superhuman,' seeing religion only as a cultural system of "symbols." I shall critically analyze this view, trying to show, among other things, how Geertz cannot really do without the notions of the 'superhuman' and 'transcendent,' after all.

Geertz and the Concept of 'Culture'

According to Michael Levine (1998: 37), "(g)iven the dominant view in religious studies which sees religion as a cultural system (Geertz 1973), it is a mistake to see gods as essential – even when present in a system." This is an extremely odd argument; it suggests that the dominant view is always the right one. Surely, in the Middle Ages some people said that given the dominant view that the earth is flat, it is a mistake to see the earth as round. McCauley and Lawson (1998: 70) quite rightly point out that, although religion can be seen as a cultural system, the crucial question remains what is distinctive about religion as a particular type of cultural system. This is recognized even by Geertz (1973: 113) himself, although he ultimately fails to distinguish religion from other cultural systems (Guthrie 1980: 183). If more or less everything can be seen as 'religion,' the concept loses its meaning and its usefulness. It no longer identifies anything. As Lawson (1999: 141) ironically writes, the advantage of such a view of 'religion' is that the scholar cannot miss his or her target: like a perfect hunter, one hits everything that one is aiming at because one never knows how the targets differ from each other.

In what follows, I analyze the view of religion as a "symbolic cultural system," put forward by Geertz, trying to show on what premises it rests and what emendations are needed if we are to sustain anything like such a view. The point is to show how the cognitive approach can contribute to Geertzian ideas and thus help us to explain religion as a distinct cultural phenomenon.

Although it may now seem self-evident to us to what kind of concept the word 'culture' refers to, it actually is not so self-evident. The word 'culture' acquired a new meaning in the 17th century, before which no such concept as the modern 'culture' existed. It was Francis Bacon who first used the word 'culture' in the sense of 'spiritual cultivation,' writing in 1605: "... so the culture and manurance of minds in youth hath such a forcible (though unseen) operation ...." (Bacon 1963: 2nd book, XIX.2., p. 184). The word 'culture' derives from the Latin '*colo/colere*' (<PIE *$k^w el$-, 'to turn,' 'to be busy with' [Buck 1949: 494, 724]), which has had many meanings, such as the following:

- 'To live in, inhabit', 'to live, dwell' (of gods worshipped in a particular place);
- 'To till, cultivate' (land);
- 'To look after, keep going, tend' (things);
- 'To decorate, adorn, embellish;'
- 'To worship;'
- 'To pay constant attention to' (persons) and 'to cultivate friendship';
- 'To practice religion;'
- 'To maintain, foster' (laws etc.);
- 'To promote the growth or advancement of, develop.' (Oxford Latin Dictionary 1968: 354-355.)

Thus the concrete basis of the abstract concept of 'culture' seems to lie in agriculture, the cultivation of land (see also Gudeman 1986: esp. 129-139; Mithen 1996: 248-259; Pyysiäinen 1996a: 42-43). Anthropology as a science of culture, distinct from ethnology, emerged during the period from 1850 through 1880, following advances in philology and paleontology. Culture was at first defined as something "superorganic" (Herbert Spencer) and was explained within an evolutionary theoretical framework. Within the British tradition, E.B. Tylor and James Frazer were the great comparativists who put forward grand theories of cultural evolution, soon to be challenged by such American cultural anthropologists as Franz Boas, Alfred Kroeber and Robert Lowie, who emphasized that general theories must be based on particular ethnography. (Voget 1975: 41, 111, 136-140, 320-329; Silverman 1-53; Pals 1996: 236-237.)

Tylor (1994) and Frazer based their theories on assumptions concerning the human mind, took religious beliefs literally, and explained them as springing from the human need to explain various natural phenomena (see Lawson and McCauley 1990: 32-41; Boyer 1993a: 15; Horton 1993: 53-62). Later, the emerging new traditions of social and cultural anthropology shifted their emphasis to the collective level of "cultural systems" and "the social," which also placed religion in a new frame of reference. It is typical of these views that culture is understood as an autonomous level of reality, which should also be studied as such and not "reduced" to anything else. Yet this is merely presupposed, not carefully argued for. (Tooby and Cosmides 1995; Boyer 1993a: 8-13; 1994b; McCauley and Lawson 1996.) Roger Keesing (1974) has distinguished four forms of this view of culture as a specific level of reality: cultures as adaptive systems, ideational theories of culture, cultures and sociocultural systems, and cultures as ideational systems. It is also to be noted that anthropology is a strongly interpretive science, lacking theoretical concepts of its own (Sperber 1996b: 9-18), and that anthropologists do not share a common paradigm, various national research traditions differing from each other considerably (Barrett 1988: 3, 69-72, 97-99, 214-217. Also Spiro 1968: 85).

This is also the background of Geertz and his approach to religion, which belongs to what Keesing (1974: 79-81) calls "ideational" theories of culture, represented, besides Geertz, by such writers as Louis Dumont and David Schneider. Geertz was raised within the American tradition of Boas and others, and especially as a student of Talcott Parsons. Parsons, himself influenced by Max Weber's *Verstehen* ('understanding') approach to social behavior, had developed further the (structural)-functionalism of the British anthropologists Bronislaw Malinowski and E.E. Evans-Pritchard. He influenced Geertz especially in two respects: the emphasis on the meaning of an action to people who engage in it, and the idea of three levels of organization in human groups: the individual personality, the social system, and the cultural system as a network of values, "symbols," and beliefs. (Pals 1996: 238-240.)

In his influential paper "Religion As a Cultural System," originally published in Banton (1968), Geertz (1973: 90) defines a religion to be:

> (1) A system of symbols which acts to (2) establish powerful, pervasive, and long-lasting moods and motivations in men [*sic*] by (3) formulating conceptions of a general order of existence and (4) clothing these conceptions with such an aura of factuality that (5) the moods and motivations seem uniquely realistic.

I shall try to show that each of the five parts of this "definition" includes problems which derive from the vagueness of Geertz's concepts of 'culture' and 'symbol,' and which cognitive considerations can help to solve. Briefly:

(1) Symbols are neither a class of phenomena, nor form a system on the cultural level;

(2) "Moods and motivations" cannot be understood as mere "dispositions;"

(3) Ideas of a general order of existence are tied to an idea of a counter-intuitive reality;

(4) The "aura" of factuality cannot be explained without a psychological argument;

(5) "Moods and motivations" cannot be made to seem realistic without the activation of some psychological mechanism.

I start by analyzing Geertz's "semiotic" understanding of 'culture,' leaving the idea of symbolism to be dealt with in the next section. For Geertz (1973: 89), culture is "an historically transmitted pattern of meanings embodied in symbols, a system of inherited conceptions expressed in symbolic forms by means of which men communicate, perpetuate, and develop their knowledge about and attitudes toward life." Culture is, shortly, a web of significance, and its analysis is "not an experimental science in search of law but an interpretive one in search of meaning." Cultural analysis, "guessing at meanings," or sorting out the structures of signification, is much like the work of a literary critic, rather than like deciphering codes. The anthropologist's data thus consist of "our own constructions of other people's constructions of what their compatriots are up to." (Geertz 1973: 5, 9, 20.)

In other words, the anthropologist "reads" a culture like a text, and thus grasps its meaning by his or her intuition. A culture is a public, "acted document." Although it is "ideational," it, nevertheless, does not exist "in someone's head." It is "unphysical" and yet not in any way "occult." Geertz begs the ontological question that thus arises by saying that it is "wholly misconceived." The thing to ask about symbolic behaviors is not their ontological status; it is "the same as that of rocks on the one hand and dreams on the other – they are things of this world." (Geertz 1973: 10, 12.)

Thus, although we ought not to ask ontological questions about culture, Geertz is eager to provide answers: at least cultures do not exist in someone's head, and are neither superorganic nor "brute patterns of behavior." Despite this, Geertz insists that the ontological status of culture is the same as that of dreams. For him, the crucial ontological distinction is between things of "this world" and other kinds of things (whatever they might be). Saying that culture is of this world suffices for Geertz as an ontological analysis, although he seems to think that there is nevertheless some ontological difference between the rocks and the dreams of this world. In the final analysis, however, Geertz only says what culture absolutely is not, not what it really is. (Geertz 1973: 10-11. See Sperber 1996b: 79-80.)

Geertz explicitly refuses to discuss in any detail the criticism directed against the "privacy theories of meaning" he invokes to back his argument. He merely declares that, although cultures are structures of meaning, they are no more psychological phenomena than a Beethoven quartet, Tantrism, genetics, the progressive form of the verb, or the Common Law. (Geertz 1973: 11-13.) Let us stop here to consider this claim in some detail, starting with the progressive form of the verb.

We should note, first of all, that the progressive form of the verb is a much more precise notion than a cultural phenomenon such as for instance Tantrism. As Boyer (1993a: 11) remarks, cultural phenomena do not even approach the standards of stability and certainty which are familiar to linguists. It is therefore misleading to assume, without evidence, that cultural "structures of significance" really exist as something specific and definable, yet independent of psychology. And even linguistic structures, although much more specific, do not exist irrespective of human cognitive constraints, i.e. irrespective of psychology. (See also Spiro 1968: 86.)

Elman et al. (1998: 129-147) provide a detailed discussion of the acquisition of the English past tense by the developing child, as modeled by a connectionist network. Here the particular problem is how the child is able to learn both regular and irregular forms. Some authors have supposed that they are dealt with by two separate cognitive mechanisms; thus the child first learns only separate forms, such as 'smiled,' 'hit' or 'went,' and only later discovers that some forms are based on a rule. Rule-governed forms are then handled by one representational mechanism, and irregular forms by an other. Elman et al., however, show how a single neural net mechanism can learn to produce the correct past tense forms of the overwhelming majority of English verb stems to which it has been exposed. No rules are needed. The regular and irregular verbs are represented in a distributed fashion throughout the network. Moreover, Elman et al. have also shown how the verb forms in English have developed, i.e. how the language got to be the way it is.

This example shows that verb forms cannot be understood as abstract entities independent of human cognitive mechanisms. On the

contrary, it is the cognitive constraints that affect the formation of linguistic forms which exist as mentally represented. We therefore have
good reason to presuppose that other cultural phenomena too are by
no means independent of our cognitive make-up. As Lawson and
McCauley (1990: 188) say, symbolic-cultural systems are empirically
tractable only through our mental representations of them. The metaphysical question of whether or not culture is a separate ontological
level is of course a difficult one (see Pihlström 1996: 250-287), but here
we are only interested in whether the assumption of culture as a specific ontological level is useful in empirical research. According to
Boyer (1993a: 6, 9-13), for example, it does not produce explanatory
schemes that could not be produced simply by studying people's actual ideas and actions (see also Abu-Lughod 1991).

One problem is that, were culture to constrain people's thoughts, it
should have a causal influence on them, and this is only possible if culture is something physical. But, in the Geertzian view, culture does
not seem to emerge from any particular material body. It is, in fact,
more natural to consider that culture is not a physical state or event at
all, but a metaphorical name for a precipitate of mental and public
representations. Thus it cannot be used as a causal explanation of
anything. (Boyer 1994b: 87, 265; Sperber 1996b: 7-18; 97. See Tooby
and Cosmides 1995.)

Geertz's lack of precision on this issue means that he cannot handle
in any coherent way the relationship between the individual and the
cultural, but merely presupposes that individuals simply passively
internalize the "cultural" ideas they happen to come across. No explanations are put forward as to the mechanisms of concept acquisition
and transmission. This is a problem, as it leaves too much room for
empty speculation about cultural transmission. If the cultural is considered to emerge from the material via the psychological, we should
at least have a theory of how this happens. (Bloch 1989; Boyer 1994b:
3-28.)

According to Sperber, culture is made up of "contagious" ideas as
well as of all human productions whose existence permits the propa-
gation of ideas. Cultural representations are widely distributed, lasting
representations that have both a mental and a public aspect, in the
sense that a mental representation results from the interpretation of a
public representation which is itself the expression of a mental representation. Thus socio-cultural phenomena are kinds of ecological patterns of psychological phenomena: social facts are defined in terms of

psychological facts, but are not reduced to them. "Culture is the precipitate of cognition and communication in a human population." (Sperber 1996: 1-10, 13-16, 25-26, 31, 33, 5697, 115. Quotation from p. 97. See also Tooby and Cosmides 1995: 24.)

In such a view, "patterns of meaning," "systems of symbols," "worldviews," etc. are selective abstractions from peoples actual mental representations, not ready-made schemes implanted in individual people's heads like copies of a computer program. People cannot simply share common "worldviews" or "cultural models," because some important aspects of cultural representations are not culturally transmitted at all. They derive from intuitive ontologies, which thus constrain culture in an important way, and consequently psychology is by no means irrelevant for anthropological research. (Boyer 1994b: 113-118; 1998; 1999: 70.)

The idea that symbols form *systems* also now becomes suspect. Geertz in no way explains what he means by a system, although this assumption seems to be important in his argument. He merely says that symbols are woven "into some sort of ordered whole" (Geertz 1973: 129). In general, systems are understood as either bounded units of nature or groups of interacting variables, which have an output that is somehow dependent on a specific input (see e.g. Laszlo 1975). It is difficult to see how "symbols" can form a system in this sense. It is the human cognitive mechanism that forms a system, rather than symbols or culture.

However, Brian Malley (1995; 1997) has recently claimed that the recurrent patterns normally understood as religious should be regarded as including systems-level emergent dynamics. Religious models are cognitive entities, and religious systems emerge from socially connected cognitive systems. Thus we have "socio-cognitive" systems, from which performance, communication, end evolutionary dynamics emerge as recurrent types of order. Explaining these systems requires complexity theory, as not all such religious systems allowed by our cognitive constraints have actually developed. Cognitive explanations thus cannot be enough. (Malley 1995: 7-8, 16; 1997: 389.)

Complex systems have three characteristics: they are self-organizing; they evolve toward criticality (an example of this is a pile of sand on a circular platform which at some point, as it grows in size, begins to avalanche in cascades); and they maximize the computational utility of their constituent ideas. This third feature is especially apparent in religion, as religious concepts are highly evocative and thus have almost unlimited explanatory power. (Malley 1995: 17-19; 1997: 390-391.) Boyer (1996b), however, has made four comments in refutation of this: that religions are not unified systems, that the order found in religious representations can be explained by referring to organizing principles that are not themselves religious or unique to religious phenomena, that systems-level theories are mere morphological descriptions, and that they prevent us from isolating important causal factors (see Malley 1997: 390-391).

I believe that, while Boyer is at least partially right in each case, there is still room for other kinds of explanations than causal cognitive ones. No matter how we draw the line between religion and non-religion (or whether we draw it at all), the fact remains that there is emergent order in people's representations that cannot be explained merely causally (see Clark 1997: 179-192; Varela, Rosch, and Thompson 1996). The relevance of complexity theory in explaining this order is yet to be shown, but there is also a third alternative, besides the models of Boyer and Malley: the content-specific cognitive psychology developed by Pertti Saariluoma (1995; 1997). What is important here, however, is that all these three models far exceed Geertz's interpretations in specificity, complexity and empirical testability.

According to Saariluoma (1995: 98-99), the notions of attention and memory cannot answer all important questions regarding selectivity in thinking. Since they are capacity-oriented, they cannot explain why mental representations have a certain kind of content rather than another kind. Capacity cannot make any difference between the content of thoughts. We need a content-specific cognitive psychology, i.e. "a theory that explains human behavior in terms of the contents of the required representations and processes needed in constructing these representations." Such a psychology explains why any given thoughts have a definite set of elements linked together into a whole as well as why some other and apparently equally possible set of elements is not included. (See also Saariluoma 1997: 104-108.)

Thus mental representations are analyzed with reference to their self-consistency. Any element present in a system of representations must be "senseful," in the sense that there is a reason why it is there. They are not "meaningful" because they do not necessary have any meaning, like for example a good move in chess, but they make sense when considered in relation to other elements in the system. Saariluoma has revived Leibniz's old concept of 'apperception' to refer to the conceptual perception or construction of semantic representations.

Apperception assimilates the perceptual stimulus and conceptual information in memory into a semantically self-consistent representation, and thus accounts for the fact that people can control the contents of their mental representations. It is apperception that provides the representational system with a senseful structure. (Saariluoma 1995: 99-103.) In this model, the systematic properties are thus to be found on the level of the individual mind.

Whether the representations entertained by individual minds can show systemic properties on a collective level is an interesting question I do not attempt to solve here. I merely point out that one option, which Malley (1995) too seems to have in mind, would be to see cultural evolution as based on emergent self-organization, as in Stuart Kauffman's (1993) view of biological evolution (see also Elman et al. 1998: 47-106). This view is a disputable one, however (Wilson 1998: 88-90, 125-163). It would also require considerable empirical work to show that people's mental representations actually manifest an emergent order that cannot be explained by the properties of individual minds. Here, however, the important point is that Geertz has in no way tried to account for the supposed systemic nature of symbols, or even to describe such systems *as systems*. I suspect that this would not even in principle be possible without psychological considerations. Thus the idea of culture as an independent level of reality is useless as an explanatory concept.

Geertz and Symbolism

In this section, I deal with Geertz's view of cultural symbols. Geertz's view includes the following three assumptions: (1) that there are such special entities as "symbols," (2) that these symbols have intrinsic meaning, and (3) that these meanings can be somehow "inherited," this process of "inheriting" being so obvious that it does not have to be explained at all. These, as I will try to show, are all highly dubious assumptions. I will first deal with symbolism and then with the idea of "inheriting" views and conceptions.

"Symbolism" is, of course, a famous paradigm in anthropology, and is represented – besides Geertz – by such scholars as Claude Lévi-Strauss and Victor Turner. I shall not discuss these theories here, as Sperber (1995) already has published an excellent critique of the basic assumptions on which they rest. Sperber rejects such "semiological" views which take symbols as a class of phenomena that have a hidden meaning. In this view, a "symbol" consists of a signifier (*signifiant*) and a meaning (*signifié*) which together act as the signifier of a symbolic meaning (see Barthes 1986: 109-127).

"Symbols," however, cannot form such a language-like system, because we are not able systematically to substitute one kind of symbol for another kind of symbol, although in language we can replace most words by a definition. On the other hand, if symbols do not form a language of any sort and yet have meaning, we should be able to substitute a verbalized meaning for the symbolic meaning, which is not the case. The interpretation of symbols always tends to change their meaning. It is not the case that to each symbol there corresponds a fixed set of interpretations, or the other way around. Exegesis is not an interpretation but rather an extension of the symbol. As symbols are not a specific class of phenomena, meaning cannot be restricted to some particular class of phenomena either, and all objects of perception and thought would have to be said to "mean" as well; this, as we will see toward the end of this section, leads to absurdity. (Sperber 1995: 1-15, 34.)

Geertz, whose views are not analyzed in Sperber (1995), developed his idea of 'symbol(ism)' inspired by the views of the philosopher Susanne Langer (1942; 1953) regarding such concepts as 'meaning,' 'sign,' 'symbol,' 'communication,' etc., saying that it is time for the anthropology of religion to "become aware of the fact" that these are the dominant concepts of our time (Geertz 1973: 80-81, 89, 91 n. 5, 100 n. 21, 111 n. 38). Geertz, however, does not offer any systematic treatment of Langer's views, merely referring occasionally to some detail in Langer's work. Langer herself draws heavily on aesthetics, and considers that the function of artistic symbols, as distinct from mere signals, is to express ideas. They articulate and present concepts. Symbols do not form a language, nor do they have any fixed reference in reality. Rather, they are articulate, non-discursive significant forms of human feeling. (Langer 1953: 26-40, 50-51, 67, 369-391).

Interestingly, also the historian and philosopher of religion, Peter Munz, has applied a rather similar theory of symbols to religious materials, although he refers to Langer only in one of his later works, and only in passing (Munz 1973: 108).[7] Munz, to whom Geertz does

---

7   Both Langer and Munz own to a considerable extent to Ernst Cassirer's work on symbolism (e.g. Langer 1953: 81, 186-189, 236-241, 378, 394; Munz 1973: 92-97, 106).

not refer, considers that symbols are the "objective correlates" (T. S. Eliot's term) of human "feeling-states," "subjective states of mind," or "states of consciousness." Yet there is no one-to-one relationship between a feeling-state and its symbol. The symbol does not stand for the feeling-state. Rather, in the objective symbol the subjective feeling-state becomes objective in an expressive manner, and there is thus no way to check whether the symbol really corresponds to the feeling-state. This is because feeling-states have objective existence only as symbolized. (Munz 1959: 50-58, 61, 127; 1964; 53-65; 1973: xi-xii, 59-65, 92-97.) Religion, for Munz, is a way of interpreting symbols in the light of the idea of a divine agent (Munz 1959: 71, 82-83, 175, 215; 1964: 209).

Geertz, for his part, means by a symbol "any object, act, event, quality, or relation which serves as a vehicle for a conception," the conception being the symbol's "meaning" (Geertz uses quotation marks here). Symbols are "tangible formulations of notions, abstractions from experience fixed in perceptible forms, concrete embodiments of ideas, attitudes, judgements, longings, or beliefs." In other words, a symbol is anything concrete by which people communicate their ideas. Importantly, Geertz emphasizes that such symbols are "social events," public and observable. Therefore, in the study of cultural activity, the scholar should not "enter into a mentalistic world of introspective psychology," or "wander in a haze of 'Cognitions,' 'Affections,' 'Conations,' and other elusive entities." (Geertz 1973: 91.)

Culture patterns are complexes of symbols that serve as "extrinsic sources of information." As such, they provide "a blueprint or template in terms of which processes external to themselves can be given a definitive form," although symbols are not identical with or constitutive of their referents, as Ernst Cassirer mistakenly held (see n. 7). Symbolic culture patterns only provide "programs" for the institution of social and psychological processes. Such extrinsic sources of meaning are important because human behavior is only loosely determined by genetic information. As (unlike for example beavers) we do not have an instinct to build dams, we can only obtain a conception of what it is to build a dam from some symbolic source. (Geertz 1973: 92 and n.7., 93.)

There is, however, a double aspect to cultural symbolism. Cultural patterns are both models of and models for, in the sense that, on the one hand, they can be manipulated to bring them "into parallel with the pre-established nonsymbolic system" (model of reality). On the other hand, the nonsymbolic system too can be manipulated "in terms of the relationships expressed in the symbolic," as in building something according to a blueprint (model for reality). For example, genetic programs, which for Geertz represent nonsymbolic information, are only models for. Only "culture patterns" have the intrinsic double aspect of being at once models of and models for. They "give meaning" to social and psychological reality "both by shaping themselves to it and by shaping it to themselves." (Geertz 1973: 93.)

Here Geertz comes very close to a somewhat psychologically realistic description of symbols and culture; unfortunately, he goes astray because of his wish to emphasize that culture cannot be reduced to psychology. He says that material symbols are only vehicles for conceptions and ideas and that they are shaped by psychological (and "social") factors, while they in turn also shape psychological and social reality. In principle, this sounds like a plausible account. If I give my wife a rose to let her know that I love her, she may consider the rose a symbolic expression of what I supposedly feel. The rose as a symbol is shaped by my psychological state. Furthermore, when I see my wife's happiness in receiving the rose, my own feeling assumes a new quality of happiness, and in this sense the symbol has also shaped my psychology. It has served as a vehicle for a message and as an "embodiment of an idea." This seems to be in perfect agreement with what Geertz says in his essay. But this example does not entail that the rose 'means' my love (see Sperber 1995: 21-22). The meaning – contrary to what Geertz thinks – is not in the rose, but in my and my wife's thoughts.

Geertz says that, as cultural symbols are public and observable, the scholar studying them should not "enter into a mentalistic world of introspective psychology," but should study symbols as complexes that form cultural patterns; "meanings can only be 'stored' in symbols" (Geertz 1973: 127). This presupposes that the so-called symbols somehow embody meaning in themselves. They are not merely "vehicles" that have been used and then abandoned, but have as it were an *intrinsic* meaning. Therefore they can "give meaning" to psychological processes. This, as Boyer (1994b: 25 *et passim*) notes, comes close to being a magical account of cultural transmission: the mere presence of a symbol can implement meanings in people's minds. Geertz's account inevitably leads to such a conclusion, as he has no theory of learning or concept acquisition or therefore of cultural transmission. Like many anthropologists, he seems to assume that people just somehow absorb ideas from 'culture' or cultural objects.[8] (See Sperber 1995: 1-16; Bloch 1989; Boyer 1994a: 396; 1994b.)

Although Geertz has to admit that "symbols" both give meaning to and express psychological reality, he nevertheless considers that psychological factors are irrelevant for the anthropological study of symbols. The anthropologist should study "(c)ultural acts, the construction, apprehension, and utilization of symbolic forms" as "empirical totalities," not such "elusive entities" as cognition. Yet Geertz admits that the "symbolic dimension" of these phenomena is a theoretical abstraction *like the psychological one.* (Geertz 1973: 91.) In other words, a rose for example is something empirical, but the scholar's interpretation of the rose as a symbol of love is something abstract and is made by the scholar, i.e. is based on his or her cognitive processes.

Now, why would the idea of psychological processes in the background of this symbolism be more elusive than the idea of symbolic meanings? The ontology of "meanings" and "cultural patterns," as we have seen, is after all much vaguer than the ontology of psychological factors. The elusiveness of the idea of "cultural symbolism" becomes apparent when Geertz (1980: 103-105) says that the Balinese do not express their ideas as beliefs but rather put them into symbols, and that it is hard to try to summarize their cultural ideas on the basis of symbolism. The difficulty derives from the presupposition that "cultural patterns" are something that the members of the culture share but which nevertheless are somehow independent of people's minds, as though meanings were entities rather than relations between a subject and an object. Public meanings seem to have no corresponding mental representation, which is simply an absurd assumption (Sperber 1996b: 79-81).

It is of course necessary to use abstractions in describing the life and practices of a given population, but it is these abstractions that are elusive entities, not the psychological processes that can be used to explain why certain ideas become widely distributed in a population. "Cultural patterns" are abstractions made on the basis of such widely

---

8   One could of course try to argue that Geertz does not want to explain anything, only to interpret. Yet he himself (Geertz 1973: 4, 24, 87-88) is worried that no theoretical advances have been made in contemporary anthropology, and that anthropologists draw only from a narrowly defined intellectual tradition, not paying attention for instance to the "harder sciences." A "theoretically more powerful concept of culture" is needed to replace Tylor's "most complex whole," and anthropology asserts itself, although timidly, to be a science.

distributed ideas; they do not constitute an explanation for the recurrence of these ideas. Since Geertz is interested in "culture," not in
individuals, he wants to study meanings as cultural entities riding pig-
gy-back on empirical symbols. This idea, however, is based on the
mistaken assumption that in communication we first transform our
ideas without residue into verbal or other signs, after which the signs
are decoded by the listener(s); if the act of communication has been
successful, the listener(s) end up having received the sender's idea as
such. It is as though we could just "pack" and "unpack" signs and
symbols with meanings. (See Sperber and Wilson 1988; Boyer 1994b.)

Sperber and Deirdre Wilson, and also Boyer, however, have per-
suasively argued that in communication only some degree of resemblance is achieved between the thoughts of the communicator and the
audience. Rather than a semiotic process of symmetrical coding and
corresponding decoding of a message, we are dealing with an inferential process even when codes are used. Communicators produce pub-
licly available tokens that are expected to affect the audience's mental
representations in a predictable way. Such cultural "reifications of
ideas" as texts, paintings, etc. do not actually reify ideas, but constitute
cues likely to trigger similar inferences in a population of individuals.
Mental representations that recur frequently in a culture are inferred
by individuals from a perceptual input on the basis of preexisting conceptual structures, and their recurrence can be explained by certain
kinds of biases inherent in the human cognitive make-up. We do not
"inherit" ideas and meanings from our ancestors through the medium
of symbols. (Sperber and Wilson 1988; Sperber 1996b: 58, 81-83;
Boyer 1994b: 283-288.)

It is important to realize that the act of inference involves active
mental processing on the part of the subject. "Meanings" are not
merely absorbed from symbols in some mysteriously inexplicable way.
Cultural objects, texts included, do not have any intrinsic meaning.
They merely provide cues that direct people's attention, thus under-
determining their own interpretation. It is the specific properties of
the human mind that make certain inferences from material cues
more likely than others. Even texts do not have an intrinsic meaning.
Rather, they provide cues that direct people's attention in such a way
that the inferences readers draw from them are highly predictable. As
Varela, Rosch, and Thompson (1996: 179) put it, cultural knowledge
"does not preexist in any one place or form but is enacted in particular situations."

It would be a magical belief to hold that material tokens can generate particular assumptions in people irrespective of the latters' cognitive capacities. Material objects in themselves are mute, although they can be used to extend the information processing capacity of the brain, a process Andy Clark (1997: 45-51, 59-69, 179-218) calls "scaffolding." We can for example write things down, use all kinds of material tokens, including even computers, to improve our capacity to remember and carry out mental processes such as calculation. There is thus no sharp dividing line between the brain and the external world, although it ultimately is our brains that thus make also the external world smart.[9] An interpretive anthropologist who writes for example that the innermost part of the royal palace is a world axis (Geertz 1980: 114) does not find this meaning in the material object, the palace, but ascribes it to the object on the basis of his personal knowledge and cognitive capacities. Psychological considerations can thus contribute significantly to the interpretation and explanation of cultural ideas. (Boyer 1994b: 259-261. See Sperber 1996b: 26, 43, 75, 83; Dennett 1997: 66-73.)

As Sperber explains, cultural representations are widely distributed, lasting representations that have both a mental and a public aspect. This view of culture and communication also means that religious symbolism cannot be understood as a property of certain objects and events, in the sense that they have somehow acquired a capacity to "establish powerful, pervasive, and long-lasting moods and motivations in men" (Geertz 1973: 90). Rather than a property of material objects, symbolism is a property of human cognition. The fact that "symbols" can evoke all kinds of feelings and ideas in humans is not determined by properties of symbols alone but by the ways our minds work in relation to certain kinds of stimuli. This is precisely because the material environment without an observer is mute. Objects of perception or thought have meaning only in so far that they serve as the basis for someone's cognitive process.

This problem of meaning has been encountered in artificial intelli-

---

9   Clark (1997: 61) suggests, on the basis of connectionist modeling and theory, that we can mentally simulate external reality and thus also internalize cognitive competencies that are rooted in manipulations of the external environment. An example this would be for example writing something down in order to remember it better. Clark then remarks that the basic error of classical rule-and-symbol-based AI might be regarding such combinations of human cognitive powers and manipulation of external reality as an inherent property of the human mind alone.

gence, whose representatives want to argue that computer programs carry just as much meaning and are just as intentional as human minds. According to John Searle (1980; 1995), however, meanings can only be derived from conscious human intentions. Only the human mind can have intrinsic meaning, computer programs having only derived meaning, just like a written sentence or a configuration of beads on an abacus – or, I would add, a "symbol." We could also say that programs only provide direct evidence for the *information* to be conveyed, whereas in genuine communication we provide direct evidence of our *intention(s)* (Sperber and Wilson 1988: 23). This is precisely the direction pointed at by Sperber's (1995) criticism of symbolic meaning. Symbols do not carry meanings because they are not the material tokens of specific intentions.

The proponents of strong artificial intelligence, however, argue that we need not presuppose any intrinsic meanings, since one kind of derived intentionality can be derived from another kind of derived intentionality, and human intentions are just as derived as the intentionality of computer programs. (Dennett 1997a: 66-73; Churchland 1995: 244-246.) This is central in the "functionalist" account of cognition, as we have seen in Chapter 1: calculating that $2+2 = 4$ is the same kind of representation as taking up two plus two beer cans and putting them together. Both processes support the same kind of causal process. It is the functional relations that establish meaning. You may be more intelligent than your pocket calculator but that is actually a difference of quantity, not of quality.

This account, however, presupposes that consciousness is here irrelevant. What we call consciousness supposedly can be reduced to various psychological functions only, one psychological process deriving its intentionality from other psychological processes. The intentionality of mental states is relative to their functions. (E.g. Dennett 1993.) Searle (1980; 1995), however, insists that intentionality is related to consciousness; only conscious beings can have intentional beliefs, and consciousness can only emerge from biological brains. David Chalmers, for his part, claims that although the phenomenal consciousness arises from functional organization, it is not a functional state. It is an organizational invariant, a property that remains constant over all functional isomorphs of a given system. Thus, despite Dennett's claims to the contrary (see also Dennett 1997b), consciousness is more than mere functional organization. But contrary to Searle's claims, the biological brain is not the only material basis that can

support consciousness. Any material system with the "right" functional organization will do, and thus also an appropriately programmed
computer could be conscious.[10] (Chalmers 1997: 15-22, 174, 247-249,
313-323. Cf. Churchland 1995: 187-252; Jackson and Pettit 1996.)

This, however, cannot be a causal explanation of consciousness for
the simple reason that computational simulations are not causal
explanations. They are interpretations we as conscious beings make.
Nothing is a computation inherently. Computations do not exist as
natural facts, but are abstract entities by which we conceptualize natural processes. (Searle 1995: 218-219; Revonsuo 1994. See also Scott
1995.) This, then, also means that neither computer programs nor
"symbols" of any kind can be said to have intrinsic meaning. Intrinsic
meanings only belong to conscious experience. (But cf. Chalmers
1997: 315-320.) Selmer Bringsjord and Michael Zenzen (1997) have
also presented a rather detailed argument showing that phenomenal
consciousness cannot be computational (as Chalmers and the functionalists claim) because computations are reversible while consciousness is not[11].

As meaning does not reside in isolated objects, such as works of art,
texts, or buildings, but is the property of a conscious cognitive process,
symbolism is best viewed as a cognitive mechanism that participates in
the construction of knowledge as well as in the functioning of memory. It is not an instrument of social communication or a property of
phenomena that can be considered apart from this mechanism. (Sperber 1995: xi-xii, 146-147.)

Sperber explains this by first distinguishing between semantic and
encyclopaedic knowledge. Semantic knowledge is about cognitive categories, not about the world. Encyclopaedic knowledge is about the
world. For example 'The lion is a dangerous animal' is encyclopaedic

---

10   Chalmers (1997: 276-308) eventually opts for panpsychism and claims that even
a thermostat has rudimentary conscious experience because the structure of experience is the structure of a phenomenally realized information space. Yet he also recognizes that he would not be surprised if his idea turned out to be entirely misguided;
this is in his opinion even more likely than the opposite (Chalmers 1997: 310).
11   Bringsjord and Zenzen (1997) show that while any series of computations in a
Turing machine can be logically reversed in a useful way, states of consciousness cannot. One cannot for example have the experience of listening to Beethoven's ninth
backwards step by step. This is both a practical and a logical impossibility both at the
levels of phenomenology and of neural processing. Bringsjord and Zenzen also point
out that it may be possible some day to put forward a scientific explanation of consciousness without that it is possible to implement consciousness in a computer or a
robot.

knowledge (it concerns lions), whereas 'The lion is an animal' is
semantic knowledge (it concerns the concept of 'lion'). In practice, it
may often be difficult to decide to which category some piece of
knowledge belongs, although in principle the distinction expresses an
important difference. Symbolic knowledge resembles encyclopaedic
knowledge, but there are also important differences. Symbolic knowledge for example allows for incoherences and contradictions of a kind
that we usually try to avoid in encyclopaedic knowledge. (Sperber
1995: 91-95; see also Boyer 1994b: 48-49.)

This does not result from a random set of faulty reasonings, but
from a systematic relaxation of constraints. Whereas encyclopaedic
statements like 'John is the son of Bob' are compared to other statements expressing encyclopaedic knowledge in order to assess their
truth-value, symbolic statements like 'Jesus is the son of god' are not in
such a way assessed. They can be considered to be true without the
believer necessarily even understanding them. They are metarepresented in the form '"Jesus is the son of god" is true,' with "Jesus is the
son of god" being "half-understood," symbolic knowledge. It is thus
possible to believe that '"Jesus is the son of god" is true' without knowing what 'Jesus is the son of god' means. (Sperber 1995: 98-99; 1996b:
69-74, 96-97, 119-150.)

Symbolic knowledge thus is neither about semantically understood
categories nor about the world, but about encyclopaedic entries of
categories in the memory. It is knowledge about knowledge, or meta-
encyclopaedic knowledge. While the representation 'the fox is wild' is
encyclopaedic knowledge, and 'the fox is an animal' is semantic
knowledge, 'cunning as a fox' is symbolic knowledge. In this case,
what is known or believed about foxes is put in quotation marks and is
used to express something else by means of that knowledge or belief.
Symbolicity thus is the property of conceptual representations of acts,
utterances or objects. (Sperber 1995: 108-112.)

Conceptual representation normally consists 1) of focal statements,
describing some item of new information, and 2) of auxiliary statements, linking the new information to the encyclopedic memory. In
the case of symbolic knowledge, either the focal statements fail to
describe new information or the auxiliary statements fail to link it to
encyclopaedic memory. When for example one hears for the first time
that 'Jesus is the son of god,' one may not be able to understand that
piece of information and/or may fail to relate it to entries in one's
encyclopaedic memory; whereupon the symbolic mechanism is acti-

vated and starts to search for any such representations in memory whose truth would make 'Jesus is the son of god' understandable. This mechanism does not attempt to "decode" the information, or to find its meaning, but to invent a relevant place for it in the memory. A representation is symbolic precisely to the extent that it is not entirely explicable. (Sperber 1995: 112-113, 120-121.)

This symbolic process has two aspects: a displacement of attention, or focalization, and a search in memory, or evocation. In focalization, attention shifts from the new information in question to the unfulfilled conceptual conditions. In evocation, the new information is reviewed and tested against the information in one's long-term memory. In other words, when the invocation of relevant background information fails, evocation begins. Alternatively, the failure of the sequential process triggers a parallel process, in which information may be revived that turns out to be more interesting than the representation in quotation marks or the focal condition.[12] The symbolic mechanism creates its own pathways in the memory, and the symbolic process may become endless. Religious representations for example are never given a final solution, the symbolic exegesis being an endless process. Otherwise the evocation can end in recognizing the metarepresented idea as a mere fiction, or in giving it a non-symbolic interpretation, such as a scientific one. (Sperber 1995: 119-123, 141-145. Also Boyer 1994b: 48-49; Atran 1996: 250-252.) It is this evocation that is substituted for 'meaning' in this model: the meaning of a "symbol" is the same as its evocative processing. Thus for example the "meaning" of the image of the cross consists of all the individual evocative searches that people undertake for a relevant place in memory for this piece of information.

In this light, the interpretations of symbolic anthropologists themselves are symbolic. The anthropologist observes some such custom, such as for example the ritual penis-bleeding of the Gnau of New Guinea, and cannot find any such representation in his or her memory that would make it understandable. Thus the symbolic mechanism

---

12 This seems to correspond to Edward de Bono's (1990: 236-245) "lateral thinking," which he contrasts with "natural," "logical," and "mathematical" thinking (ibid. 220-235). Lateral thinking is concerned with making the best possible use of existing information in long-term memory by rearranging it in insightful ways. On the whole, de Bono's idea about the brain as a "memory surface" seem to be an interesting anticipation of connectionism (his book was published in 1969 and contains no notes or bibliography).

is activated and starts to reorganize the anthropologist's encyclopedic knowledge database, so that the strange custom can be connected to it. The anthropologist may for instance consider the possibility that penis-bleeding symbolically stands for menstruation. But then he or she has to explain why the Gnau themselves explicitly deny this, which might be done by having recourse for instance to Freudian interpretations (see Sperber 1995: 34-47). Or, the anthropologist may argue, like Gilbert Lewis, that "human beings respond to certain natural aspects of their experience of the human body in like ways," which are not conscious and which therefore constitute "natural symbolism" (cf. Douglas 1970), stimuli to which we react intuitively and emotionally. This then can be combined with the view that the Gnau seek by penis-bleeding to fulfil some social function they attribute to the phenomenon of menstruation. (Lewis 1988: 106-120.) Such interpretations clearly are not explanations for the customs observed, but are themselves acts of symbolic exegesis.

In the next section, I deal with the rest of Geertz's "definition" of religion, as involving certain kinds of "moods and motivations" that relate to human attempts to understand the surrounding reality.

Geertz on Religion as a Symbolic Cultural System

In defining religion, Geertz speaks of *a* religion, not of 'religion' as a general concept. Any religion is a system of symbols which serves the *function* of establishing moods and motivations in people. It accomplishes this task by formulating conceptions of the order of existence and by making these conceptions seem realistic. It is noteworthy that Geertz seems to imply that a system of symbols can formulate conceptions by itself. Obviously, his anti-psychologism and his willingness to see culture as an independently existing level prevents him from saying that ideas are formulated by *people*. Saying this would also bring him dangerously near to the idea that religion consists of false but convincing conceptions that the clergy have fooled people into believing in.

Let us see how Geertz himself explicates his definition. He starts by noting that "sacred symbols function to synthesize a people's ethos and worldview." By ethos he means "the tone, character, and quality of their life, its moral and aesthetic style and mood;" by worldview, "the picture they have of the way things in sheer actuality are, their most comprehensive ideas of order." (Geertz 1973: 89, 126-127.) In the background, the idea thus figures strongly that "symbols" have the power to unify people's thoughts and emotions.

Geertz's distinction also recalls Gregory Bateson's (1936) distinction between ethos and eidos, to which, however, Geertz does not refer. By ethos, Bateson meant the kind of "precipitate" of emotions, attitudes and instincts that typify a culture. Eidos, for its part, referred to a similar precipitate of cognitive processes. More recently, anthropologists have largely substituted 'worldview' for Bateson's 'eidos.' Quite interestingly, however, Bateson acknowledged that the Iatmuls of New Guinea he had studied did not seem to have any coherent "worldview" or "cultural model" concerning cosmology and related matters. (See also Vesala 1995: 2-13.)

However, according to Geertz (1973: 89-90):

> "(I)n religious belief and practice a group's ethos is rendered intellectually reasonable by being shown to represent a way of life ideally adapted to the actual state of affairs the world view describes, while the world view is rendered emotionally convincing by being presented as an image of an actual state of affairs peculiarly well-arranged to accommodate such a way of life.

Thus ethos and worldview are so related that a particular worldview *intellectually* legitimates a particular ethos. The worldview in turn is made *emotionally* convincing by the fact that it pictures reality as such that the prevailing life-style seems an especially rational choice. This apparently is what Geertz means by his claim that a system of symbols establishes powerful moods and motivations in men (*sic*). This means that religious symbols shape reality by "inducing in the worshipper a certain distinctive set of dispositions" (Geertz 1973: 95-96).

In seeing moods and motivations as dispositions, Geertz leans on Gilbert Ryle's (1990) logical behaviorism, according to which there is no such separate thing as 'mind.' The ontology of the concept of 'mind' is similar to the ontology of such abstract concepts as 'university:' there is no such thing as 'the university' apart from certain individual buildings, playing fields, museums, offices, etc. Similarly, what is erroneously called 'mind' is actually merely a collection of certain kinds of dispositions. There is no such 'place' as the 'mind.' (Ryle 1990: 13-20.) Mental dispositions are probabilities of activities, in the sense that for example being pious merely means being liable to perform pious acts. This dispositional view of "mental traits" gets them "out of any dim and inaccessible realm of private sensation" into the public realm of facts. (Geertz 1973: 95-96. Cf. Ryle 1990: 112-147.)

A motivation is, for Geertz, a persisting tendency or inclination. Motives are neither acts nor feelings, but liabilities to perform certain kinds of acts or to have particular classes of feeling. Moods, for their part, are feelings or emotions that acquire their meaning from the conditions from which they are conceived to spring, whereas motivations become meaningful with reference to the their ends. (Geertz 1973: 96-97.) It is the task of religious symbols to establish powerful, pervasive and long-lasting moods and motivations in men.

This view involves three important problems. First, "symbols" cannot have any tasks apart from the people who use them, or "induce" anything in people irrespective of the latters' cognitive constraints. Second, symbolic systems as cultural patterns cannot be causal factors because they are mere abstractions. Cultural patterns are not physical states or events, but highly selective summaries of ideas entertained in a population, and thus cannot explain why people have certain kinds of moods and motivations. (See Boyer 1994b: 87, 265; Sperber 1996b: 7-18; 97.) Third, the dispositional view of the mental is not satisfactory, as it leaves unexplained what causes people to act in certain ways. What does it really mean for instance that a person has a tendency to act piously? How is the tendency represented? What does it consist of? How does it cause pious behavior? All these questions presuppose cognitive considerations of the kind that Geertz wants to avoid.

It would not make sense to say that a person has a tendency to act piously if he or she did not have a long-term memory in which the tendency is somehow represented, consciously or unconsciously. Connectionism provides one way of conceptualizing how this happens. It allows for a "bottom up" approach, explaining "cultural patterns" as abstractions from individual mental processes, in contrast to Geertz's "top down" approach in which mental processes are seen as mere individual "copies" of cultural programs. A tendency to act in a certain way can be said to consist of a specific configuration of synaptic connections or of activation levels in neurons, whose outward manifestation is observable behavior (see Churchland 1995: 3-53; Damasio 1999: 219-223, 331-332). While it is true that both mental and public representations can evoke strong emotions in people, this should nevertheless be explained as an interactional process between cognitive constraints and cultural input. This will be discussed in more detail in

Chapter Five. Here I move on to a consideration of what makes moods and motivations religious.

According to Geertz, the religiosity of a mood is due to the fact it "springs from entertaining a conception of all-pervading vitality like mana and not from a visit to the Grand Canyon." A religious motivation is directed toward the achievement of an unconditioned end like nirvana and not a conditioned one. Religious symbols are symbols of "some transcendent truths." Yet religion cannot be defined with reference to "belief in spiritual beings." A minimal definition of religion, rather, is constituted by what Salvador de Madariaga has called "the relatively modest dogma that God is not mad." (Geertz 1973: 98-99.)

I must say I am rather perplexed by these characterizations. They are so vague, so confused and so enigmatic that it is almost impossible to gather what Geertz is actually trying to say. Why can't supernatural beings be used as a defining characteristic of religion, since 'god,' after all is, brought into the definition? It is difficult to understand the difference between Tylorianism and "Madariaganism" because of the anecdotal nature of the argument. Some kind of transcendence seems, however, to be a necessary element in Geertz's understanding of religion, although he does not explain its nature in any way. Rather, he seems to be on the one hand denying its relevance, while on the other hand he speaks of transcendent truths.

Geertz explains, quoting Langer, that people cannot tolerate chaos and lack of explanation, and therefore always attempt to bring anomalous events and experiences within the circle of the explicable, despite the limits of their analytic capacities. Although this, as Geertz admits, sounds like Tylorianism, it cannot be denied that most humans cannot leave unclarified problems unclarified, but have to develop some notion as to how such things might be reconciled with more ordinary conceptions. Geertz even has to admit that his "more animistically inclined informants behaved like true Tylorians." They seemed to be constantly using their beliefs to "explain" phenomena, or to convince themselves that even strange phenomena were in principle explainable, even if it was a matter of argument which explanation might turn out to be the true one. That which lies beyond accredited knowledge places human experience in a permanent context of metaphysical concern and creates suspicions that the world we live in may, after all, be an absurd one. (Geertz 1973: 99-102. Cf. Horton 1993: 53-62.)

What Geertz fails to appreciate is that in cases where ordinary explanations turn out to be insufficient, people in general are prone to apply counter-intuitive explanations. What Geertz refers to as "transcendent truths" might better be called 'counter-intuitive' truths. Some kind of counter-intuitive order of things is brought to explain various kinds of anomalous things, i.e. things that are somehow at odds with common knowledge. (Cf. Spiro 1968: 109-110.) Geertz himself provides a very good example of this, although he seems to regard the example as something that in his view actually should not happen.

In the example, the Javanese studied by Geertz (1973: 101) were quite astonished to see how rapidly a large, peculiarly shaped toadstool grew within a few days (or, according to some, within a few hours) in a carpenter's house. People came from miles around to see it and had all kinds of "animist" and "animatist" explanations for it. Yet the toadstool was not of any real significance to anyone. In growing five times as fast as the usual, it was merely an odd and uncanny thing. In other words, it was something counter-intuitive and therefore attention-demanding.

When we thus replace the concepts of 'transcendence' and 'supernatural' by the concept of 'counter-intuitiveness,' the problems with the Tylorian vocabulary vanish and Geertz's observations become intelligible. The anomalies he speaks of can be understood as deviant phenomena in given intuitive domains (see Sperber 1996a; Anttonen 1996; 2000). The idea of such counter-intuitive phenomena, especially counter-intuitive agents, can in principle solve Geertz's problem with the notion of 'transcendence:' phenomena that cannot be explained within the boundaries of intuitive knowledge call for a counter-intuitive explanation. Counter-intuitive explanations, for their part, are available simply because they emerge quite naturally from intuitive ontologies. It is not necessary to presuppose that this function of religion is also a cause for the existence of religion.[13]

Geertz argues that religion, by means of symbols, formulates an image of a genuine order of the world such that it can also account for all kinds of ambiguities, puzzles and paradoxes. Religious symbolism relates "man's sphere of existence to a wider sphere within which it is conceived to rest." Geertz then asks, what makes a religious perspec-

---

13 According to Spiro (1968: 109-110), religious beliefs are held because, in the absence of competitive explanations, they satisfy the human need to know, understand, and find meaning in existence.

tive different from other kinds of perspectives and how men come to adopt it. As the "outcast discipline" of psychology is the most troublesome of all for Geertz, he has to find a solution that does not refer to psychological processes, and thus ends up with social action as a solution. (Geertz 1973: 108-109, 113.)

First, he says that the religious perspective differs from the common-sensical, the scientific, and the aesthetic in that it "moves beyond the realities of everyday life," to what is "really real" and nonhypothetical. And how do religious representations acquire their unquestionable status? For Geertz, it is in ritual that "this conviction that religious conceptions are veridical and that religious directives are sound is somehow generated." Rituals involve a symbolic fusion of ethos (moods and motivations) and worldview (metaphysical conceptions) that shapes "the spiritual consciousness of a people." (Geertz 1973: 110-113.)

It would actually be quite natural to conclude that rituals involve strong emotions that enhance the recall of the representations transmitted in the ritual, and that these representations in turn evoke strong emotions (Pyysiäinen 2001b). I shall deal with this issue in Chapter 5. But Geertz, who did not have proper psychological tools available, prefers to speak of "the spiritual consciousness of *a people*," as though it were a less troublesome concept than the concept of a psychological process in an individual mind! For him, the acceptance of religious authority "flows from the enactment of the ritual itself." A ritual induces a set of moods and motivations (an ethos) and defines a worldview by means of a single set of symbols. How this actually happens, remains a mystery. (Geertz 1973: 118.)

Yet this is the crucial point in Geertz's argument. If it really is the ritual that – by its mere enactment – induces in people the moods and motivations that seem realistic in relation to the conceptions of general order put forward in the ritual, it would be quite important to know how this happens. In other words, Geertz is saying that a religion is a system of ritual symbols that in itself formulates a worldview with an aura of factuality, which then establishes in people peculiar moods and motivations that seem realistic given the truth of the conceptions that form the worldview. Rituals "shape the spiritual consciousness of a people" (*sic*), i.e. make the people believe in a certain image of the order of the world. Yet Geertz carefully avoids speaking of individual people believing something because of emotional reasons. What he is interested in is rituals that just happen – so it seems – without active

participants; and a worldview that just exists, without being represented by anyone.

Secondly, Geertz also tries to avoid speaking of superhuman agents
and transcendence (remember also Levine!), although ultimately he
cannot really do completely without such concepts. I have shown the
utter necessity of including the belief in counter-intuitive agents in any
"definition" of religion, but Geertz tries to get by without them by
introducing a distinction between "pure" and "applied" religion.

According to Geertz (1973: 119-120), the dispositions that rituals
induce in people have their most important impact in influencing people's daily lives outside the ritual context. Religious belief as a pale,
remembered reflection of what was experienced in ritual is a slightly
different thing, and confusing the two, according to Geertz, has led to
strange views about "primitive mentality." How can "primitive man"
be at once as rational as described by Malinowski, and yet as illogical
as described by Lévy-Bruhl?

Here Geertz is once again very close to a probable solution, but
fails to draw the right conclusions. Counter-intuitive beliefs form a
specific domain of knowledge and do not affect people's reasoning
powers in other domains, because human intelligence is domain-specific. Believing for example that ghosts can fly on banana leaves does
not entail that one's general reasoning abilities are somehow inadequate, because there is no such thing as general reasoning. Reasoning
is always domain-specific; what counts as an explanation for the
behavior of humans, for instance, does not normally count as an
explanation in the case of physical objects. And what works in the
domain of religion does not work in the domains of intuitive ontologies. The point is not that strange beliefs adopted in a ritual context
somehow become a bit more rational in the context of everyday life,
but that religious beliefs belong to a distinct domain. Even one who
believes in Providence takes out an insurance policy; not because he
or she at that moment has almost forgotten his or her religious belief,
but because believing in Providence and taking out insurance actually
are not mutually exclusive for the believer. Geertz cannot account for
this because he did not have access to the right cognitive psychological
tools. Sperber, for his part, does.

According to Sperber (1995: 93-95), the Dorze of Ethiopia for
example believe that the leopard is a Christian animal and observes
the fasts. Yet the Dorze guard their animals on fast days as carefully
as always, because they know from experience that leopards are dan-

gerous every day. From their tradition, on the other hand, the Dorze know that the leopard fasts on Wednesdays and Fridays, i.e. it does not eat meat. For the Dorze there is no more paradox involved than there is for the Christian who believes that Jesus is descended through Joseph from Abraham, and who at the same time also believes that Joseph was not the father of Jesus. If pressed on the matter, the Christian may say for instance that Joseph was a relative of Mary's (although this is not said in the Bible), and the Dorze man may say for instance that perhaps the leopard merely does not eat meat killed on fast days.

The important thing is that the believer fails entirely to see any paradox in such cases, because the symbolic mechanism works by metarepresentation. It is always possible to believe that "'p' is true" by inventing new interpretations for 'p.' No criticism of 'p' can get the believer to give up his or her belief, because his or her metarepresentational reasons for accepting 'p' seem intuitively compelling (Sperber 1994: 62). If one has a strong faith in the Church, or in science, one is prone to accept even religious, or scientific, claims that run counter to one's intuition.

A paradox would only be involved if an assumption A inevitably activated an assumption B, which in turn inevitably activated A and so on. Let A be 'Jesus is descended through Joseph from Abraham' and B 'Joseph is the father of Jesus' (which is known to be untrue). In this case we would have a genuine paradox only if A followed from B as a deductive inference, which, however, is not the case. The beliefs do not form such an inferential sequence, but are separate items related only abductively. (Boyer 1994b: 238.) By abduction is here meant a form of reasoning in which such conjectural assumptions are put forward that, if they were true, would account for the data in question. In abduction, a new empirical rule is invented to render predictable what would otherwise be mysterious. (Boyer 1994b: 146-147. See also ibid., 147-151, 215-218, 223-342, 251-258, 287-288; Oatley 1996.)

Here we have a much more precise answer to the problem than Geertz's (1973: 121-122) distinction between "religion pure and religion applied:" People are not consistently "religious" in all matters of life, as this would be quite impossible. It is also not the case, as Geertz insists, that the bias religion gives to ordinary life varies with the religion involved. The general bias, based on violations of intuitive ontologies, is based on a universal mechanism, although the specific contents it produces of course vary.

In sum, if we want to regard religion as a cultural and symbolic phenomenon, Geertz's "definition" needs the following qualifications:

- Symbolism is not a property of cultural objects but a form of knowledge.
- It is doubtful that symbolic representations form cultural systems.
- The notions of 'counter-intuitiveness' and 'counter-intuitive beings' are necessary.
- Emotions play an important role in the transmission of religious ideas.

It is quite natural to see religion as a cultural phenomenon in the sense that many religious representations are shared by many people. In this sense, we can speak of recurrent patterns of religious representations. This does not necessitate a "top down" approach to religious representations, in the sense that we would have to take them to form systems that could be studied apart from individual minds, as a computer program can be studied apart from the specific individual computers in which it is implemented. On the contrary, the pattern is merely an abstraction from various individual representations, which together constitute culture in the sense of a "precipitate of cognition and communication in a human population" (Sperber 1996b: 97).

Thus religion is at once cultural and individual, public and private, individual representations being based on public ones and these in turn being expressions of individual representations. Within this scheme symbolism is best understood as a form of knowledge, which cannot actually be said to form a system at the level of culture. At least Geertz himself has not in any way explained in what sense religion is a *system* of symbols.

The notion of counter-intuitive agents also seems to be a necessary element if we want to see religion as different from other forms of culture. Moreover, people seem to react to counter-intuitiveness emotionally, mainly with fear, which enhances the recall of counter-intuitive ideas. This question will be the subject of investigation in Chapter five.

Summary

'Religion' cannot simply be equated with 'culture;' such a merging of two very vague concepts merely produces one which is even more vague. 'Cultures' are merely abstract summaries of the thoughts and behaviors of individuals, not identifiable wholes that can be empirically explored. By the same token the idea of cultural *systems* becomes suspect. Furthermore, if religion is seen as one cultural system among others, we have to be able to specify what is distinctive about religion.

Geertz's influential view of religion as a symbolic cultural system was analyzed in the light of these problems. His views of culture, its systematic nature, and its use of symbolism turned out to be too vague to offer any sure ground for theories about religion. The problems largely derive from Geertz's dogmatic anti-psychologism. Although he claims for example that in rituals "moods and motivations" are established that make religious beliefs appear realistic to believers, he avoids discussing the psychological processes involved in this.

I deal with the emotional aspect of rituals, and of transmission religious ideas in general, in Chapter five. Here I argue, along with Sperber and Boyer, that the transmission of culture cannot be understood without a proper theory of concept acquisition and representation; all communicative processes are inferential and meanings thus cannot be transferred as fixed entities, via the medium of "symbols." Meanings do not reside *in* "symbols" but rather are ascribed *to* symbols. Symbolism is best understood as a mechanism of the mind, in the manner suggested by Sperber: half-understood information initiates a search in memory for information that will fit with the information that activated the search mechanism. It is here, as well as in connection with the emotional aspect of religion, that cognitive theories can offer a proper starting point for putting forward testable hypotheses about religion as a cultural phenomenon.

By means of the concept of 'counter-intuitiveness' it is possible to delimit the range of cultural phenomena studied within comparative religion: we study recurrent patterns of thought and behavior involving counter-intuitive representations. Religion thus is a phenomenon based on the human ability to form counter-intuitive ideas, metarepresent them, and treat them symbolically. The problem that remains is that, as we saw in Chapter one, not all counter-intuitiveness can be assumed to be religious. This will be discussed in more detail in Chapter seven.

CHAPTER FOUR

RELIGION AND THE SOCIAL

In this chapter I move on to consider Durkheim's approach to religion, which suffers from the same kind of shortcomings as Geertz's: the arbitrary use of the notion of symbolism, and a lack of attention to the psychological mechanisms of religious representation. Where Geertz's emphasis was on culture and meaning, however, Durkheim is interested in the social, and he uses the concept of the 'symbol' only as an *ad hoc* way out of a threatening impasse.

On The Sociological Background of Durkheim's Theory of Religion

Durkheim (1937) spends 638 pages to put forward a relatively simple, although ingenious, theory of religion. This theory can be summarized as follows:

Society, although part of nature, yet is something *sui generis*. It is a kind of collective consciousness, a synthesis of all individual states of consciousness, or a consciousness of consciousnesses. It contains collective representations that are not mere abstractions from various individual representations, but exist independently of them. Religious beliefs and rituals are a symbolic expression and a shaper of this collective consciousness. They evoke in us mental representations laden with such "psychic energy" that has the capacity to make us obey the demands of the collective consciousness. Thus reverence toward religious representations is in fact unconscious reverence toward the society. The sacredness of religious representations derives from the fact that they manifest the preconditions of our cognitive abilities: the social that is the source of all categories of understanding. A coherent system of sacred things that does not include any other system as one of its elements is a religion. It unites all its adherents into a single moral community, a "church." The sacred is the social, the religious is the sacred, and thus the religious is the social (see also Pals 1996: 115).

Before turning to a more detailed analysis of this theory, I first briefly situate it in its proper intellectual milieu. In its time, Durkheim's emphasis on the social was something new. As Daniel Pals (1996: 88) puts it, up to then 'society' had mainly been associated with "upper-class manners and the dinner parties of the wealthy," and sociology did not exist as an independent discipline. By the turn of the century, however, the idea of sociology had acquired such popularity that in 1900 Durkheim could say that it was "on everyone's lips." (Lukes 1977: 392-398.)

Various theories (or myths) of the "social contract," whereby human beings had supposedly shifted from a state of nature to one of civilization, had been put forward by philosophers during the 17th and 18th century (e.g. Hobbes 1985; Rousseau 1980). In 18th century Britain the new discipline of political economy also emerged, within which the large-scale interactions of human beings were for the first time explained by empirical observation and reasoning, without the use of theological argument (e.g. Smith 1952; cf. Luhmann 1982b). In France, such Enlightenment philosophers as the Marquis de Condorcet and others had paved the way for August Comte's new science of sociology, in which, however, conceptual analysis was still preferred over the study of empirical facts. Durkheim has been seen as an heir to this tradition. (See Lukes 1977: 392-393; Pals 1996: 91-92; Belier 1999: 26; Wilson 1998: 14-44.)

Durkheim's theory of religion reflects his earlier ideas about the division of labor as the basis of solidarity and morality (see Giddens 1978: 81). According to Durkheim (1926: 1-2, 26-27), Adam Smith (1952: 3-12) was the first to attempt a theory of the division of labor. Smith and John Stuart Mill saw the division of labor as "the supreme law of human societies and the condition of their progress," while Comte was the first to understand that the division of labor was not an economical phenomenon alone. All great political societies are able to maintain their equilibrium only because of the specialization of tasks based on the division of labor, which is the principal source of social solidarity. Such division extends to all areas of social life, including politics, art and science, and is the very basis of the existence of those societies.

This hypothesis, says Durkheim, is irreconcilable with Rousseau's (and others') idea of a social contract. Such a contract would imply that at a given moment in the state of nature all individuals suddenly agreed on the development of a social organization, which is impossible. A moral consensus can emerge only gradually, with a division of labor that keeps on assuming increasingly subtler forms.[14] (Durkheim 1926: 178, 379; 1966: 121-122.)

---

14   Here Durkheim seems to be right. There is no evidence even of a single case of a state's being formed by such "social contract" (Diamond 1999: 283. See also Huxley 1996: 407-410).

In the primitive, collective, society, all members are alike and are linked directly to one another. The links that thus bind the individual to the society are wholly analogous to the links that attach things to persons: the society owns its members. In such cases, the collective consciousness, the "society living and acting within us," can totally envelop the individual conscience, and solidarity can only grow in reverse ratio to personality. This form of solidarity Durkheim calls "mechanical." Its counterpart, "organic" solidarity, belongs to societies with a division of labor. The members of such societies are individuals with varying personal characteristics, and they depend upon the society because they depend upon the parts of which it is composed. The society is a system of different, special functions which are united by specific relations, like a body with many different organs (hence the term "organic" solidarity). In such societies, it is the division of labor, the "source of civilization," that has assumed the role that was formerly filled by the common conscience. It creates a sense of solidarity among people, this solidarity being a social fact which nevertheless exists in the "physical and psychic constitution" of individuals. (Durkheim 1926: 12, 19, 31, 36, 98-102, 147-148.)

This category of social facts consists of "ways of acting, thinking, and feeling, external to the individual, and endowed with a power of coercion, by reason of which they control him." These constitute a *sui generis* type of phenomenon: "the social," or "social facts." Social facts are not simply something we find in every individual consciousness. Collective states of consciousness are "reincarnated in the individual," but their origin is in the social and they are independent of their individual manifestations. "(T)he social fact is a thing distinct from its individual manifestations," exercising an external constraint on the individual. (Durkheim 1966: 3, 6-7, 13; 1937: 301, 331.)

Religious beliefs and rituals are "symbolic" and "metaphoric" expressions of this fact that the society has moral authority over its members. When we recognize someone or something as a representative of that authority, we form of him or it an idea that is invested with a "psychic energy" (*l'énergie psychique*) that makes us do whatever the authority demands. No purely private states of consciousness can attain such intensity. On the contrary, each individual representation bears all the power of the innumerable other individual representations. Thus social pressure affects us "through mental pathways" (*par des voies mentales*) by which the group is "incarnated" in the individual. In our consciousness there are two circles of mental states: one that consists of representations arising from ordinary sensory experience, and another consisting of representations arising from collective influences, the influence of the society. (Durkheim 1937: 296-304, 322-323.)

Durkheim admits that societies are made up of individuals,[15] and that in this sense the "first origins" of sociological phenomena are psychological. Although solidarity is a social fact, in order to exist it "must be contained in our physical and psychic constitution." Social life is dependent on its (material) substrate, just as the mental life of the individual is dependent on the brain and the whole organism. But "the social" is a new, emergent (although Durkheim does not use this precise term) phenomenon, just as life for example is an emergent phenomenon in relation to inorganic matter as its ultimate basis. In this sense, the whole is not the same as the sum of its parts, and a society is not merely the sum of its individual members. Emerging from individual consciousnesses, the social is a "specific reality which has its own characteristics," a reality *sui generis*. Although in individualistic cults for example religion seems to belong totally to the interior sphere of the individual, it is the society that is the vital source that nourishes religion. (Durkheim 1926: 31; 1966: 102-103; 1937: 22, 605-607.)

Thus, according to Durkheim, a social group actually has its own "consciousness" (*conscience collective*) or "soul" (*l'âme collective*), which is not merely the conscience of all individual consciousnesses, but a "common soul of society in its living parts," and a "group condition repeated in the individual." It is a *sui generis* synthesis of particular consciousnesses and as such the highest form of psychic life. The society is not a personal being, but "something special," a "psychic individuality of a new sort." Collective emotions that suddenly burst forth in a crowd, for example, do not merely express what the sentiments of its individual members had in common, but are "something entirely different." Individual consciousnesses echo the collective sentiment because of the "special energy" residing in it. (Durkheim 1926: 97-98; 1966: 8-10, 103; 1937: 605, 633.)

Thus any explanation of a social phenomenon by a psychological

---

15   Peter Beyer (1984: ix-x) notes that anthropology has given rise to a humanistic tradition within which societies are considered to be made up of individuals. In contrast, the German sociologist Niklas Luhmann, who has inspired Beyer's work, sees social systems as consisting of communicative acts. Only the communicative acts in which human beings engage are included in the social system, not the individuals themselves.

phenomenon is false. Collective emotions, tendencies and representations are caused by the conditions in which the group is placed, not by states of individual consciousnesses, which on the contrary are molded by social factors. For this reason, social facts have to be explained by other social facts, not by psychological ones. (Durkheim 1966: 104-106, 110, 113.) Here Durkheim (1966: 102) employs a rather strange argument: social life has to be explained by the nature of society itself, because when an individual dies society alone remains. If Durkheim means that when one individual dies the society remains, this is true but trivial, and does not establish the necessity of rejecting psychological explanations of social behavior. If, on the other hand, he means that even if all its individual members died the society would still go on living, the argument is absurd.[16]

Nevertheless, Durkheim insists that the causes of social facts should be sought in the nature of the "collective individuality," not in the separate individualities from which it emerges. He notes, however, as though anticipating Carl Hempel (1965: 297-330), that to "show how a fact is useful is not to explain how it originated or why it is what it is." A fact can exist without being at all useful. In explaining social phenomena, we have to seek separately the efficient causes which produce them and the functions they fulfill. Yet Durkheim claims that a fact must be useful in order that it may maintain itself. To explain a social fact, we not only have to seek the cause on which it depends; we also have to show its function in the establishment of social order. The function of a social fact should always be sought in its relation to some social end. (Durkheim 1966: 90-91, 95-97, 104, 110-111. See Lukes 1977: 462-477.)

Religion and Society

For Durkheim, religion is an expression of the collective consciousness. The totemic idea of the great god for example derives from the

---

16 I simply do not understand Luhmann's argument when he writes that the concept of the 'collective consciousness' can be made convincing because everyone can distinguish between knowledge that disappears with the knower and knowledge whose meaning and content is co-guaranteed by the consciousness of others. (Luhmann 1982a: 366 n.8.) This distinction is simply the distinction between my knowledge and that of others, and in no way necessitates speculations about a collective consciousness.

"tribal sentiment" (Durkheim 1937: 423). God is "nothing but the figurative expression (*l'expression figurée*) of the society;" and "are not god
and the society one (and the same thing)?" (Durkheim 1937: 323,
295). These quotations express the two premises on which
Durkheim's theory of religion rests: his theory of collective consciousness and the claim that religion expresses this consciousness in a "symbolic" or "metaphorical" way. In religion, the members of a society
"symbolically" worship that very society.

As the society is the basis of human culture, and as our categories of
understanding and feelings of moral obligation derive from the society, religion becomes the source of all cognition and morality. According to Durkheim, "... when a more or less powerful conviction is
shared by the same community of men, it inevitably assumes a religious character." All penal law for example is more or less religious
because its "soul" is respect for a superior force. (Durkheim 1926: 110,
143.) Thus the first systematic representations constructed by human
beings about the world and themselves had a religious origin, and
even philosophy and the sciences were born out of religion.
(Durkheim 1937: 12.)

The whole human capacity conceptually to grasp reality is based on
religion, since for Durkheim such categories of understanding as time,
space, class, quantity, cause, etc. have emerged within religion, and
the "soul" of religion is the idea of society. The categories of understanding do not arise out of experience nor do they exist a priori in the
mind, but are derived from the collective consciousness. Only because
humans are social beings, can they transcend the bounds of immediate experience in their thinking. (Durkheim 1937: 12-28, 598-599.)

Religion, i.e. religious beliefs and rituals, is not an undivided entity,
and religious phenomena are not restricted to organized religions, but
can be found for example in various folk traditions. Religion is best
characterized by the distinction between the sacred and the profane.
This is an absolute distinction, in the sense that the sacred and the
profane have nothing in common, and are distinguished only by the
fact that they are considered to be different. We divide all things into
these basic categories, which are also thought to form two distinct and
irreconcilable worlds. Sacred things are superior to profane ones, and
are protected and isolated by prohibitions. The most sacred thing is
such that it cannot even be touched by a profane thing without conse-
quent punishment. There are also two kinds of sacredness, auspicious
and disastrous, which correspond to collective well-being and malaise

respectively. Religion thus is a "system of beliefs and practices related to things sacred, i.e. things set apart and forbidden, beliefs and practices that unite all those who adhere to them into one single moral community, called a Church." (Durkheim 1937: 49-58, 65; 584-592.)

The stable and permanent systems of ideas and practices that constitute religion can only be based on the psychic force of the collective consciousness. No natural phenomenon can arouse the powerful emotions that characterize religion, the course of nature being too uniform and predictable to awaken in us any sense of wonder. As science has not yet had a chance to teach modesty to primitive man, he thinks that he is in control of things and believes that he can raise the wind, force the rain to fall, stop the sun, etc. It is therefore impossible for religion to have emerged from the theosis of natural phenomena. Moreover, if that were the case, the first natural phenomena to have become divine should have been the most majestic ones, the sun, the sea, etc., and not mere humble plants and small animals. (Durkheim 1937: 118-122.)

This claim is an especially important move in Durkheim's reasoning. What he is really claiming is that nothing is supernatural for primitive man, because he has no concept of the natural either. Not knowing the natural order of things, he considers nothing supernatural. The idea of some mystical dimension of reality only appears very late in the history of religions, and is completely unknown to primitive peoples and to all peoples that have not reached a certain degree of intellectual culture. Such peoples consider it perfectly natural that humans can for example slow down the movement of stars or stop the rains. Ideas of religious forces are not derived from ideas of physical forces but the other way around. (Durkheim 1937: 33-36.)

Although there are also unpredictable natural phenomena, such as for instance an eclipse, there is no reason to think that primitive man would have regarded them as due to some supernatural causation. That would require that he considered them to be impossible from the natural point of view, which cannot be the case since primitive man had no idea of natural order. The idea of order in nature has only been introduced by the sciences. Religion therefore has nothing to do with the uncommon and unknown, but rather with what is stable and orderly. (Durkheim 1937: 36-40.)

Durkheim also has another argument against the idea that religion has sprung from a belief in the existence of some kind of supernatural beings: as such beings do not exist, religion would have to be an illu-

sion and an error, which is impossible to accept if we consider the
ubiquity and persistence of religion in all cultures. No human institution can be based on an error or a lie, and even the most obscure rites
and myths are expressions of some human need or some social view-
point. The theory of animism for example must be erroneous because
it entails that religious beliefs are hallucinatory representations, with
no objective foundation and serving no useful end of any kind. It is
impossible to accept the idea that religion might thus be merely a tissue of illusions. What science could have as its ultimate goal the nullifi-
cation of its very object? How could such a fantasy have so strongly
shaped the human consciousness? If the animist theory were right,
and people came to know it, they would stop believing in what they
would now know to be illusions, which, for Durkheim, obviously is
something rather impossible to imagine. (Durkheim 1937: 3, 97-99,
123-124.)

Yet even Durkheim himself describes religion as "delirious" (*une
espèce de délire*) and as having meaning only in relation to the society,
not to the individual or to physical reality (Durkheim 1937: 124).
Believers talk about gods and spirits and the like, thinking that their
religious experiences are about these beings, although in reality the
whole of religion is about the society. Because of the social pressure
that affects them through mental pathways, believers have created the
idea of some external power on which they are dependent. Without
the teaching of scientific analysis, people feel that they are acted upon
but do not know by whom. Thus the idea of a god or gods is actually
an idea of the society. The society is all that is needed to arouse the
experience of the divine. God and the society are one and the same
thing, and the moral authority of god is the authority of the society.
We obey that authority because our ideas about it are invested with
"immanent psychic energy" that springs from the collective consciousness, intensive religious life always involving psychic excitation. In this
way, the society is "incarnated" in the individual and its idea
expressed in religion. (Durkheim 1937: 294-304, 323-324.)

To solve the obvious problem of the fact that believers do not themselves understand their religion in this way, Durkheim employs the
concept of "symbolism." The idea of god is a symbol, or a metaphor,
a material expression of something else, the society. Religion is a system of ideas by which people metaphorically and symbolically understand the society. (Durkheim 1937: 294, 322-323.)

Religion As Symbolic of the Society – A Critique

Durkheim's theory involves three major problems: the idea of a collective consciousness, the assumed but unexplained symbolic relationship between religion and reality, and the claim that the idea of another, "supernatural," reality is not a necessary element in religion. I first
discuss Durkheim's idea of a collective consciousness, and then consider his claims about the supernatural and about symbolism.

It should be emphasized that although consciousness studies are
now a distinct field of their own, for Durkheim 'consciousness' was
merely an intuitive folk category. Although it is very central to
Durkheim's thought, he does not provide any clear formulation of it,
merely claiming that the collective consciousness is a reality *sui generis*,
without explaining how it emerges from lower levels of order.
Durkheim's only attempt at an explanation is his brief example of collective emotions in a crowd. According to him, they are something
more than just the sum of all individual emotions. Using rather figurative expressions, Durkheim then claims that our mental representations of the society have "immanent psychic energy," and that the
sacred beings we respect appear in our consciousness as representations that are charged with high mental energy due to the emotions
they arouse in us. (Durkheim 1937: 296-304, 322-323, 453; 1966: 8-9.
See Lukes 1977: 462-463, 523-524.)

Here we encounter the same problem as earlier with the concept of
'culture:' 'culture,' 'collective consciousness,' and 'social fact' are
abstract summaries, not actual entities. "The mental," emotions, cognitive functions, and consciousness are all phenomena that ultimately
have a physical basis in the brain and in the rest of the body, whether
we understand the mutual relationship of consciousness and the physical in any of the hitherto proposed scientific ways. By the same token,
they are also phenomena that exist in the *individual*, the fact that they
can also be shared being based on the human ability to communicate.

There are differing views as to the nature of consciousness, as we
saw when dealing with intentionality in Chapter 3. It has been
explained for example as a "software" running on the hardware of the
brain, to which it is connected by "myriad microsettings" (Dennett
1993); as nothing more than so many neural computations, presented
as a unified conscious content in the intralaminar nucleus in the brain
(Churchland 1995); as a natural phenomenon naturally (but not logically) supervening on the brain and based on certain fundamental nat-

ural laws, which, however, are not physical (Chalmers 1997); and as a biological phenomenon based on the brain as the organ of consciousness and as transcending altogether the old Cartesian dichotomy between "body" and "mind" (Searle 1995). This latter, philosophical, view is now strongly supported by empirical neuroscientific research which has yielded a truly empirical theory of consciousness (Damasio 1999) which I accept as my working hypothesis and discuss in Ch. 5 below. Within none of these theories has the possibility of a collective consciousness been raised.

We could, in principle at least, imagine the conscious minds of a group of individuals interacting in such a way that they begin to manifest certain self-organizing properties on the collective level, and also having a feedback effect back on individual brains. To the best of my knowledge, however, nothing like this has so far actually been shown to exist. For anything in the environment to affect an individual, it must first be represented, consciously or unconsciously, by that individual. And, as we have seen, no thoughts or emotions can be directly transferred from one mind to another. Communicating individuals can only produce various kinds of material signs, which serve as cues from which other individuals draw inferences. The relationship between an individual and any group of other individuals is thus much more complex than the relationship between consciousness and the brain – which is complicated enough! –, and Durkheim has done nothing to clarify this relationship. He merely claims that collective emotions and consciousness exist, but has in no way explained the mechanisms whereby they are implemented in individual minds. 'Psychic energy' and 'mental pathways' are merely vague metaphors.

This, of course, casts serious doubts on Durkheim's basic thesis that religion is an expression of the collective consciousness. But there is also another problem. Durkheim describes religion as a "symbolic" or "metaphorical" expression of collective consciousness, and yet provides no explanation of symbolism or metaphor. He seems to have been forced to resort to these concepts only because religious people themselves do not say that by means of their beliefs and practices they express how much they honor the authority of the society. Thus the relationship between religious representations and the society must be a "symbolic" one (see also Boyer 1993a: 4). What it actually means, however, remains unexplained.

It is obvious that Durkheim uses the concept of symbol in another sense than Geertz. It is not the concrete form of an inner state of mind, but rather a substitute for something else, in the sense that for example '$' is the symbol for the American monetary unit. Religious beliefs and rituals are symbolic expressions of the fact that the society has moral authority over its members. The problem with this is well illustrated by Perner's (1993: 51-65) criticism of Piaget's use the concept of 'symbol.' Piaget observed his daughter Jacqueline at the age of 1 year and 3 months when she saw a cloth whose fringed edges vaguely recalled those of her pillow. Jacqueline seized the cloth, sucked her thumb and lay down on her side, laughing and keeping her eyes open but blinking every now and then. Then she cried: "Nono." Should we say that little Jacqueline pretended to sleep on her pillow?

Here 'pretend' can mean either that Jacqueline symbolically substituted the cloth for the pillow, or that she merely acted as if it were the pillow. These are two different things. Acting "as if" merely requires the ability to distinguish between two situations, reality and pretense, and can be done within what Perner calls a "situation theory" (see below p. 212). But for Piaget pretend play means that the cloth was turned into a symbol for the pillow, which is a different thing and requires more sophisticated cognitive operations. It is one thing that a cloth can be merely substituted for a pillow, and quite another that it can be used symbolically to represent the pillow. Such symbolization requires a capacity for metarepresentation, in the sense that one has to be able to represent the representation of a cloth as being a representation of the pillow. (Ibid.)

Now, if religious ideas were either "as-if" ideas or "symbolic" representations of the society, this would mean that religious people either know that their ideas are mere "pretend play," or that they are meant to represent something else. But this is clearly not so (see also Hinde 1999: 44). One who believes for example that god loves the world does not – at least in most cases – think that 'God loves the world' is a symbolic expression of the fact that the society has authority over its members. If beliefs were "symbolic" in this sense, the symbolism would have to be unconscious, and the conscious motives of believers would have to be irrelevant to our understanding of religion. But neither Durkheim nor anyone else has shown what unconscious cognitive mechanisms could make such symbolism possible (see also Lawson and McCauley 1990: 33-43; Boyer 1993a: 23-27). Therefore the whole argument sounds like an *ad hoc* one (cf. Lewis 1988: 106-120).

Substituting 'metaphor' for 'symbol' is no solution either. Saying that all talk for instance about gods is a metaphorical way of speaking of society involves the problem that religious people themselves do not know that they are using such a metaphor, and there is no such thing as an unconscious metaphor (except for "dead metaphors"). Again Durkheim does not specify any mechanism that is responsible for the translation of ideas about society into ideas about gods. Moreover, in light of gathered evidence, it is very doubtful that counter-intuitive beliefs serve to organize human relationships in small hunter-gatherer bands without any bureaucracy and hierarchy of settlement (Diamond 1999: 267-270, 277; see Ch. Five).

It is a different thing that religious beliefs have also social functions in organized societies. That much is obvious. As Durkheim himself observes, however, one cannot reason from function to cause; and, as Guthrie (1993: 5) notes, showing that religion may be useful does not show why it arises and is believed. Carl Hempel (1965: 297-330) tried to show in the 1960's that functional analysis can never establish that p is the cause of Y because from p fulfilling a certain function in relation to Y it does not follow that Y could only be brought about by p. Functional explanations can only show that, for Y to exist, there has to be some such thing that serves the specified function X. In other words, the cause of Y must be some phenomenon {g, h ...r} having the function X. (See also Guthrie 1993: 16-19.)

In Durkheim's case, this means that we cannot reason from the fact that beliefs about counter-intuitive agents often tie a group of people together as a "church" to the conclusion that such beliefs have been invented for the purpose of increasing social cohesion. This would not explain why, of all possible things, it is precisely counter-intuitive agents that have come to serve that purpose. In other words, Durkheim fails after all to explain the persistence of religion, as the same functions could be served by other kinds of beliefs and practices. Or, if the argument is that only a belief in counter-intuitive agents together with the related practices can serve the purpose of establishing social solidarity, then Durkheim fails to explain why and how this is so. What in my theory are the specifically "religious" features of religion, are quite inconsequential in his theory.

This brings us to another problem, namely Durkheim's dismissal of ideas about "gods" and "transcendence." As we have seen, his main argument was that primitive religions supposedly could not contain any ideas about another reality because primitive man did not make any distinction between the natural and the non-natural. My claim is the contrary: such beliefs are a necessary (but not sufficient) defining characteristic of religion, and they can persist without always being useful, the reason for their persistence being that they are memorable and attention-demanding and therefore easily distributed. This view is based on Boyer and Ramble's (in press) and Barrett and Nyhof's (2001) empirical evidence, and it avoids the logical problem inherent in functionalism: every social phenomenon must serve some positive function in order to survive, and if it does not survive it could not have had any useful function. In other words, functional explanations are immune to all counter-evidence, and thus cannot be scientific. (See Sandbacka 1987: 101-125; Boyer 1987: 56; Guthrie 1993: 18-19.)

In the cognitive view, it is quite natural for beliefs about gods to survive even without any specific function. They survive because they are possible and have "attention-grabbing potential" (Boyer 1999: 58), and people therefore feel obliged do something with them in order to prevent a chaos in consciousness. This view naturally entails that people have had ideas about counter-intuitive agents for about as long as they have had their other higher cognitive capacities in place (see Mithen 1998: 198-202; Guthrie 1980: 182). Durkheim is naturally right in saying that the ideas of god(s) and of the transcendent as distinguished from the natural *in a scientific sense* are not universal. But to claim that primitive man had no idea whatsoever of a natural order of things, and that he really believed himself to be capable of stopping the sun and getting the rains to fall, etc. is absurd. Early humans would not have survived at all had they not been capable of knowing what is possible and what is impossible, what is dangerous and what is not. They had to know for example that they had to eat, that they could not leap safely from a high mountain, that some animals were dangerous to them, etc. Everything that countered these intuitive beliefs was exceptional and attention-demanding.

Thus, from the cognitive point of view, Durkheim is just plain wrong in saying that for primitive man everything was natural, that the idea of the supernatural only appears very late in the history of religion, and that therefore the idea of supernatural powers is not relevant to religion, the idea of physical forces being derived from religion and not the other way around (Durkheim 1937: 33-40). What is natural and what is not is determined by biologically based intuitive ontologies, and everything that is not in accord with these ontologies is counter-intuitive and unnatural. This, then, is the starting-point for religious beliefs: counter-intuitive representations are taken as evidence for the fact that an exhaustive description of reality cannot be based merely on intuitive knowledge and common sense. This means that for the believer there are agents and forces acting upon us that cannot be fully understood, explained or controlled (cf. Guthrie 1993).

On a closer reading, it is apparent that Durkheim himself could not really eliminate counter-intuitive agents in his theory of religion. He says that, after all, explaining religion means explaining the "quasi-divine principle" that dominates totemism. The totem is a material symbol of the "totemic principle," or "god," and by the same token of the society. (Durkheim 1937: 293-295.) The idea of the soul, in turn, is the idea of the totemic principle within individuals, a tiny bit of the divine in us (Durkheim 1937: 343, 366-386). What exactly is the difference between a quasi-divine agent and divinity in its "precise and strict" sense (Durkheim 1937: 40) is not explained.

According to Durkheim (1937: 298-299, 322-323), however, the ideas of efficient moral powers external to the individual are merely personifications of social pressure, whose true nature and mechanisms people do not understand as long as they are ignorant about science. They know that they are being acted upon but do not know by what, and therefore have to themselves invent the idea of these powers. But society is clearly not the only thing, and possibly not even the one most difficult to understand, that determines our existence. As Guthrie's (1993) perceptual schema theory implies, the perceptual ambiguity of the *natural* environment has caused humans to postulate the existence of all kinds of invisible intentional agents. As I see it, quite irrespective of whether or not all such ideas have had survival value for the species, the *capacity* for agent detection has been an evolutionary advantage. Postulating the existence of counter-intuitive agents may merely be parasitic on this ability and the ability to form cross-domain representations. (See Pyysiäinen 2001b.) This in turn means that, besides the perceived natural environment, the conceptual reality constructed by humans is also always partly ambiguous and contains slots that people are tempted to fill by representations of counter-intuitive agents (see Pyysiäinen 1999b). (See Beyer 1984: xxxv.)

But for such representations to affect people's behavior, they must be the object of serious belief. It is important to realize that it is not necessary for them to be true, only for them to be considered to be true. This is a distinction Durkheim failed to make, in insisting that an illusion could not persist. Yet he also clearly realized that religious representations must be believed (and not just be objectively true) in order for them to be able to create solidarity among believers. He is absolutely right in writing that mythological beings can only affect human minds if people believe in them, and that such beliefs only can function if they are shared by a group (Durkheim 1937: 607). He admits that religion is not merely a system of signs, but also a collection of the means whereby the specific attitude of belief is created. Agreeing with William James that religious beliefs are based on a specific experience, and that it is the task of rituals to create and sustain such mental states, Durkheim admits that religious representations can only do their job if people firmly believe in them. (Durkheim 1937: 13, 596, 607.)

This is also reflected in Durkheim's conviction that if animism were true and people came to know this, they would abandon their religious beliefs. But ironically this also applies to Durkheim's own theory: if shown that religion is actually about society, people turn from religion to science as the "more perfect from of religion" (Durkheim 1937: 613, 625). Durkheim does not explain, however, why people would abandon their beliefs if they were shown to be not literally true, if the only important thing in them were their social function. If Durkheim is right about the importance of literal belief in religion, he cannot be right about the unimportance of belief in counter-intuitive agents in religion.

His argument is problematic for at least two reasons. First, although there was still lots of religion around in the world in Durkheim's time, the history of religions also knows many gods that were no longer believed in at the beginning of the 20th century. Thus, although religion in general still persists, many individual beliefs have died out. Second, there actually are many individual people who have ceased to believe in the god(s) in whom they used to believe, even if that particular religion as such is not dead. People who can no longer believe that gods and demons exist must either in practice abandon their traditional religion or attempt to find new interpretations for it (see Lawson and McCauley 1990: 159; Hinde 1999: 36). In the west, the first alternative is known as "secularization" and the second as "liberal theology."

That religion in general has persisted is due to two reasons. First, religious representations are evocative (Sperber 1996: 73), are characterized by counter-intuitive claims, complex concepts with no one clear interpretation, and involve inferential gaps, which means that people are often uncertain about the propositions that can be directly derived from religious statements they regard as being true (Boyer 1994: 42-49). It is therefore always possible to find radically new interpretations for religious beliefs which are challenged by some piece of evidence. But when people no longer can believe in the real existence of counter-intuitive beings, religion loses its power.

Second, religion may persist because people do not know of the scientific arguments against its truth, because they cannot understand those arguments, or simply because they prefer to believe the priest, guru or shaman rather than the scientist. Why bother with complicated metaphysical arguments when it is often much more convenient and helpful to keep one's religious beliefs? In other words, there is one point that Durkheim did not take into account: it does not directly follow from the truth of a scientific theory that all people will find that theory easy to accept. Even if animism were true, believers would not immediately recognize and accept this and abandon their religious beliefs. There is after all a host of non-religious illusions that persist merely because they can be known to be illusions only by a careful study of extremely counter-intuitive scientific arguments (see Wolpert 1994).

In the final section of this chapter, I briefly outline ways in which some of Durkheim's basic ideas can be embedded within a cognitive theory about religion.

Religion and Society Reconsidered

If we accept the existence of representations about counter-intuitive agents as an essential part of religion, and if we likewise do not deny the relevance of psychology in explaining religious phenomena, the coercive power of what Durkheim calls collective representations can be explained within a coherent scheme. There is no way of explaining the "sacred" status of certain representations without an explanation of why they have such a powerful effect on people. This entails explaining both the special nature of these representations as such, i.e. their counter-intuitiveness, and their psychological effects on people. Here I merely offer some brief comments on the social aspect of these effects, the psychology of emotion in religious belief being the subject of the next chapter.

My claims are of course not completely novel. That religion includes "fabulous," "mythical," or "supernatural" representations and a collective respectful attitude toward them has been part of many accounts. C. Scott Littleton (1965) for example has presented a scheme for the classification of folk narratives which is based on two continua: a factual – fabulous continuum and a secular – sacred continuum. Here factuality means that a narrative is "based upon objectively determinable facts or scientifically acceptable hypotheses," and sacredness means that a narrative "expresses ideas that are central to the magico-religious beliefs and ideology." Thus myths are "extremely sacred and patently fabulous," while history is both factual and secular. Folk tales, for their part, are fabulous but secular; and sacred histories are sacred but factual. Legends, or sagas, are in the middle of both continua.

Within the sociology of religion, two contrasting views have been held: that the supernatural is a subset within the set of sacred things (e.g. Hammond 1986), and that the sacred is a subset of the set of supernatural things (e.g. Berger and Kellner 1978) (see Raiskila 1995). What is problematic here is that both the concept of the 'supernatural' and that of the 'sacred' have been used mostly as intuitive folk categories, and their mutual relationship has therefore been difficult to establish.

If, however, we replace 'supernatural' by 'counter-intuitive,' Vesa Raiskila's (1995) proposed solution that in religion the sacred and the supernatural overlap is easy to accept as being right to the point. There are many kinds of counter-intuitive representations, some of which are religious, some fictional, some related to mental disturbance, and some even scientific (see Chapter Seven.) We might thus claim that religious counter-intuitive representations and behaviors are differentiated from the rest by the fact that they are considered to be sacred. It seems to me, however, that the only theories about the notion of the 'sacred' that purport to meet scientific standards are those put forward by Paden (1992; 1996; 1999) and by Anttonen (1996; 2000). I myself shall adopt a simpler solution in the concluding chapter of this book, and attempt to differentiate religious counter-intuitiveness from other types of counter-intuitiveness by the criteria of serious belief, agent-representation, and socially shared ways of using religion in "life management." Here I shall have to take these arguments for granted for a while, and proceed to assess some of Durkheim's ideas in this light.

We may assume that when people believe that religious counter-intuitive representations testify to the existence of a hidden and mysterious, counter-intuitive, dimension of reality, they naturally have to take all possible precautions against the possibility that these counter-intuitive agents and forces might be harmful. Moreover, they will also try to get onto as friendly terms with these agents and forces as possible, and to get these forces to act for their benefit. But as religious counter-intuitive ideas are the product solely of human reasoning powers, not of empirical observations, their content is derived from human conceptual resources alone (which are of course not independent from observations that people have made in natural contexts). Counter-intuitive agents themselves cannot be observed. It is therefore only natural that counter-intuitive agents and forces resemble those natural agents and forces that are known to the particular group of people in question from natural contexts.

This, however, is not to say that in gods people actually worship their own society. Believers are quite clear about the fact that there are counter-intuitive agents that live in another world, which may to some extent resemble the society of humans. But this similarity is not identity. Therefore beliefs about counter-intuitive agents and forces are the primary data of the scholar. It is only by unduly confusing data and theory that the scholar can insist that the data are actually constituted by "the social" and not by beliefs about counter-intuitive agents. Without any first hand empirical evidence, such a move can only result in theoretical speculation (Durkheim's way of using studies of totemism as evidence is notoriously sloppy [see Lukes 1977: 477-482, 524-529; Giddens 1978: 101-102; Pals 1996: 116-117]).

It is of course not possible within the present confines to develop any new kind of sociology of religion. I must be content merely to point for example to the work of Niklas Luhmann (1984) and of Peter Beyer (1984; 1994), in which religion is treated as communication about a supposed other reality that has interesting sociological effects. The main point I want to make here is that the social effects of religion would not be possible in the absence of a belief in agents that have counter-intuitive capacities to bless, condemn, revenge, save, protect, etc.

What seems to be happening, however, is that, although some religious movements are gaining increasing support in the modern West, at the same time "secularization" and "liberal theology" are advancing as well, as people become more and more educated (see Wiebe 1991). It is in this respect remarkable that Durkheim based his theory of religion on materials from a primitive society with mechanical solidarity, yet implying that the theory was just as applicable to societies with organic solidarity, even though two completely different kinds of social structure are involved. As he himself wrote, it is the division of labor that in the modern society has assumed the role that was formerly filled by the common conscience (Durkheim 1926: 148; see Horton 1993: 75). If religion is based on the common conscience, what, then, is the "division of labor" between religion and division of labor in creating solidarity in a complex society? Division of labor clearly implies a functional differentiation of the society (see Luhmann 1982c) in which religion no longer is the sole provider of social cohesion. (See also Lukes 1977: 519; Giddens 1878: 99-104.)

This is at the heart of Luhmann's and Beyer's sociological theories of religion. For Luhmann, society consists of various subsystems that evolve in part by reacting to their environment, i.e. to other subsystems. In such a functionally differentiated society, religion is just one functional subsystem among others, each of which has its own rationality. Economics and science for example having their own standards of rationality, religion can no longer be the basis of all rationality. Therefore within religion the existence of other subsystems is experienced as a problematic denial of religion. Luhmann describes the relation of religion to other subsystems in a modern society by the Greek word *diakonia* ('service'). It signifies all those services that, under the umbrella of "religion," are meant to respond to problems engendered but not solved in other subsystems of society. As long as religion dominated the society, social life was understood as a striving for a perfection exemplified by the concept of 'god.' But now that religion is merely one subsystem among others, the economy is no longer conceived of as a subsystem, and the whole society has become "economicized." And within economics there is no ideal of perfection, only endless open-ended development. Under these circumstances, the idea of divine revelation can no longer determine the relationship of religion to other subsystems, and theology is in danger of suffocating in an endless process of self-reflection. (Luhmann 1984; 1982b: 222; Beyer 1984.)

Consequently god as a counter-intuitive agent tends to become something highly abstract, to the extent that people merely recognize that "there must be something greater behind this all" (see Pyysiäinen 1998: 182; 1999b). This, however, is a question on which more empirical research is needed. In such research, the sociological and cognitive perspectives should be combined in order to achieve a proper theory to be properly tested. An appropriate subject for research, for instance, would be people's ideas about the proper domains of application of various kinds of counter-intuitive concepts.

Thus religion is a special way of using counter-intuitive ideas, both individually and socially. Durkheim was by and large right about the social uses of religion and of the importance of belief as a psychological attitude that emerges in social practice, but he could not correctly account for the historical and psychological origins of religion, or explain the psychological mechanisms involved in religious belief. In the next chapter, I attempt to develop psychological arguments for the origins of religious ideas and for the nature of religious belief. These arguments can help us to understand the specific "moods" or states of consciousness that supposedly dominate religious rituals, helping to maintain religious belief.

Summary

Durkheim's seminal work has influenced various attempts at explaining religion as essentially an expression of "collective consciousness" and of social categories. An analysis of Durkheim's basic claims shows that this idea is a rather insufficient account of religion; yet it contains relevant insights. Religion cannot be understood as merely a symbolic expression of the fact that members of a society feel this society to have moral authority over them. Yet an examination of this view can contribute to solving the problem of why only some counter-intuitive ideas are regarded as religious.

The first problem in Durkheim's account is that the concept of 'collective consciousness' is totally unspecified. Durkheim does not explain what it is and how it emerges from individual consciousnesses. Nor is there any compelling evidence for the existence of any such entity.

Secondly, the claim that religious representations are a "symbolic" expression of the society is problematic because Durkheim does not explain what he means by "symbolic." It could in principle mean that believers use religious representations pretending that they are representations of the society, or that they use them as "symbolic" substitutes for the idea of the society. This latter case involves a metarepresentation of religious representations as being a representation of the society. The first alternative is out of the question, as believers do not regard their religious beliefs as mere make-belief play. The second alternative is also implausible; Durkheim has not shown by what mechanism the idea of the society is translated into ideas of gods etc. As believers do not understand their religious ideas in this way the mechanism would have to be an unconscious one, but no evidence for the existence of such a mechanism is presented.

Third, Durkheim's claim that our mental representations of the authority of the society contain "immanent psychic energy" and therefore evoke emotions in us needs to be specified. 'Psychic energy' is a mere metaphor; energy is a form of existence of matter ($E=mc^2$), and there can thus be no "psychic" energy. However, it is true that religious representations can evoke strong emotions in us. In order to understand why and how, we must study human psychology and its neural basis (which I discuss in the next chapter); a consideration of "social facts" is not enough.

Fourth, Durkheim's denial of the existence of the supernatural in all but more advanced forms of religion is erroneous and prevents us from seeing why religious representations evoke emotions. Substituting 'counter-intuitive' for 'supernatural,' we are in a position to argue that, beginning from the Pleistocene hunter-gatherers, all healthy human beings have had intuitive expectations of how entities normally behave, and that the related ability to form counter-intuitive representations is at least several tens of thousands of years old. Counter-intuitive representations thus belong to all known religious traditions. In the next chapter I argue that it is precisely counter-intuitiveness that evokes emotions in us.

Fifth, although Durkheim says that to "show how a fact is useful is not to explain how it originated or why it is what it is," he nevertheless seems to think that his theory also explains how and why religion has originated. To the extent that it is only a theory of the ways in which religion is useful, however, it can be made compatible with cognitive theories about religion. If we consider that counter-intuitive representations have emerged as a by-product of a cognitively fluid mind, and that not all counter-intuitive representations can be considered religious, Durkheim's theory provides a useful perspective in which to look at the question of what makes counter-intuitiveness religious. The central issues here are serious belief and the way representations are used in social life. I return briefly to this in Chapter Seven.

CHAPTER FIVE

RELIGIOUS BELIEF, EXPERIENCE, AND RITUAL

We have now seen how central a position the idea of ritual occupies in the work of Geertz and Durkheim, as the special context in which religious beliefs are either generated or affirmed. Despite his antipsychologism, Durkheim could not but conclude that religious beliefs are based on specific experiences created in rituals. Likewise the other antipsychologist, Geertz, concluded that it was in ritual that the conviction that religious conceptions are veridical was somehow generated. It is in ritual that the fusion of ethos and worldview takes place, shaping "the spiritual consciousness of a people" (Geertz 1973: 113). The acceptance of religious authority "flows from the enactment of the ritual itself" (Geertz 1973: 118), a ritual inducing a set of moods and motivations (an ethos) and defining a worldview by means of a single set of symbols. Religious belief is a pale, remembered reflection of what has been experienced in ritual.

Thus Durkheim and Geertz have to postulate some kind of religious experience to fill a gap in their accounts of religion: rituals supposedly create an emotional reaction in participants, such that all of a sudden all kinds of odd beliefs begin to seem realistic to them. Roy Rappaport (1999: 24, 378) has likewise argued that the Holy and its elements are generated in and integrated by ritual. How exactly this happens is not explained by Durkheim or Geertz, who leave the assumed process shrouded in mystery. Likewise Rappaport's (1999: 431) "cybernetics of the holy" lacks an indication of the mechanism through which this cybernetics works.

Here Boyer's cognitive approach is of no help either. Although he explains in detail how religious concepts are acquired and mentally represented, he has so far paid little attention to religious truth claims and the phenomenon of religious belief and experience (but cf. Boyer in press Ch. 9). Boyer (1994b: xi) writes: "I certainly have no model or hypothesis as regards the religious 'experience,' the various subjective, particularly emotional, states associated with religious practice, though it is a fascinating and barely understood domain." This neglect of emotion and experience is also found in Sperber's (1995; 1994; 1996) work. The cognitivist, or functionalist, account of the nature of the human mind focuses on symbolic thought processes alone, leaving little room for emotions as a necessary concomitant of all sane cognition (Damasio 1996). (Pyysiäinen 2001b.)

It is my purpose here to try to bridge the gap between the Boyerian account of religious thought and recent neuroscientific work on the nature of emotions and consciousness. We have already seen how cognitive considerations can help us to correct earlier views of the nature of religious concepts and their acquisition and transmission. It is now time to revisit that favorite old topic of many scholars of religion, "religious," or "mystical" experience, and to see how the advancement of neuroscience can correct that picture. In what follows I first discuss two more recent versions of the argument that it is in ritual that religious experiences are cultivated, and then try to put forward a more precise view of what emotions actually are. Finally, I present a neuroscientific explanation of religious and mystical experience and of their role in religion at large.

Ritual and Emotion

'Religious experience' and 'mysticism' are terms that scholars of religion often use but rarely explain (Pyysiäinen 2001b). It is not only 'religiousness' and 'mysticism' that are vague concepts, but also 'experience.' The common sense view is that if something is an experience, then it is not just a cold thought but something more. It is personal, emotional, and vivid, and it usually has a strong impact on the subject in question. Although this may be to the point, it is difficult to construct a scientific theory of religious experience on this basis alone. Such a theory might be possible by taking as a starting-point Whitehouse's (2000) recent theory of an "imagistic mode" of religion, although here I can only provide a preliminary outline of the implications of Whitehouse's theory for our understanding of religious experience. My main interest here is in emotions as an important characteristic of religious experience.

The basic implication of Whitehouse's theory is that religious experience may not be determined primarily by emotions but by the way something is cognitively encoded. As I understand the concept, an 'experience' is a personally important event in whose cognitive encoding episodic memories have primacy over the doctrinal schemes available in a particular tradition. It is therefore encoded in episodic, not semantic, memory. In such case, one vividly remembers a particular episode with all its details, whereas non-experiential knowledge is encoded in the form of general schemata ("then and there I accepted Jesus as my personal redeemer" vs. "[According to the Church] Jesus is our redeemer.") (Whitehouse 2000.)

In the imagistic mode of religion strong emotions are an important characteristic of religious experience, although they may also figure in its opposite, the doctrinal mode (see below). What ultimately distinguishes the two modes is the form of codification, i.e. whether it is the semantic or episodic memory that is activated. It is interesting that, just as Durkheim and Geertz insisted that religious belief was created in rituals, so also Whitehouse has constructed his theory of the two modes by focusing on how religious representations are transmitted in rituals. Rituals that are often repeated do not involve high emotional arousal of the subjects; it is the sheer repetitive sermonizing that guarantees a faithful transmission of the doctrine. Rarely repeated rituals, however, employ emotional shocks instead of repetition: the events in question are vividly recalled but only as isolated personal memories. There is no general schema to combine the memories into a doctrine.

The two modes are to be understood as "basins of attraction," and thus as not forming a strict dichotomy. Rituals are geared towards either doctrinal or imagistic effects (otherwise they die out due to a tedium effect), but a mixture of typical characteristics is also possible. It is thus quite possible for a person to undergo a strong emotional experience, and for the experience to be then subjected to doctrinal interpretation. In such case, the episodic memories of the experience may be gradually overwritten by doctrinal interpretations; one finally ends up with a "theologically correct" (Barrett 1999), schematized memory of what was experienced. But it is also equally possible for some doctrinal formulation to be reinterpreted in the light of some strong personal experience; doctrine is thus transformed into personal episodic memories.

In the following, I approach the problem of emotion in religious experience by first considering 'ritual' as a concept in comparative religion; I then compare Whitehouse's and McCauley's slightly different theories of ritual and emotion. In the later sections, I develop a concept of religious experience that is based on neuroscientific theories of emotion and that is applicable both within and outside ritual contexts.

Theories of ritual

'Ritual' is almost as vague a concept as 'religion.' It is used in a variety of senses, and religious and other types of rituals are sometimes differentiated and sometimes not. In everyday parlance, 'ritual' refers to all kinds of repeated and formalized, stylized, actions. This is typical of ritual from the scientific point of view as well. (Zuesse 1987; Hinde 1999: 109). Rappaport (1999: 24, 33-36) for example defines ritual as "the performance of more or less invariant sequences of formal acts and utterances not entirely encoded by the performers." In scholarly studies, rituals have been seen as acts of communion, as an early attempt at technology, as a form of collective representations, as an example of repression, as a social function affirming the status quo, and as an 'anti-structure' in a structured society (Lawson and McCauley 1990: 45). Typically the emphasis has not been on ritual as kind of action, anthropologists having been more interested in other kinds of functions and meanings that rituals have been thought to reveal (Houseman and Severi 1998: 165). Rappaport's (1999: 27-32) theory is an exception; he defines ritual neither through its contents nor through its function, but with reference to its form. Meanings and effects only follow from ritual's universal form.

As my purpose here is merely to examine the role of emotions in religious rituals, I shall not discuss earlier theories of rituals in much detail, restricting myself merely to a few comments (see Lawson and McCauley 1990: 12-14, 32-60; Bell 1997; Houseman and Severi 1998: 165-202; Rappaport 1999: 23-58). In comparative religion, after the pioneering works of Müller, Tylor, Frazer, Robertson Smith and Durkheim, the most influential interpretations of ritual have been those of Arnold van Gennep and his follower Victor Turner. Van Gennep's famous *Les rites de passage* was published before Durkheim's *Les formes élémentaires*, in 1909, but it became influential only after it was translated into English in 1960. Meanwhile, Durkheim's legacy had continued in British social anthropology in (structural) functionalism, and rituals were viewed in the light of their social (Radcliffe-Brown) or bio-psychological (Malinowski) functions (Pals 1996: 113; Bell 1997: 27-28). From such a functionalist point of view, van Gennep's failure was thought to be that he was not a proper functionalist; he did not focus on any particular society, and he "rushed into global generalizations" (see Anttonen 1992: 16-17; Honko 1979: 371-372; 383).

But Van Gennep's (1977) point was neither to provide an exhaustive description of the rituals of any particular society nor to claim the existence of a universal pattern, but rather to provide a conceptual scheme within which to analyze cross-culturally recurrent processes. He tried to show that shifts in time, space and social position have always been ritualized, using the imagery of spatial movement as an analogue. The inherent logic of these shifts is best described by the threefold structure of separation, marginality and aggregation. (See Anttonen 1992: 15, 18-20; Houseman and Severi 1998: 168-170).

Later, Turner (1969; 1981) developed van Gennep's ideas into an analytical tool for showing how symbolic structures serve both to maintain social equilibrium and to introduce novelties. Turner paid special attention to Van Gennep's concept of *marge*, on the basis of which he developed the notion of 'liminality' (and 'liminoid' in modern societies). Liminality is a state between two social positions, after the one has been given up and the other has not yet been attained; a position in which the subject is separated from what is familiar and habitual. Those who are undergoing this transition form a "communitas" with its own (anti)structure, in contrast to the normal structure of the society, a state where people are receptive for instance to religious experiences. By thus temporarily questioning the social structure, rituals serve ultimately to affirm it. Of the different types of ritual proposed, Turner (1981: 7-10, 19) recognizes only two, life-crisis rituals and rituals of affliction, which he sees as "prescribed formal behavior for occasions not given over to technological routine, having reference to beliefs in mystical beings or powers." (See Lawson and McCauley 1990: 49, 145-146; Bell 1997: 39-46, 93; Houseman and Severi 1998: 170-172.)

The classification of rites according to their functions (see Jackson 1979) is also central in the work of Lauri Honko (1979: 373-378). Honko divides rites into three categories: rites of passage, calendrical rites, and crisis rites. Rites of passage are organized by the society to move individuals from one status to another. They are non-recurrent from the individual's point of view, i.e. one undergoes a given rite of passage only once, and they are always anticipated. Calendrical rites are group-oriented cyclical rites located at the turning points of the socio-economic seasons. They are also recurrent and anticipated. Crisis rites, finally, are occasional rituals, organized by an individual or a group at unexpected times of crisis. Honko classifies them as non-recurrent and non-anticipated, since the catastrophes and misfortunes due to which they are organized are experienced as unique events, and since such catastrophes usually cannot be anticipated.

It is important to realize that this classification is not based on types of ritual activity or on a specific behavioral *mode*, but on specific behavioral *contexts*, i.e. on the purposes for which rituals are used. There seems, however, to be a host of such behavioral contexts, which do not necessarily have anything in common except for the ritual mode of behavior which is used. (See Boyer 1994b: 188-191.)

It should also be emphasized that Honko's division is to be seen as an analytical tool; it does not imply that every rite must fall neatly into just one of the three categories. Rites of passage, for example, may in some instances have a calendrical nature (e.g. the habit of baptizing infants on Easter Sunday), and they are recurrent from the point of view of the group, although not of the individual. Some recurrent calendrical rites, on the other hand, may not be recurrent from the individual's point of view if they are performed rarely enough. Crisis rites are non-recurrent and non-anticipated only if we regard each catastrophe and misfortune as unique and emphasize the point that people usually cannot foretell the precise occurrence of a famine or flood. On the other hand, as Anthony Jackson (1979: 417) points out, crisis rites are anticipated in the sense that people have developed such rituals precisely because they know that *sometimes* such catastrophes may take place, just as they know (although usually with much more certainty) that sometimes a given rite of passage will be needed. There is also no obstacle to arranging a particular crisis rite more than once, although the recurrence does not usually take place on any regular basis.

Neither symbolist, structuralist nor intellectualist theories of religion alone offer a satisfactory starting point for the scientific study of rituals, as Lawson and McCauley (1990) argue. Symbolist interpretations (e.g. Turner) have been especially popular in history of religions, psychology, theology and the social sciences (see Lawson and McCauley 1990: 46-50), and I have already discussed their inherent problems in connection with Geertz and Durkheim. I might add the work of Edmund Leach (1979), who has offered a theory of rituals as a form of symbolic communication which can be understood in the light of theories of language as communication. Leach speaks of the similarity between the grammatical rules of a language and the grammatical rules of symbolic-cultural systems (Leach 1979: 10), but has not in any way tried to describe what those rules might be. (Lawson and McCauley 1990: 54-55.)

As to structuralism: what is missing for example in the analyses of Lévi-Strauss (e.g. 1979) is a unified theory and an indication of the specific underlying principles that might order structural analyses. Without these, an analysis may be insightful but it is purely intuitive; it does not achieve the systematic unity that should characterize a true theoretical explanation, and it lacks generality (see also Sperber 1995: 51-84). Lévi-Strauss does not offer a unified theory of his structural principles, nor does he describe the criteria for their application with sufficient specificity. Thus structuralism fails to specify the constraints on the possible forms of symbolic materials, and the empirical testing of structuralist suggestions is not possible. (Lawson and McCauley 1990: 41-43, 173-174; Boyer 1993a: 16-17.)

Intellectualists, such as Horton (1993), see ritual as proto-technology, just as religion in general is an attempt at explaining and controlling reality theoretically, albeit in a naïve fashion. But although it is true that people seem to use religious beliefs to explain things, this cannot be their real *raison d'être*, since people also seem to hold religious beliefs to be true quite irrespective of how things in the world turn out to be. Lawson and McCauley, however, share with the intellectualists the view that religious systems embody cognitive models which *seem* to explain reality, although their applicability does not depend on their reference to the world. (Lawson and McCauley 1990: 33-37, 51, 156-157; Boyer 1993a: 15-16; Pyysiäinen 1996a: 57-59.)

Finally, according to Frits Staal (1989), rituals do not carry any meanings but form a purely formal system, with no interpretation or semantics. Rituals have a syntax that is independent of semantics and has a transformational-generative structure. The syntactic forms of ritual and natural language are isomorphic. However, Staal neither specifies the smallest units of ritual acts nor explains how they could in principle be recognized. His denial of the semantic dimension of rituals stems from his view that rituals do not refer to anything outside of themselves, which Staal takes to entail that rituals have no meaning whatsoever. Instead, rituals have exactly the same biological basis as the ritualized behaviors of animals: they are compulsive patterned behavior anchored in some biological function. In the same vein, language too is a distant descendant of animal rituals. Thus rituals should be clearly distinguished from religion, orthopraxy having nothing to do with orthodoxy. Yet, as Lawson and McCauley point out, many linguists regard language as biologically based and yet are not at all inclined to deny the semantic dimension of language (e.g. Pinker 1994). (Lawson and McCauley 1990: 56-59, 166-169.) In the following, my own cognitive theory of emotions in rituals will be related to those put forward by Lawson and McCauley (1990; McCauley 2001) and by Boyer (1994b: 185-223), although I do not restrict the role of emotions to rituals alone.

Ritual form and emotions

The question of why some rituals are accompanied by strong emotions while others are not is currently explained by two competing hypotheses: the hypothesis of ritual frequency (Whitehouse 1992; 1995: 193-221; 2000) and the hypothesis of ritual form (Lawson and McCauley 1990; McCauley 2001). According to Whitehouse (1992; 1995; 2000), it is the frequency of performance that determines how much sensory pageantry and emotional excitement a ritual involves. Rarely performed rituals have to appeal to the emotions to ensure that the participants will be able to remember the details of the ritual, while frequently performed rituals need not involve such emotional coloring, as the sheer frequency of performance guarantees that the details are remembered. This assumption is perfectly in line with what we know about the psychology of memory.

To give an example: the Pomio Kivung and its splinter group, studied by Whitehouse in East New Britain in Papua New Guinea, had two strategies for preserving their ideology unchanged, and for sustaining unity – on the one hand frequent mechanical repetition of the doctrine, on the other (in the splinter group) occasional emotional outbursts. These techniques correspond to two modes of religiosity: a doctrinal mode, based on verbal language and logical coherence, and an imagistic mode, based on non-verbal imagery and receiving its persuasiveness from emotional and sensual stimulation. (Whitehouse 1995: 174, 183-184, 191-221. Cf. Rubin 1997; Pyysiäinen 1999a).

The mainstream institutions of the Pomio Kivung were not sufficient to account for the enduring popularity of the movement. On the contrary, the main stimulus for renewed commitment came from temporary attempts to break away and perform isolated climactic rituals to produce the millennium. In these rituals, compelling and moving images of eschatological themes were cultivated in an emotional atmosphere of fear and mystery. Such emotional outbursts enriched and deepened people's experience of orthodox practice and created enduring solidarity. The religious experiences of the participants produced "revelations," which were capable of being sustained long after the rituals had ceased. (Whitehouse 1995: 150-152, 174-185.)

Although Whitehouse has written for example that the participants in repetitive rituals have an "explicit goal to create a single, unified system of ideas," and that therefore every detail of the religion is "drummed home" to the community at large (Whitehouse 1992: 785), he insists that these are unintended consequences of rituals, established through selectional processes, and do not necessitate any functionalist interpretation. (Whitehouse 1995: 4, 205.) One way of putting the matter is to say that, of all infrequently performed rituals, those involving emotional stimulation are – *ceteris paribus* – more likely to survive, whether or not the people in question are aware of the reason for this.

McCauley (2001), however, finds the frequency hypothesis as insufficient as an explanation of what kinds of rituals are likely to involve emotional stimulation. The hypothesis does not explain why some rituals are performed only infrequently; furthermore, there are rarely performed rituals, such as the Hindu *agnicayana*, which do not involve emotional stimulation. Yet McCauley agrees with Whitehouse that emotional provocation makes a ritual more memorable than it would be otherwise, and that people find rituals with sensory pageantry emotionally provocative. His own ritual form hypothesis is based on the theory of rituals of Lawson and McCauley (1990).

McCauley (2001) claims that emotional provocation only belongs to such rituals in which the active agents are "culturally postulated superhuman agents" (CPS agents), and which therefore are not repeated for any one individual. That only gods can do something once and for all, is based on Lawson and McCauley's (1990) idea that CPS agents put a stop to an otherwise endless regression of rituals; this is in my opinion a sound principle, just as it is sound to claim that the presence of CPS agents tends to provoke strong emotions. I, however, would rather speak of counter-intuitive agents. Moreover, the idea of *cultural* postulation needs to be critically assessed in the light of Sperber and Wilson's and Boyer's views of cultural transmission as an inferential process. The reasons why counter-intuitive agents provoke strong emotions also has to be more clearly explained. In the following I first present the basic idea of Lawson and McCauley's ritual theory, and then try to show how the concept of counter-intuitiveness can help us to explain why the supposed direct intervention of a CPS agent is emotionprovoking.

Lawson and McCauley (1990: 146-155) give Lévi-Strauss credit for having realized that the only meaning one can find in mythologies is

the meaning that lies in the way a myth's various elements are combined, not in the isolated elements themselves. In other words, some
symbolic-cultural systems may be completely self-referential. Likewise, Sperber (in his early work, 1995) and Staal seem to be aware of
this, but they draw the wrong conclusion: that this implies that religious and/or ritual systems have no meaning at all. This view cannot
be sustained unless one is willing to extend this conclusion to natural
language as well; it too requires holistic semantic analysis, yet is not
usually thought to be meaningless. Therefore symbolic-cultural systems too should be considered to have meaning arising out of some
sort of collective self-reference. Religious conceptual schemes can
order a wide range of human experience which may otherwise be
alien, chaotic, or incomprehensible. This is precisely because religious
representations have no clear reference outside their own discursive
context, and therefore can be applied to explain any conceivable state
of affairs.

Otherwise Lawson and McCauley agree with Sperber's (1995) criticism of the "cryptological" view of symbolism, which I have discussed
in Chapter 3. They too want to avoid suggesting an isomorphism or
complete analogy between natural language and ritual. They also hes-
itate to claim that there are substantial biological constraints on religious ritual systems, in the manner of Sperber's (1995; 1994) innate
symbolic mechanism. The real point is to show that Chomsky's com-
petence approach is highly relevant to the study of symbolic-cultural
phenomena, Chomsky's own contrary opinion notwithstanding. We
should study minds rather than symbol systems themselves, and see
how ritual structures are mentally represented by people. Thus we can
make our way bottom-up from the cognitive to the cultural. If there
are no biological constraints on the representation of rituals, the
observed uniformity of ritual behavior can only be explained by social
and cultural forces, which, however, must always be represented 'in
our heads.' Yet Lawson and McCauley acknowledge that the representation of ritual structures is based on the (biologically determined)
human ability to represent the structure of behaviors in general,
which either is partly innate or based on very early developed capabilities (see Ch. Seven). (See Lawson and McCauley 1990: 85, 180-184.
Cf. Lawson 1999; 2001.)

These generalities of the mental representation of action include
such things as an agent as the necessary initiator of action, an object
or a patient that is acted upon (not necessary), and an instrument that

is used. There can for example be no drinking of beer without an agent who drinks, beer that is drunk, and some instrument, such as a glass or a bottle, for drinking. From these kinds of regularities Lawson and McCauley build up their theory of the representation of religious ritual systems. To begin with, they differentiate religious rituals from other types of ritual by observing that in certain rituals there is always involved a CPS agent, a fact that obviously forms a cross-culturally recurrent pattern which is quite naturally taken as being religious. Moreover, it is doubtful whether other types of rituals form any coherent whole at all. This means that ritual action is made religious by the fact that a specific type of conceptual scheme, involving CPS agents, is used in its formation. The ultimate basis of the form of religious rituals is agent causality; the whole structure of ritual action can be understood against the specific role played in ritual action by superhuman and other agents. (Lawson and McCauley 1990: 87-89, 176. Cf. Boyer 1994b: 185-191.)

Ritual structures can be formally described by means of a formation system and an 'object agency filter' (a cognitive principle which excludes ineligible entities functioning as agents). The formation system includes the following slots or nodes:

Participant
Action complex
Agent
Object
Quality
Property
Act
Action Quality
Action Property

The formal structures that can be generated from these principles describe actions, which are analogous to sentences in Chomskyan theory. The analogy, however, only concerns the functional roles of these units within their respective theories. Representations of ritual actions reflect the structure of action, just as representations of sentences reflect sentential structures. This, however, in no way necessitates a sentential account of cognitive processing. (Lawson and McCauley 1990: 84-93.) In what follows, I shall not try to present Lawson and McCauley's whole theory, but shall focus on what is relevant to my own argument, i.e. the role of the CPS agent.

The crucial thing is that performances of actions usually presuppose an earlier performance of some other action. You cannot for example go out unless you have first come in; you cannot be fired if you have not first got a job. Normally such chains of actions can be traced backwards *ad infinitum*, but not so with religious ritual actions. Although they also presuppose previous "enabling" actions, there are unequivocal limits to their number. A priest for example is capable of ritually pronouncing a couple man and wife *because* he has himself undergone the ritual or ordination. The bishop who ordained him was able to do so *because* he himself had been ordained. Thus a chain of ordination rituals can in principle be traced back to St. Peter, who was ordained by Jesus (Jesus had the authority of god because he was god). But it is with god that the chain stops. God does not need any enabling rituals to be able to establish "super-permanent" effects. This fact about Christian rituals serves as one instance of the more general principle that CPS agents terminate an otherwise endless regression of enabling rituals. It is because of this that rituals in which the actor is a CPS agent need not be repeated. Their results are permanent. (Lawson and McCauley 1990: 95-98, 165.)

Two important universal principles are involved: the principle of superhuman agency and the principle of superhuman immediacy. The first of these says that the most central rites in any religion are those where the agent in the ritual is a CPS agent. The other principle says that the fewer enabling actions to which appeal must be made in order to implicate a superhuman agent, the more fundamental the ritual is to the religious system in question. Thus the most basic religious rituals in any religious system are those whose efficacy does not presuppose the performance of other rituals. (Lawson and McCauley 1990: 124-126.)[17]

The relationship between ritual action and religious conceptual schemes, however, may be more complex than Lawson and McCauley seem to think. Their formal action descriptions are not inductive generalizations from actual actions, but rather are based on a deductive framework. The theory entails that a religious conceptual

---

17   Theodore Vial (1999) has tested Lawson and McCauley's theory in his study of the change in the baptism ceremony in Zürich in the 1860's; he finds that the theory well explains what was at stake in the baptism debate, although it cannot explain why the government requested a change in the ritual and why the debate was so heated. I think, however, that the heatedness too can be explained by the modified principle of counter-intuitive immediacy I introduce in Chapters 5 and 7.

scheme serves as the basis for giving content and assessing the value of such abstract sequences as for example [agent + act + object], which thus can represent for example 'the shaman slaying a goat.' While it is true that a ritual cannot be understood without some knowledge of the religious beliefs of the participants, it does not follow that we are dealing with a systematically related doctrinal system and its behavioral expression. Although the participants, if requested, can cite a host of traditional beliefs to account for their ritual behavior, this is often purely *ad hoc*, since ritual action is not intentional in the same sense as ordinary action. (Boyer 1994b: 196-197.)

Non-ritual behaviors are scripted and goal-directed in the sense that for example the action complex of 'going for a beer' consists of various sub-actions whose interconnections are determined by the goal of drinking beer in a pub, possibly with good friends (see Rubin 1997: 24-28). It is also easy to decide whether or not the action has been successful: you either got to the pub and got the beer, or you didn't. If for instance you realize, when already in the pub, that you have no money, the intended action complex is interrupted. You almost got your beer.

This is not so with rituals.[18] Although baptizing an infant for example seems to be a goal-directed action, the action is not instrumental in terms of an external goal. A ritual is successful only on condition that it is properly performed; we cannot judge its success by its consequences. We cannot for example examine the infant to see whether it really has been properly baptized. It all depends on whether the ritual itself has been "well-formed." This entails that one also cannot perform a ritual only partially. One either performs it or not. There is no such thing as a half-performed ritual, or such a being as a half-baptized infant. (Boyer 1994b: 210.) I think this explains the formal and stylized nature of ritual action. In not being governed by any intentional goals, ritual action can only be defined by its own form. It is as self-referential as religious semantics.[19]

---

18   After writing this passage, I realized that George Homans had likewise argued that ritual action is not instrumental in any ordinary sense. It does not produce any practical result on the external world, and that is precisely why we call it a ritual. (Quoted in Rappaport 1999: 56.)

19   Rappaport (1999: 52-58) uses the notion of self-reference to describe how rituals "indexically" express the participants' physical, psychical and social states. In addition to this, they also carry "canonical" information which is not entirely coded by the participants. In other words, to the extent that there is room for variation in the traditional sequence of actions, not entirely coded by the participants, a ritual also reveals something about the performers' themselves.

Robert A. Hinde (1999: 110), however, insists that rituals may involve genuine goals, such as for instance healing a sick person. But it is impossible in such cases to evaluate the efficacy of the ritual by referring to any empirical evidence. For example, the simple fact that the sick person does not recover is not in itself any indication of the failure of the ritual, because there are many other ways of interpreting the situation. The believer does not have to consider that the ritual did not work or that the counter-intuitive agent(s) were unable to heal the sick person, because religious representations are typically compatible with all possible states of affairs. If the patient does not get better, then either the ritual was not correctly performed, i.e. was not actually a ritual at all, or the counter-intuitive agent(s) in their great wisdom decided not to heal the person for some inscrutable higher reason.[20] (See Boyer 1994b: 207-209.)

This means that there are no comprehensive systematic links between rituals and religious belief systems. It is for this reason that people cannot usually explain why they perform the kinds of rituals they do; or, if they do offer an explanation, the reasons given are rationalizations that are in no way necessary to the representation and performance of the action in question. They are merely conjectures based on abductive reasoning, assumptions that can be imagined to have a causal connection with the action in question, not deductions from any coherent "worldview" or "cultural model." Thus the religious belief tradition in question seems to provide some but only some of the missing background in the representation of ritual sequences. While it is true that in religions with a systematic theology (see Pyysiäinen 1999a) there exist more or less detailed explanations for the *raison d'être* of rituals, these explanations have only little to do with the actual behavior of the majority of believers (cf. also Barret and Keil 1996). Systematic theology may not constitute an exhaustive explanation of a ritual behavior even for specialists. (Boyer 1994b: 212-222.)

Thus ritual behavior is an actional parallel of religious belief, although there is no one-to-one relationship between them. Interestingly, this parallelism suggests that Lawson and McCauley's (1990) idea of the structuring role of counter-intuitive agents may also figure

---

20   The theologian Vincent Brümmer (1984: 1) for example writes: "If the efficacy of prayer can in principle be known from experience, does it not follow that we should be able to conduct an experiment to test the claim that prayers are efficacious? To many the very idea of such experiment sounds irreligious and even blasphemous."

in the representation of religious beliefs, not only in rituals, in the sense that according to people's intuitions the most clearly religious beliefs are such that directly involve a counter-intuitive agent. Actually, Jesus instituting the Church, for instance, is a myth rather than a ritual. I return to this below and in the last chapter.

It is on this theory of ritual form that McCauley (2001) bases his argument, according to which the crucial determinant of whether a ritual is emotionally provocative is its specific form. Sensory pageantry and emotional stimulation only belong to rituals where the agent of action is a CPS agent. Only such rituals can produce those kinds of super-permanent changes that characterize for instance ordinations, baptisms, weddings and funerals. And the changes being permanent, there is no need to repeat such rituals. One only needs to be baptized once. It is only CPS agents that can bring about such permanent changes, not humans by themselves. It is this once-in-a-lifetime nature of these kinds of rituals that, according to McCauley, explains why they and only they are accompanied by emotional provocation. It is not the frequency of performance but the type of the ritual that determines whether or not it involves sensory pageantry and emotional stimulation. Although rituals with a CPS agent as the active agent are not repeated for one and the same individual, it is not this non-repeatability that is here the determining factor, but the form of the ritual.

Here McCauley is actually presenting two different explanations. On the one hand, he seems to be saying that emotions are provoked when a CPS agent is experienced as doing something super-permanent, although McCauley does not explain why this should be so. On the other, he argues that emotional stimulation is consciously used to make people remember the ritual, which is felt to be so important that the participants must be convinced that something profound and super-permanent has occurred. It is the emotional stimulation that serves to convince the participants that they have taken part in something absolutely unique, and to remember that occasion vividly. This, however, comes close to saying that it is after all the fact that the ritual is only performed once, i.e. is not repeated, that determines the presence of emotions. Moreover, this shifts the emphasis from the form to the *function* of the ritual: emotional arousal belongs to rituals which are important for the individual (or for the society). The crucial question is whether the event is important because of the counter-intuitive agents, or whether the counter-intuitive agents are summoned because the event is important.

In order better to come to grips with what is at stake here, let us imagine a secular parallel. If an ordinary Joe Sixpack for example goes, along with 200 other people, to listen to the President of the United States give a speech on some occasion, a little but probably not very much emotion is provoked, at least if Joe does this on a regular basis. But if the President himself came to congratulate Joe on his fiftieth birthday, that would surely be an emotion-provoking and most memorable event. Not because he does this seldom, and not because everybody wants Joe to remember the event, but simply because he is the President.

Religious rituals differ from this example in that the presence of powerful counter-intuitive beings cannot be observed. We are dealing merely with the *believed* presence of counter-intuitive agents, on occasions that are somehow important for the people in question. Shifts in time, space and social position have everywhere been ritualized not only using the imagery of spatial movement as an analogue (van Gennep 1977; cf. also Anttonen 1996) but also by performing the relevant actions in the name of counter-intuitive agents that are evoked in situations that involve danger or conceptual ambiguity. Rites of passage usually involve questions of conceptual ambiguity: how one becomes a person (baptisms); the ontological status of the deceased (funerals); how one acquires the specific essence of a religious specialist, such as a shaman (see Boyer 1993b; 1994b: 155-184) (ordinations). Calendrical rites deal with conceptual problems that relate to the nature of time, but they are also devoted to coping with various socio-economic dangers. Crisis rites, for their part, mainly deal with concrete dangers relating to disease, natural disasters and social problems.

It seems that all these rituals can involve strong emotions. A crisis always provokes emotions, and even some calendrical rituals may appeal to the emotions, such as for example a Lutheran service arranged specifically for veterans of the Winter War on Finland's Day of Independence. It is important to realize, however, that in these cases it is not the ritual form that makes the event emotional, but contextual factors such as illness, famine or painful memories. Only in rituals that deal with conceptual ambiguities is it the ritual form that seemingly generates the emotional reactions of the participants. This, however, does not necessarily exclude contextual emotion-provoking factors from these rituals; a funeral for example calls forth emotions of sadness, fear, etc. not only because god is the active agent in it but because the participants are sad about the loss they have suffered.

McCauley is right in that an intimate relationship with a counter-intuitive agent is emotion-provoking, although this does not mean that it is the only factor determining the emotionality of a ritual. The crucial factor seems not to be the fact that it is the counter-intuitive agent that, in a way, approaches the patient of the ritual, but the intimate relationship between the patient and the counter-intuitive agent. Surely Joe would be quite emotional even if it were he who approached the President in the Oval Office, as long as the situation involved an experience of intimacy between the participant(s) and a powerful authority. There are many kinds of religious rituals in which the participants approach a passive counter-intuitive agent in quite an emotional way. Examples can be found in the meetings of various revivalist movements, such as the "Toronto Blessing" or the "Laughing Revival" (see Poloma 1997).

I do not, however, think that the explanation for this is that only counter-intuitive agents can produce the super-permanent effects that typify this kind of ritual, and that this is why the people in question remember the event so well. It is rather that certain things in life are, by natural or social necessity, permanent and happen only once: one is born only once, one becomes an adult only once and is usually given only one name, and one also dies only once. Consequently it is more natural to consider that this is the reason why counter-intuitive agents are appealed to on such occasions, not the other way around. It is not gods that make such transitions unique events. Dying for instance is a super-permanent event regardless of whether gods are summoned to witness it or not. The presence of counter-intuitive agents is merely a consequence.[21]

McCauley could of course argue that although dying as a biological phenomenon is a permanent change, he is not talking about that but about the religious effect brought about by the funeral ritual. After all, people commonly consider that one is not properly dead if the funeral rituals have not been properly performed, even though biological death is an obvious fact (see Pentikäinen 1968). But the reason why we think like this must be based on the natural fact that living beings die and that the ontological status of the deceased is in part mysterious to us. A corpse cannot be treated as an ordinary person, but it cannot be treated as a mere object either (cf. Merleau-Ponty 1992: 82, 98, 198).

---

21 After having written this chapter, I realized that Boyer (in press) had come to a very similar conclusion about this.

The idea of a dead person is counter-intuitive, in the sense that the deceased is considered to have some of the properties of a person but yet to lack the biological and even physical properties of living persons. Thus it is in some sense natural that representations concerning the counter-intuitive are activated in funeral rituals, due to an associative mechanism that connects the representation of the corpse with other counter-intuitive representations present in one's database. Since the change from a living person to a dead one is known to be permanent it cannot but be accepted, and therefore also interpreted as being the will of those counter-intuitive beings or forces that are believed to control our lives. From this, it is a short leap to the conception that a ritual must be arranged in which the new status of the deceased is actively established by a counter-intuitive agent. The same holds, *mutatis mutandis*, for other such transitions and the related rites of passage. They deal with the ontology of conceptual categories.[22]

Thus it is not only the ritual form that provokes emotion, but the fact that something important and permanent is happening. Moreover, if the crucial determinant of ritual form is whether the counter-intuitive agent appears as the agent or as a the patient of the ritual, then the ritual form is not so relevant for deciding whether emotion will be provoked by the ritual in question. The important thing seems to be whether the participant(s) experience an intimate relationship with the counter-intuitive being(s). A ritual form (if we may call it such) that allows for this is a consequence of contextual factors, in the sense that the most intimate experiences of being in a relationship with counter-intuitive agents take place in situations that are felt to be somehow important and critical. This also means that it is not so much the specific ritual mode of behavior that provokes emotion, but the nature of religious representations. Yet in some cases a specific mode of behavior, such as repetitive drumming or dancing, can also produce in the participants changes that involve emotional arousal (see Siikala 1978; Pyysiäinen 1996a: 80-92). This kind of autosuggestive stimulation can be accompanied by various kinds of contextual stimuli that likewise provoke emotional reactions.

It is, however, not necessary for the encounter with counter-intu-

---

22   Boyer (in press), independently of my reasoning, explains this by the supposed fact that a corpse activates in the mind two incompatible reasoning mechanisms: one dealing with physical objects and the other with persons. This is perfectly in line with what I have said here, and also goes a good deal deeper in explaining what is at stake.

itive agents to take place in a social context of ritual. It can also happen in solitude. But although it is possible to have a religious experience in one's own solitude, such experiences do tend to be ritualized even if they do not become socially shared. As there is no established way of dealing safely with counter-intuitive agents whose existence is taken seriously other than the rituals known in one's community, they are the obvious source of exemplary reactions. If for example one thinks that one has just seen a ghost, one may recite a prayer and make the sign of the cross. Elements from communal rituals are borrowed for private use in situations where one cannot control one's behavior by natural intuitions.

Private rituals have sometimes been compared to obsessive-compulsive disorders, and there are obviously real similarities to be observed. Both religious rituals and obsessive-compulsive behavior are typified by what Hinde (1999: 114-115) calls the "just right syndrome:" both involve for instance arranging objects in highly circumscribed ways, doing things in precisely the right manner or repeating sequences of actions always in the same order. This also involves beliefs about all kinds of misfortunes that are apprehended should the relevant ritual behavior fail to obey the supposed scheme. (See Dulaney and Fiske 1994.)

People can also go on performing rituals when counter-intuitive beings have been deprived of their majesty; this results in dry and routinized rituals with no emotional arousal. As Max Weber (1966: 187-188, 193-195) realized, only in newly established religious movements are charismatic leaders important, and the members of the movement are also expected to strive towards the kind of experience(s) the leader is capable of. Only when the movement becomes institutionalized and a hierarchical organization is developed are the subjective experiences of the members replaced by "institutional grace" (*Anstaltsgnade*). It is now enough for the members to accept the organization and its doctrine, personal mystical experience being regarded as a sign of distrust in the institution's capacity to distribute grace to all. Thus not only doctrinal questions but emotional reactions as well are brought under institutional control. (See also Poloma 1997.)

In order really to come to grips with what is at stake here, we have to explain why the principles of superhuman agency and immediacy work as they seem to do. In the light of the theories of Antonio Damasio (1996; 1999) and Joseph LeDoux (1998), to be discussed in the next section, it is apparent that emotions can be provoked by both conscious and unconscious stimuli. Conscious stimuli involve an appraisal of the stimulus in question, while unconscious stimuli provoke either basic, biologically determined emotions or emotions based on forgotten earlier experiences. This, however, shifts the emphasis from ritual to religion in general. If the crucial factor in conscious stimuli is the direct action of a counter-intuitive being in a critical situation, emotions should be provoked whenever people experience the presence of counter-intuitive agents in a moment of danger or despair; and this seems to be the case.

It is important that the biological function of emotions is to prepare us to cope with dangerous situations. A dangerous situation may activate the idea of counter-intuitive beings (e.g. "Help me, God," or "thanks to God I was saved"), but likewise the idea of counter-intuitive beings may activate emotions of fear or of reassurance ("God, please forgive me," or "I fear nothing when God is with me"). To paraphrase William James (1884), we do not pray (only) because we are afraid, but are afraid because we pray. Fear can be caused both by environmental factors and by religious representations themselves, and both stimuli can enhance each other. Ritual form and contextual factors interact.

For example, the role of snakes both in mythology and in religious cults (see Williamson and Pollio 1999) can on the one hand be explained by biology; on the other hand, the biological facts are influenced by mythology. We know that both humans and rhesus monkeys have such an innate tendency towards a fear of snakes that when the child for the first time observes its caregiver responding to a snake with marked fear the child immediately develops a permanent fear of snakes. Thus the biologically based tendency to fear snakes can explain – at least in part – why in various mythologies the serpent so often represents evil. At the same time these mythologies have obviously strengthened the human fear of snakes. (LeDoux 1998: 237; Hinde 1999: 118; Wilson 1998: 71-81.) Religious and other emotion-provoking stimuli can enhance one another.

It is important that we cannot restrict the role of strong emotion in religion to ritual contexts alone, although much of explicit religious beliefs is transmitted in rituals, while rituals serve to enhance religious belief. Although McCauley is right about the emotion-provoking quality of counter-intuitive agents, they are not encountered only in rituals. With the exception of certain autosuggestive or meditative techniques, emotional reactions also do not follow from ritual behavior per se, but from the fact that in rituals beliefs about counter-intu-itive agents are activated. Ritual is an enactment of religious belief, even though this enactment is not systematic due to the evocative nature of both the belief system and of rituals themselves.

What is Emotion?

So far the word 'emotion' has been used more or less as a folk-psycho-logical concept. It is now time to be more precise about it. René Descartes viewed emotions as a kind of thought; they were distin-guished from other kinds of thoughts by their great confusion and by the fact that they were caused by physiological states of the body (see Alanen 1989). Damasio seems to be wrong in claiming that Descartes's sharp distinction between operations of the mind on one hand and the structure and operation of a biological organism on the other is the probable source of the twentieth-century idea of the mind as a sort of disembodied computer program. For Descartes, the "pas-sions of mind" were evidence for the fact that the mind is in close interaction with the body. (Alanen 1989; Damasio 1996: 249-251.)

In 1884, James (1884) presented his famous theory of the interac-tion between body and mind in emotion. According to James, physio-logical changes are not caused by emotional states of mind but the other way around: bodily changes follow directly from the perception of some fact, and emotion *is* nothing but our feeling of these bodily changes as their occur. This theory was challenged in the 1920's, when the physiologist Walter Cannon insisted that the physiological responses that accompany different emotions are the same regardless of the particular emotional state that is experienced. In other words, although emotions always involve bodily responses, different kinds of emotions do not involve different kinds of physiological reactions as James had suggested. Cannon, however, agreed with James that emo-tional responses, for instance running away, were not caused by emo-tional experiences, such as being consciously afraid. For Cannon the response was simultaneous with the conscious experience, while for James it determined the experience. (LeDoux 1998: 42-46, 85; Dama-sio 1999: 290-291.)

In the early 60's, after the decline of behaviorism, Stanley Schachter and Jerome Singer (1962) published an article in which the Aristotelian and Cartesian conception of emotion as cognitive interpretation was revitalized. Schachter and Singer claimed that it was thoughts, or cognitions, that provided the specificity of various emotions, the bodily reactions being – as Cannon had insisted – non-specific. The physiological responses in emotion inform the brain about a state of arousal, and contextual information about the situation, physical state and appropriate emotional reactions is used to label the emotion in question as 'fear,' 'love,' etc. Emotional feelings result when we interpret and explain emotionally ambiguous bodily states to ourselves. This was seemingly confirmed by Schachter and Singer's experiment, in which emotional arousal was artificially produced in subjects by injections of adrenaline, after which the situation they were in was framed as being either hilarious, fearful or neutral. The subjects clearly interpreted the physiological reactions caused by the adrenaline as being either joy, fear or nothing in particular, according to their interpretation of the social situation in question. Although this theory was criticized on many points, it paved the way for the purely cognitive view of emotion which started to emerge during the 70's. By 1980 it was just about the only approach available; LeDoux comments that "emotion has not been a very popular topic in brain science," and that cognitive scientists have been prone to view emotions as mere "cold cognitive processes." (LeDoux 1998: 11, 20, 46-53, 304.)

There were problems with Schachter's and Singer's theory, however, and one was that it did not explain what generates emotional reactions in the first place. A new view started to emerge when Robert Zajonc (1980) published his important paper, arguing that emotional preferences could be formed without conscious awareness. Thus emotions were not the same as cognitive judgements. His experiments have been replicated many times, and it is now clear that the emotional meanings of stimuli can be processed unconsciously. The actual cause of an emotion can be different from the reasons we adduce to explain the emotion to ourselves or others after the fact. (LeDoux 1998: 49, 53-67.)

According to LeDoux (1998: 68-70) himself, emotion and cognition are separate but interacting mental functions mediated by separate but interacting brain systems. In other words, he approaches emotion from a neuroscientific point of view as a series of brain events that make us feel the different emotions. Although we can learn from computer simulations of emotions, they are merely simulations of some aspects of emotion, not emotional feelings. A similar neuroscientific approach has also recently been presented by Damasio (1996; 1999).

Others too have considered the neurophysiological basis of emotion, and the dominant view of it has come to be the limbic system hypothesis. LeDoux (1998: 73-103), however, rejects the often-held view that the "emotional brain" is constituted by what is known as the "limbic system" in the brain (cf. Damasio 1996: 28, 118). According to LeDoux, no good way has been been found of identifying what parts of the brain make up the limbic system. Older theories relied on the now obsolete assumption that the cortex contains older (in an evolutionary sense) and more recent parts, and identified the limbic system as consisting of the phylogenetically old cortex together with anatomically related subcortical areas, or of brain areas connected with the hypothalamus. But the distinction between older cortex and neocortex has now broken down, and the hypothalamus has been found to be connected with all levels of the nervous system, including the neocortex. Thus the brain may contain not be just one but many emotional systems. (LeDoux 1998: 99-103.)

It is good, however, to bear in mind that the brain as a whole does not have any specific function of its own. Rather, it is a collection of systems, or modules, each with different functions, evolutionary changes taking place at the level of individual modules (see Ch. Seven below). Our emotional life too is based on brain mechanisms that have evolved in the course of phylogeny and thus some of our emotional systems in the brain are the same as in many vertebrates. (LeDoux 1998: 105-107.)

This has led some psychologists to search for certain basic emotions, defined by facial expressions that are similar across many different cultures. Silvan Tomkins for example proposed in 1962 the existence of eight basic emotions: surprise, interest, joy, rage, fear, disgust, shame and anguish. Later, Paul Ekman listed six basic emotions: surprise, happiness, anger, fear, disgust and sadness.[23] For Tomkins (1980: 142), affects are sets of muscular and glandular responses located in the face and also widely distributed throughout the body, which generate positive or negative sensory feedback. These responses are triggered at subcortical centers where specific "programs" are located for each distinct affect. The programs are innately endowed and have been genetically

---

23 Later, Tomkins (1980: 142) listed interest or excitement, enjoyment or joy, surprise or startledness, distress or anguish, fear or terror, shame or humiliation, contempt, disgust, and anger or rage.

inherited; they are not learned. When we become aware of our facial
and/or visceral responses, we are aware of our affects. The affect system provides the primary blueprints for cognition, decision, and
action. Affects can be activated both innately and by acquired stimuli.
(LeDoux 1998: 112-113; Damasio 1999: 50-53, 285.)

Other scholars, such as Robert Plutchik and Nico Frijda, have considered facial expressions to be too narrow a basis for classifying emotions, and have compiled their own lists, which both overlap with and
diverge from those of Tomkins and Ekman. Philip Johnson-Laird and
Keith Oatley have analyzed the words we have for various emotions,
coming up with a list that is similar to Ekman's but without 'surprise.'
Besides basic emotions there are assumed to be mixed emotions,
which result from cognitive operations. Plutchik for example distinguishes types of blends of basic emotions, according to how near the
two emotions in question are to each other on his circle of the eight
basic emotions (e.g. joy + acceptance = friendliness). (LeDoux 1998:
113-114; Plutchik 1980.)

Others, however, want to deny the reality of such primitive and
biological emotions. According to these writers, emotions are psychological constructions that arise from interpretations of various situations and are socially determined. Thus there are no universal types of
emotions. One major proponent of this view is James Averill (1980).
These scholars argue for example that in other cultures than the modern western one behavior patterns occur that we would want to classify as abnormal and "sick," but which in those cultures are considered
normal. They have their own specific labels that cannot always necessarily be translated, nor can they be explained with reference to biology because they are socially constructed. It is also pointed out that
even within western culture there is variation in the labels assigned to
different emotions. (LeDoux 1998: 115-116.)

Here we should first of all differentiate between how emotions are
labeled and how they are behaviorally expressed. Secondly, cases of
variation between cultures do not rule out the possibility that some
emotions are the same across cultures. Ekman (1980) for example distinguishes between universal, especially facial, emotional responses,
which are spontaneous, not learned, and other bodily movements,
which constitute acquired responses and vary from one culture to
another. Moreover, even universal facial expressions can to some
extent be consciously controlled and thus culturally regulated.
(LeDoux 1998: 117-118.)

Ekman tested his hypothesis by studying the facial expressions of American and Japanese subjects while they were watching an emotion-arousing film (Ekman 1980: 94-95; see LeDoux 1998: 118.) The subjects were tested in their own countries under two conditions: sitting alone and sitting while being watched over by an authoritative-looking experimenter. Their facial expressions while watching the movie were videotaped and then coded by an observer ignorant of what the subjects were watching. In the private viewing situation there was striking similarity in the emotions expressed by Japanese and American subjects. When the white-coated experimenter was present, however, the Japanese looked more polite and showed more smiling and less emotional diversity than the Americans. But slow-motion analysis of the video revealed that the smiles and other polite facial expressions of the Japanese subjects were superimposed over brief, prior-occurring facial movements, which Ekman took to be the basic emotions leaking through. The socially learned display rules were as automatic as the basic emotional expressions, but could not completely cover them, still less replace them. (See also de Sousa 1980.)

Now the important question emerges, what is actually meant by 'emotion.' Andrew Ortony and Terrance Turner (1990) for example ask why there is so much disagreement among theorists of the basic emotions as to what these basic emotions are. There is no satisfactory criterion of 'basicness,' and one scholar's basic emotions are for another not emotions at all. Ortony and Turner then suggest that what is basic, and may even be innate, is not emotions as such but certain more general response components that can be utilized in the expression of emotions as well as in non-emotional reactions. Emotions always involve higher cognitive processes, which organize the various responses that are appropriate to the situation faced by the organism. Thus the component responses are biologically determined, while emotions belong to the world of psychological determinism. (See LeDoux 1998: 119.)

The philosopher Paul E. Griffiths (1997) has aptly summed up the discussion of emotions, noting that the major divide is between "feeling theories," or "affect program theories," and "propositional attitude theories." Affect program states, such as those described by Ekman, are phylogenetically ancient, informationally encapsulated, reflex-like responses that are insensitive to culture. Other kinds of emotions are aspects of higher cognition, which differ across cultures due to the role played by culture in psychological development. In

Griffiths's view, the differing research traditions reflect the fact that there are actually two kinds of things referred to as 'emotions.' They have different phylogenies, different adaptive functions, different neuroscience and different roles in the human psychological make-up. Griffiths goes so far as to say that these are such different phenomena that lumping them together under the umbrella term of 'emotion' is not scientifically justified. The category of 'emotions' may actually break down into three separate parts: 1) universal, short-term, salient cases of anger, fear, disgust, sadness, joy, and surprise,[24] for which studies like those of Ekman's provide a satisfactory account; 2) socially sustained pretenses that have "no more in common with other emotions than a piece of playacting has in common with the behavior it imitates," and which are explained by social constructivist theories; and 3) a wider range of emotions, discussed by constructivists and evolutionary psychologists, emotions that partly vary and partly resemble each other across cultures. (Cf. Damasio 1999: 285-286.)

On the Neurophysiology of Emotion

LeDoux (1998: 69-70) summarizes his key arguments for the neurophysiological view of emotions as follows:

- When a certain region of the brain is damaged, the person in question loses the capacity to appraise the emotional significance of certain stimuli without a loss in the capacity to perceive the same stimuli as objects (see also Damasio 1996: 3-51).
- Normally the emotional meaning of a stimulus can begin to be appraised by the brain before the perceptual systems have fully processed the stimulus.
- Memories of the emotional significance of stimuli are processed by different brain mechanisms from those that process the cognitive memories of the same stimuli.
- The systems that perform emotional appraisals are directly connected with systems involved in the control of emotional responses.
- Due to this connection, appraisals are often accompanied by bodily sensations, which thus become part of the conscious experience of emotions.

---

24   These are the same as Ekman's list, except that Griffiths speaks of 'joy' whereas Ekman speaks of 'happiness.'

LeDoux (1998: 122-125) claims that the functional equivalence of behavior across species – even when the function is expressed in a radically different way – can only be explained by the fact that the brain systems involved in mediating the function are the same. The brain systems that underlie emotional behaviors have been preserved throughout the various stages of evolution and often take care of fundamental problems of survival. All animals have some version of these survival systems in their brains, but feelings can only occur when the system also has the capacity for conscious awareness.

According to LeDoux (1998: 126-127), starting in this way with universal behavioral functions is a better approach to compiling a list of basic emotions than starting with facial expressions or emotion words in different languages. Producing a list of the special adaptive behaviors crucial to survival will also yield a list of basic emotions. Different classes of emotional behavior represent different kinds of functions that take care of different kinds of problems and have different brain systems devoted to them. Different kinds of emotions thus are separate functional units. At the neural level, each emotional unit consists of a set of inputs, an appraisal mechanism, and a set of outputs. The appraisal mechanism has developed in the course of evolution to detect input stimuli that are relevant to the function of the network ("natural triggers"). These networks have evolved because they serve the function of connecting trigger stimuli with responses that are likely to keep the organism alive. In his research, LeDoux has focused especially on the fear system of the brain, more particularly on fear conditioning, using these as an example of emotions in general. Fear is a particularly good example for the study of religion as well, since feelings or emotions of fear play a central role in religion (see Pyysiäinen 2001b). As Walter Burkert (1996: 30) says, "to transmit religion is to transmit fear." (See also Whitehouse 1995: 151-152, and cf. Rudolf Otto's [1969] *mysterium tremendum et fascinans.*).[25]

The system responsible for our feelings of fear did not originally evolve to produce these kinds of conscious experience. It has developed to detect danger and to produce responses that maximize our chances of surviving the threat. These responses, i.e. defensive behaviors, evolved before there were conscious feelings of fear. Feelings of fear are a by-product of the evolution of two neural systems: one that

---

25   Even before Otto, David Hume wrote that "terror is the primary principle of religion" (*Dialogues and Natural History*, pp. 128, 143, as quoted in Taves 1999: 44).

mediates defensive behavior and one that creates consciousness. It is
our genes that determine which kind of nervous system we will have
and thus give us the raw materials out of which to build our emotions.
Yet the precise ways in which we act, think, and feel in specific situations are determined by many other factors as well. Some emotions,
or even many of them, have a biological basis, but social, i.e. cognitive
factors are also important. (LeDoux 1998: 128-137. See Ch. Seven
below.)

From the neurophysiological point of view, there are two separate
memory systems involved in fear conditioning: the explicit and the
implicit memory systems. Explicit, conscious memories are processed
in the cortex and the temporal lobe memory system, whereas implicit
memories are processed in the amygdala (see Damasio 1996: 69-70;
1999: 60-62) and elicit bodily responses without conscious awareness
of their cause. The implicit memory system is less forgetful than the
explicit one, to the extent that conditioned fear responses tend to be
practically permanent once established, thus making it quite common
to have implicit memories without explicit ones. If for instance I have
been in a car accident where the horn of my car got stuck, two kinds
of memories may be produced. Later, when I hear a horn of a car similarly stuck, the neural representation of the sound, which has become
a conditioned fear stimulus, goes straight from the auditory system to
the amygdala and elicits an emotion of fear. This is an unconscious
memory. But the sound also goes through the cortex to the temporal
lobe memory system, where explicit memories are activated, and
causes me to remember the accident consciously but unemotionally. It
is the implicit fear memory system that provides the physiological
emotional reaction to accompany the conscious memory. I remember
the accident consciously and feel bad. But it is also possible that I will
have only an implicit, unconscious memory of the horn being stuck.
In that case I will have the emotional reaction to the sound of a horn
without knowing why, the memory of the sound having been wiped
out from conscious memory. (LeDoux 1998: 153-174, 181, 196-197,
200-204.)

The implicit memory system is much more rapid than the explicit
one. In a rat, it takes about twelve milliseconds for an acoustic stimulus to reach the amygdala via the thalamic pathway, while it takes
twice as long to travel the cortical pathway whereby explicit memories
are processed. Thus for example if I am walking in the woods and
hear a strange sound in the grass, it goes straight to the amygdala and

prepares me for defence against a snake. Only after this does the sound go from the thalamus to the cortex, where it is interpreted as actually coming from a rattlesnake. It could equally well turn out to be merely the wind playing in the long grass. It is, however, better to mistake the wind for a snake than vice versa (cf. Guthrie 1993). (LeDoux 1998: 153, 163-165.)

There is also experimental evidence that the release of adrenaline that occurs in fearful situations helps one to remember the situation especially vividly ("flashbulb memories"), whereas adrenaline blockade is a hindrance to remembering. Such memories, however, are by no necessity perfectly accurate, the improvement affecting some aspects more than others. Extremely traumatic emotional events may also completely prevent recall, although the mechanism of this is not as yet understood. (LeDoux 1998: 206-211; Damasio 1999: 294-295.) The idea of "flashbulbs" has aroused considerable debate among psychologists, and various explanations have been put forward. Besides emotional stimulation, firsthand experience and violation of one's expectations have been proposed as causes for flashbulb memories. (See Whitehouse 2000: 7-10, 119-122.) I do not consider, however, that these necessarily need to be mutually exclusive factors: violation of expectations probably leads to emotional arousal, especially when one directly experiences the violation (cf. also Barrett and Nyhof 2001; Boyer and Ramble in press).

Memory is also state-specific in the sense that things are usually best remembered when one is in the same situation or state as when the thing in question happened. Random lists of words, for example, are better remembered if one is in the same room where the lists were first learned. As memories are stored in associative networks (see Pyysiäinen 2000), in order for a memory to appear in the consciousness the associative network has to reach a certain level of activation. If the emotional state which is stored as part of the explicit memory matches the current emotional state, the activation of the explicit memory is facilitated. (LeDoux 1998: 211-213.)

Damasio (1996: xiii-xv, 128, 158-159; 1999: 147-148) has emphasized that traditional views of rationality as distinct from emotion are erroneous. All the records we hold of the objects and events we have perceived during the course of our lives always include the emotional reactions we had at the time. It is for this reason that we cannot merely think about an object or event. The emotional coloring is always present. Human reasoning has not developed either phylogenetically

or in any single individual without the guidance of emotions and feelings that form a mechanism of biological regulation. At their best,
feelings lead us to the appropriate place in a decision-making space,
where we can put our logical reasoning to good use. But of course feelings can also just as well affect our reasoning in a negative manner in
terms of achieving our goals.

Damasio (1996: 132-133, 139, 143-145, 149-151; 1999: 35-81,
283-286) distinguishes between feelings and emotions: emotions are
defined by bodily changes, while feelings are either consciously experienced emotions or so-called background feelings, corresponding to
the body state prevailing between emotions. The most universal emotions are happiness, sadness, anger, fear and disgust. They correspond
in a Jamesian manner to preorganized bodily states. There are also
variations of these five emotions, with shades of cognitive state connected to subtler variations of emotional body state.

The essence of a feeling is the direct perception of the specific
"landscape" of the body. "(F)eelings are just as cognitive as any other
perceptual images" (Damasio 1996: 159). The neural networks on
which feelings depend are not constituted by the limbic system alone
but also by some of the prefrontal cortices, and especially by the brain
sectors that map and integrate signals from the body, the limbic system being regulated by the orbital frontal cortex (McNamara 2001; cf.
LeDoux above). Thus a feeling is a momentary "view" of a part of a
body landscape. Feelings are sensors for the match or lack of match
between ourselves and the environment. The brain and the rest of the
body constitute an indissociable organism which interacts with the
environment as an ensemble, and the physiological operations we call
the 'mind' are derived from this structural and functional ensemble.
Having a mind means that an organism forms neural representations
consisting of biological modifications due to learning; these neural
representations can become mental images which are cognitively
manipulated, and can also influence behavior. We are not, however,
conscious of all our feelings. (Damasio 1996: xvi-xix, 90, 97-108, 159;
1999: 36-37.)

Damasio (1996: 131-133) distinguishes between primary and secondary emotions. Primary emotions depend on the circuitry of the
limbic system (but cf. LeDoux), especially the amygdala, and are
hard-wired tendencies to react with emotion in a preorganized fashion when certain features of stimuli either in the world or in our bodies are perceived. Among such features are size (large animals), type of

motion (reptiles), certain sounds (growling), or certain configurations of body state (the pain felt during a heart attack). Thus one does not even need consciously to recognize a snake or an oncoming heart attack in order to be frightened (cf. LeDoux above). For a bodily emotion to emerge, it is enough that the early sensory cortices detect and categorize such key feature(s), and that structures such as the amygdala receive signals about them. This may then be accompanied by a conscious feeling of fear, which provides one with more flexibility of response based on one's previous experience stored in memory.

Secondary emotions occur when networks in the prefrontal cortex automatically and involuntarily respond to signals arising from the conscious and deliberate manipulation of mental images. The neural substrate of these images is a collection of separate topographically organized representations, occurring in varied early sensory cortices. In other words, the unconscious response is based on acquired rather than innate dispositional representations, although the acquired dispositions are obtained under the influence of innate dispositions. (Damasio 1996: 134-142.) These distinctions between types of emotion and feeling are represented in Fig. 1. below.

EMOTIONS	FEELINGS
• Bodily changes	• Conscious experience of
• Primary emotions (hardwired)	an emotion
• Secondary emotions (involuntary responses to conscious manipulation of images)	• Background feelings between emotions

---

Fig. 1. Emotions and feelings according to Damasio.

Griffiths (1997: 102-104) notes that here Damasio is clearly insisting that the primary-secondary distinction applies to both emotional stimuli and emotional reactions (input and output). Emotions can arise from unconscious, innate reasons and can be expressed unconsciously and due to innate reaction mechanisms; they can also arise and be expressed consciously and in relation to acquired knowledge. Griffiths, however, claims that Damasio has not presented any evidence for the assumption that secondary emotions necessarily involve the activation of primary emotions, and insists that the so-called secondary emotions can in many cases consist of complex conscious thoughts with very little physiological arousal. Thus higher cognitive activity needs not trigger any physiological emotions.

It is also quite possible that the input and output aspects of primary emotions may fall on different sides of the innate vs. acquired dichotomy. Highly stereotyped, pancultural emotional responses may be triggered by stimuli that reflect the organism's unique learning history. Furthermore, in Griffiths' opinion, both innate and acquired stimuli can trigger stereotypic as well as varied responses. (Griffiths 1997: 105-106.) Leaving this criticism aside for a while, I next discuss Damasio's 'somatic marker' hypothesis.

Damasio (1996: 170-173, 180-184) has developed his somatic marker hypothesis to account for the way we make decisions. He claims that – unless one has serious prefrontal damage in the brain – there is no such rationality that is free from emotional coloring. Reasoning is guided by emotion as a negative "gut feeling;" it cannot take place as mere cold calculation, for the simple reason that it is impossible to hold in the working memory the various ledgers of loss and gain that one would need to consult for comparison. The capacity of the working memory is approximately four units, and selective thinking is basically the recognition of ideas that have been stored in long-term memory and their manipulation in the working memory (Saariluoma 1995: 34-69; see LeDoux 1998: 184-186). It is therefore unavoidable that decisions are made on the basis of the gut feeling that is associated with what one has in mind. Damasio calls this feeling a 'somatic marker,' because it is a bodily state that marks a mental image. It forces attention on the negative outcome to which an action may lead, thus contributing to a cost/benefit analysis by reducing the number of options. Neurophysiologically this mechanism is located in the prefrontal cortices and the amygdala.

Most somatic markers have been created during the process of education and socialization by connecting specific classes of stimuli with specific classes of somatic states. Failures in this process result in the kinds of personality that have been labeled with the terms 'psychopath' and 'sociopath.' For these personalities, the threshold at which the emotions kick in – if indeed they do at all – is so high that their actions appear to be based on a purely calculative rationality. When such personalities achieve power in a society, the whole sociocultural system may become "sick" in this sense. Damasio mentions the Nazi, Stalinist and Pol Pot regimes as examples of this, and says that western society is frighteningly becoming yet another example of such sickness. Although the critical, formative set of stimuli to somatic pairings is acquired in childhood and adolescence, the accrual of somatically marked stimuli continues throughout life. (Damasio 1996: 177-179, 205-222.) Such markers, once learned, can – as LeDoux's research too suggests – become permanent. Although one can learn to control one's behavior in the presence of a given somatic marker, the marker itself will not change.

In the pages ahead I discuss the concepts of 'religious experience' and 'mysticism' and try to develop an explanation of the respective phenomena, utilizing the ideas of LeDoux and Damasio as well as recent research on the neuropsychology of religious experience.

Religious Experience, "Mysticism" and Emotions

Thus far, we have discussed theories of the acquisition, representation and transmission of religious concepts on the one hand, theories of emotion and feeling on the other. Now these two areas of inquiry need to be connected. I shall first discuss the concepts of 'mysticism' and 'religious experience' as they have been used in comparative religion, and then move on to build a new model of religious experience, based on the work of LeDoux, Damasio, Michael A. Persinger and Vilaya-nur Ramachandran.

Religious experience and "mysticism"

There are many kinds of religious experience. They include for example uncontrolled bodily movements (fits, bodily exercises, falling as if dead, possession), spontaneous vocalizations (crying out, speaking in tongues), unusual sensory experiences (trances, visions, auditions, clair-voyance), and "altered states of consciousness" (Taves 1999: 3). The latter are often called "mystical" experiences, although 'mystical' is sometimes also used as a synonym of 'religious' as a qualifier of experience. However, it may be better to reserve this word for those specific kinds of religious experience dealt with below.

The modern idea of the centrality of experience in religion derives from 18th century Romanticism, with its emphasis on emotion. The central figure of this movement was Friedrich Schleiermacher who greatly influenced Rudolf Otto. (Proudfoot 1985; Taves 1999.) Like Schleiermacher, Otto (1969) saw religion as being based on the human feeling of absolute dependence on something greater. Religious experience was a contact with the "Wholly Other" and religion therefore something *sui generis*. Wrote Otto (1969: 28):

> The truly 'mysterious' object is beyond our apprehension and comprehension, not only because our knowledge has certain irremovable limits, but because in it we come upon something inherently 'wholly other,' whose kind and character are incommensurable with out own, and before which we therefore recoil in a wonder that strikes us chill and numb.

According to Douglas Allen, it is precisely the phenomenologists of religion who have emphasized the experiential basis of religion, attempting to describe and systematize the "basic *structures of religious experience*." As Thomas Ryba (1991: 233) puts it: "The agreed upon end of the phenomenology of religion is that of understanding individual religions as manifestations of an underlying order of experience having its own laws and qualities." This entails an antireductionist approach, emphasizing the irreducibility and uniqueness of the religious dimension of experience. (See Allen 1978: 81, 96, 100; Pyysiäinen 2001a.)

Otto's phenomenological tradition was continued by Gerardus van der Leeuw (1986: esp. 459-462, 680-681-693), Joachim Wach (1951; 1958) and Mircea Eliade (Eliade 1976; 1959; 1961; 1951; 1974) (see Wiebe 1999: 173-190). They have not focused only on the "peak experiences" of religious virtuosos. For them, religious experience is one of the basic structures of human consciousness, and is reflected in religious life in a wider sense. This, however, is not to deny that religious experience is potentially the most intense experience of which humans are capable, as Wach (1951: 32-33; 1958: 28, 35-36, 41, 46-49) has argued. The logically most original religion was the permanent structure manifested in various experiential expressions, i.e. as thoughts, practice, and the forming of religious groups. (Wach 1946: 5, 14-34; 1958: 25, 28, 54-143.)

Eliade, who succeeded Wach as the head of the History of Religions program at the University of Chicago, identified religion and "authentic existence." The *homo religiosus* feels himself or herself to be part of a larger whole, an absolute reality not bounded by space and time. This absolute reality is the sacred, manifested within the profane in the form of "hierophanies" such as myths and rites. Thus authentic existence is characterized by the experience of the sacred, the "revelation" of reality as a totality, which offers human beings access to something greater than their contingent individual existence. (Eliade 1976; 1959; 1961: 488; 1951: 8-14; 1974: 17.)

Despite some revived interest in phenomenology within cognitive science (e.g. Varela 1996), the old-style phenomenology with its emphasis on religious experience seems nowadays to be by and large of merely historical interest in the study of religion (see Pyysiäinen 2001a. Cf., e.g., Jensen 2001; Utriainen 2001). Psychological studies of religious experience and the philosophy of "mysticism" have recently had more impact in the study of religion. The roots of this brand of scholarship are in William James' psychology of religion (which was not known to Otto). James too was influenced by Schleiermacher, although he did not consider religious feeling psychologically specific (see Proudfoot 1985: 155-169; Jantzen 1989; Barnard 1997: 94). For him religion meant "the feelings, acts, and experiences of individual men in their solitude, so far as they apprehend themselves to stand in relation to whatever they may consider the divine." Such personal experience was rooted in "mystical states of consciousness." (James 1971: 50, 366-368.) According to Ann Taves, this must be understood in the sense that religious experience is rooted in the "subconscious." This term had become a favorite explanatory concept in the new experimental psychology that had its start in Pierre Janet's discovery of simultaneously co-existent states of consciousness in a patient known as Léonie in the 1880's. (Taves 1999: 121-127, 253-284.) James is the best known representative of the tradition of psychology of religion that has centered on various kinds of subjective, "mystical" experience (e.g. Andresen and Forman 2000).

The word 'mystic(ism)' comes from the Proto-Indo-European root *mu-, referring to silence. From this root derives the word Greek word *mysterion*, which refers to the mystery cults. It was, however, only in Neoplatonism that mysticism acquired the meaning of wordless contemplation of the Eternal or The One of Plotinus. This tradition was continued by the Christian mystics. (Pyysiäinen 1996a: 68-69)

According to Grace Jantzen (1989), Schleiermacher and the Romantics, and later James, shifted the emphasis from mystical doctrine to subjective states of consciousness (see also Proudfoot 1985). This has made possible such studies of mysticism and meditation that concentrate on "altered states of consciousness" (e.g. Tart 1969). Thus mysticism is understood to consist of special kinds of subjective experiences, with various conceptual interpretations in various religious traditions. This in turn has given rise to the question of whether certain kinds of mystical experiences are "everywhere the same," differences being found only in the doctrinal interpretations that are thought to be more or less independent of the actual experiences. (Pyysiäinen 1996a: 70-80.)

Contextualists, such as Steven Katz, approach the idea of mystical experience from the point of view of mental contents; since these experiences are always experiences of some object, they are necessarily shaped and formed by the subject's culturally patterned beliefs, concepts and expectations. Thus there can be no universally identical mystical experience. (Katz 1978; 1983; 1985.)

Similarly, Hans Penner claims that 'mysticism' is a false, illusory category; once we accept that there is no direct experience of the world, independent of the social relations mediating them, there is no sense in speaking of "pure consciousness." 'Mysticism' does not refer to any particular kind of system or experience, and the study of mysticism as it has been practised has been "basically misconceived." Mystical languages cannot refer to the same Reality, because Reality is relative to a language system. (Penner 1983: 89, 94-96.)

Robert Gimello argues similarly that mysticism cannot be reduced to any single "common core of pure, undifferentiated experience," because if we subtract from mystical experience all mental contents (i.e. beliefs), all that is left is "a pattern of psychosomatic or neural impulse signifying nothing." (Gimello 1983: 62.) For Gimello, mystical experience is the psychosomatic enhancement of religious beliefs and values. Buddhist mystics, for example, have the kinds of experiences they have partly because of the discourse they learn and use. (Gimello 1983: 77, 85.) As we will soon see, this is problematic because mental content and neural processes cannot be thus separated; it is precisely the neural processes that make us experience phenomenal contents, and there cannot be meaningful experience without neural processing.

Others, such as Walter Stace and Robert K.C. Forman, claim, however, that there are mystical experiences that are everywhere the same. Stace differentiates between extrovertive and introvertive experiences. Extrovertive ones are spontaneous experiences that look "outward through the senses, while the introvertive look inward into the mind." Both "culminate in the perception of an ultimate Unity ... with which the perceiver realizes his own union or even identity." (Stace 1961: 60-62, 131-132.) The empty consciousness of the introvertive

mystical experience does not mean unconsciousness but "pure consciousness – 'pure' in the sense that it is not consciousness *of* any
empirical content." Its only content is consciousness itself, or an undifferentiated unity. (Stace 1961: 86, 110.)

This idea has recently been taken up by Forman, who describes the
"pure consciousness event" (PCE) as a contentless state of consciousness in which no changes occur, and which is not constructed by the
subject's beliefs, concepts and expectations. As "a vacuous state of
emptiness, a nonresponsiveness to the external world," it is like "a
massive forgetting." (Forman 1990: 37 *et passim.*)

Although Forman seems to be implying that during a PCE one's
consciousness is completely empty, he usually speaks of consciousness
as being especially empty of *concepts*, by which, however, he seems to
mean words. In a PCE, one takes leave of the preceding verbal mode
of experiencing, and abides empty of concepts. After the experience,
one returns to the verbal mode of experiencing and may try to
describe one's experience in so many words; all verbal accounts of the
experience, however, are contingent, in the sense that they are afterwards imposed upon an experience of which they were never a part.
(Forman 1994: 38-49.) What persists in a PCE, when all phenomenological content has been "forgotten," is *consciousness itself.* Losing all
intentional objects of consciousness does not mean becoming unconscious, since consciousness is not inherently intentional and thus can
persist even without any object. Such pure consciousness is a cognitive
state, as in it consciousness knows itself merely by virtue of being itself.
Forman calls this "knowledge by identity." (Forman 1993.)

According to this decontextualist reasoning, a PCE has no meaning
until someone retrospectively, after the experience is over, ascribes
meaning to it. PCE's are thus presupposed to be everywhere the same,
whether the subject is a thirteenth-century Dominican or a twentieth-
century Siddha Yogi. We can only differentiate between experiences
by appealing to sensory or conceptual content; if these are the same in
two experiences, then the experiences must be the same. And if there
is no content, there can be no difference. Thus PCE's are differentiated only by the interpretations ascribed to the experiences afterwards.
(Barnes 1992: 17; Forman 1993: 727.)

The PCE thesis contains both problems and a promise. The concept of 'knowledge by identity' is highly problematic, because knowing and being are two different things. A rock for example does not
know itself to be a rock merely by being a rock, because it lacks cogni-

tive processes. Consciousness, on the other hand, could be said to know itself because consciousness *is* a cognitive process, but we know as a matter of fact that conscious beings cannot be conscious of their own cognitive processes (Dennett 1993; Varela, Rosch, and Thompson 1996; Chalmers 1997; Damasio 1999).

Yet Forman insists on this, on the grounds that he knows this because he has himself once undergone a PCE while doing transcendental meditation. Upon emerging from this state he realized that he had, for a while, not been conscious of anything and yet had been awake. (Forman 1990: 28.) But this is no proof of the supposed fact that he was *conscious* during the experience. Forman misleadingly equates consciousness and being awake. In addition to his own experience, Forman has only anecdotal evidence from such ancient texts as the *Upanishads*, which do not contain any unequivocal information about cognitive processes and which thus cannot be used to prove a psychological hypothesis (see Sharf 1995; 2000).[26]

The good thing about the PCE thesis is that it allows us to view consciousness as a phenomenon independent of language, and to explore the neuropsychological foundations of "mystical" and other religious experiences, which thus cannot be reduced to culture alone. It is to such an analysis that I now turn, attempting to develop a theory of religious experience that is compatible with recent neuroscientific findings about consciousness and emotion. Two questions need to be considered: 1) what happens in the mind and the nervous system in religious experience; and 2) how religious beliefs are related to neurophysiology. I provide a partial answer to the first question by introducing Damasio's explanation of consciousness and Persinger's theory of "God Experience." After that I try to show why the relation of counter-intuitive concepts and "religious experience" is not totally arbitrary.

Neurophysiology of religious experience

Our everyday existence is conditioned by baseline nervous system activity, that under certain conditions can either speed up or slow down. In Pyysiäinen (1993: 43-46; also 1996a: 88-92) I suggested, fol-

---

26   I must plead guilty to having also myself attempted to interpret Buddhist texts in the light of the PCE thesis (Pyysiäinen 1993), although at the time I already began to realize the problems involved (see also Pyysiäinen 1998: 172-176).

lowing Forman (1990: 6), that this speeding up and slowing down can be conceptualized employing Roland Fischer's (1971; 1986) model of "ecstatic and meditative states." In this model, the "trophotropic" stimulation of the parasympathetic nervous system creates meditative states, whereas the "ergotropic" stimulation of the sympathetic nervous system brings about creative and ecstatic states. Andrew Newberg and Eugene d'Aquili (2000: 255-256) divide the results of such excitation in five categories:

1) High trophotropic activity leads to an extraordinary state of quiescence.
2) High ergotropic activity results in an extraordinary state of unblocked arousal and excitation, associated with keen alertness and concentration in the absence of discursive thought.
3) Hypertrophotropic states with ergotropic eruption at the peak of the experience.
4) Hyperergotropic states with similar trophotropic eruption.
5) Maximal stimulation of both systems (as probably in "mystical experience").

Thus we might speculate that while "mystical" experiences result from trophotropic arousal, most other forms of religious experience are due to ergotropic arousal. Both share one feature in particular: a sense of the unity of reality at least somewhat greater than the default value. This unity is then interpreted as union with god or some other counter-intuitive agent, force, or principle. Newberg and d'Aquili (2000: 262-263) interestingly speculate that such experiences tend to be interpreted impersonally when they are accompanied by neutral affect, and personally when the affect is strongly positive or negative.

The really interesting issue is what happens in human consciousness in religious, especially "mystical," experience. Damasio's (1999) theory of consciousness not only helps explain what happens neurophysiologically in a "PCE," but also provides a sound basis for a general framework for studying mysticism. (See Fig. 2 below.) According to Damasio (1999: 11, 20-26, 133, 168, 177-181, 192, 317-319), consciousness is the unified mental pattern that brings together a perceived or recalled object and the self. There are several so-called second-order neural structures with the ability to represent the proto-self and the object(s) with which it is in a temporal relationship. Such a second-order structure must involve axon pathways that receive signals from the brain sites that represent the proto-self and that can potentially represent an object. It then creates a neural pattern that describes the events occurring on the first-order maps; this pattern is experienced as a mental "image," which, however, need not be only visual. The second-order map can also signal back to the first-order maps that process objects. The main second-order structures are probably located in the superior colliculi in the midbrain, the entire cingulate cortex, the thalamus and some of the prefrontal cortices. It is thus the entire organism that contributes to the creation of consciousness, although it is the brain that holds within it a model of the whole organism (see also Clark 1997). We become conscious when our organism internally constructs and externally exhibits wordless knowledge that our organism has been changed by a perceived or recalled object.

This means that consciousness cannot be strictly distinguished from self-consciousness. The organism, as represented in the brain, seems to be the forerunner of what eventually becomes the elusive sense of self. The activity of the brain devices that represent and maintain the stability of the body state constitutes the proto-self. It is a coherent collection of neural patterns mapping the state of the organism. It is implemented in several brain-stem nuclei, the hypothalamus, the basal forebrain, and the somatosensory cortices. This is confirmed, among other evidence, by the observation that in the neonate brain most of the activity, as shown in a PET scan, takes place in precisely these areas. The neuroanatomy of the imaged account of the relationship and the enhancement of object image includes the cingulate cortices, the thalamus and the superior colliculi. (Damasio 1999: 22, 153-159, 174, 193, 266.)

From the proto-self emerges the core self, the anticipation of the autobiographical self, a transient entity that is ceaselessly re-created for each object with which the organism interacts. While we are not conscious of the proto-self, we are indeed conscious of the core self. The core self corresponds to core consciousness, which occurs when the brain's representation devices generate an imaged account of the way in which the organism is affected by the perception of an object, as well as enhancing the image of the object. Core consciousness is thus a simple biological phenomenon, which is stable across the lifetime of the organism and which is not founded on memory, reasoning or language (although working memory is an essential prerequisite for it). Core consciousness is disrupted in akinetic mutisms, absence seizures, epileptic automatisms, persistent vegetative state, coma, deep dreamless sleep, and deep anesthesia. (Damasio 1999: 16-17, 112-113, 169, 121, 174-176, 194-199.)

Core consciousness goes together with emotion and seems to be based on the same neural substrate, lack of emotion having been observed to accompany defects of core consciousness, unlike defects of extended consciousness. Both emotion and consciousness are aimed at the organism's survival, and both are rooted in the representation of the body. Background feelings and core consciousness are so closely bound together that they are not easily separable. Devices of consciousness handle the problem of allowing the individual organism to cope with environmental challenges not predicted in its basic design. (Damasio 1999: 16, 37, 100, 286, 303.)

Extended consciousness is everything core consciousness is, "only bigger and better." Extended consciousness hinges on the core self, but the self is now connected to past and future, arising in the consistent, reiterated display of some of our own personal memories. It grows throughout the process of evolution as well as during the lifetime of an individual. Extended consciousness is thus the capacity to be aware of entities and events and to generate a sense of individual perspective, ownership and agency over a large amount of knowledge. It is, quite unlike core consciousness, very much structured by language. Finally, it makes possible the existence of a conscience and thus of ethics. The autobiographical self in turn is the brain state for which the cultural history of humanity is directly relevant. It is based on an organized record of the implicit memories of past experiences of an individual organism. Although the basis of the autobiographical self is stable and invariant, its scope changes continuously as a result of experience. (Damasio 1999: 108, 173-175, 196-199, 230.)

The presence of consciousness depends on the integrity of the brain stem. Consciousness is lost in coma, which results from damage to the rear part of the brain stem, the so-called reticular formation. The reticular system maintains the cerebral cortex in an state of wakefulness and alertness. Although consciousness is more than just being awake and alert, wakefulness is its necessary prerequisite (with the exception of the special case of dream sleep). Wakefulness, background emotion and low-level attention are external signs of the internal conditions that make consciousness possible, although there are exceptional cases in which one is awake but yet deprived of core consciousness (one lacks images of knowing centered on a self). (Damasio 1999: 15, 89-90, 244-250, 260.)

One of the exceptional states of unconscious wakefulness is so-called akinetic mutism (absence of movement and speech), which results from damage to the cingulate cortex, the basal forebrain and the thalamus. These patients can pay *fleeting* and low-level attention to a *salient* event or object, but they cannot focus on objects or sustain attention over time. Both their core and their extended consciousness is severely diminished or suspended altogether. They are unable to initiate movement, because there is no conscious mind to formulate a plan; there may, however, still be slow execution of movement. When the patient recovers, he or she does not remember anything of his or her experiences while in this peculiar state with no mind. They have been awake but without consciousness. (Damasio 1999: 91-95, 101-105, 262.)

Another related phenomenon is epileptic automatism, which can appear as part of temporal-lobe absence seizures or immediately following them. In this state consciousness is momentarily suspended, along with emotion, attention and adequate behavior. In particular the absence automatisms that follow an especially long absence seizure are one of the purest examples of loss of consciousness. Those undergoing it will suddenly interrupt themselves in the middle of a sentence their movements will freeze, with the face devoid of any expression for three to some tens of seconds. The patients remain awake and the muscular tone is preserved. As the patients unfreeze, they look about, the face remaining blank, may smack their lips, fumble with their clothes, get up, turn around and walk out of the room, looking confused. When consciousness returns, the patients are bewildered and have no recollection of what has happened. There has been no content to their consciousness, although some elementary aspects of mind have been present. (Damasio 1999: 96-99.)

In sum, disruption of core consciousness (and therefore of extended consciousness) with preserved wakefulness and minimal attention and behavior takes place in akinetic mutisms and epileptic automatisms. Disruption of core consciousness with preserved wakefulness but defective minimal attention/behavior takes place in absence seizures and persistent vegetative state. Disruption of core consciousness accompanied by disruption of wakefulness takes place in coma and transient loss of consciousness caused by head injury or fainting, dreamless sleep, or deep anesthesia. (Damasio 1999: 105-106, 236-241.)

In the light of this, the introvertive mystical experience, or PCE, is most likely based on the same neurophysiology as epileptic automatisms or absence seizures. It is merely caused by deliberate effort

Type of self	Type of consciousness
Proto-self Not conscious. The activity of the brain devices that represent and maintain the stability of the body state, i.e. a coherent collection of neural patterns mapping the sate of the organism.	
Core self Conscious. A transient entity that is ceaselessly re-created for each object with which the organism interacts.	*Core consciousness* Goes together with emotions and background feelings. Occurs when the brain's representation devices generate an imaged account of the way in which the organism is affected by the perception of an object. A biological phenomenon, which is stable across the lifetime of the organism. Akinetic mutisms and epileptic automatisms: disruption of core consciousness (and also extended c.) with preserved wakefulness and minimal attention and behavior. Absence seizures and persistent vegetative state: disruption of core consciousness with preserved wakefulness but defective minimal attention and behavior. Coma and transient loss of consciousness: disruption of core consciousness accompanied by disruption of wakefulness.
Autobiographical self Based on an organized record of the implicit memories of past experiences of an individual organism.	*Extended consciousness* Everything core consciousness is, "only bigger and better." Hinges on the core self, but the self is now connected to the past and future. The capacity to be aware of entities and events and to generate a sense of individual perspective, ownership and agency.

Fig. 2. Types of consciousness and their disruptions according to Damasio.

rather than by brain injury. It is a wakeful state without consciousness. Thus no "knowledge by identity" is needed to explain a PCE. While the introvertive "mystical" experience is a kind of epileptic automatism or absence seizure, the extrovertive "mystical" experience, as well as many other types of religious experience, probably correlate with a specific kind of temporal lobe activity we will consider next.

Using a transcranial magnetic simulator that shoots a rapidly fluctuating magnetic field onto a specified patch of brain tissue, Persinger (1983) found that such artificial activation of his temporal lobes gave him for the first time in his life an experience that god exists. Since then he has run several more experimental studies on the matter, both EEG studies and various self-report surveys. All these experiments seem to support Persinger's hypothesis that religious experiences are associated with deep microseizures in the brain, known as "temporal lobe transients" (TLTs): electrophysiological changes which are brief in duration (lasting a few seconds) and focal (deep within the temporal lobe), and which can be caused for example by corticosteroid elevations due to a personal crisis, fatigue, hypoxia (lack of oxygen) or hypoglycemia. (Persinger 1983; 1987: 31-32.) It is, however, important to distinguish between Persinger's neurophysiological findings and his explanations of religious belief and behavior. There is no necessary link between temporal lobe activity and such religious concepts as 'god,' and, as I see it, Persinger has not provided a plausible explanation of their mutual relationship.

He recognizes that religion has two sides to it: on the one hand there is religious experience as generated by the functioning of the temporal lobes, on the other hand there is religious thought and behavior as generated by the intrinsic properties of human thought and language. It is thus possible to have a religious experience in the absence of traditional religious concepts or behaviors, and also to hold religious concepts and actively engage in religious activities without having religious experiences. The two aspects can of course also be combined. (Persinger 1987: 1-4, 129-132.) But if organized religious behavior is generated by the properties of thought and language, what is the role of religious experience in religion? I first consider Persinger's findings concerning TLTs and then discuss their role vis-à-vis religious beliefs and behaviors.

There are also problems with terminology. Persinger speaks of "God Experience" when he means a certain type of TLT, but this may be confusing since it is not necessary to interpret such TLTs employing the concept of 'god.' Moreover, Persinger speaks of "God Experiences" even in contexts where he actually seems to mean TLTs in general. Finally, it may be misleading to speak of god *experience*, because Persinger seems rather to mean *belief* in god. It would better to reserve the word 'experience' to what Persinger calls "extreme forms TLTs."

According to Persinger (1983; 1985; 1987: 3, 9-14, 17, 129, 138), the capacity for TLTs evolved along with the development of the temporal lobes, the hippocampus and the amygdala. It was critical for the survival of the species, because the experience of cosmic serenity could balance the newly emerged awareness of the self and the fact that the self would be extinguished in death. Thus TLTs help us to cope with incapacitating existential anxiety. Initially it may not have had any specific representation, and even today it can be labeled by such differing words as 'god,' 'nirvāna,' or the 'Great Nothingness.' All humans supposedly share the capacity for this experience, although we know it by different names and some individuals are more prone to undergo it than others.

The temporal lobe, and the hippocampus in particular, displays more electrical instability than any other part of the brain, and its cells are prone to repeated firing long after the initial stimulation has ceased. The amygdala and the hippocampus also display state-specific learning, in the sense that specific electrical patterns can come under the control of the conditions under which they were first experienced. Once conditioning has taken place, the presence of such places as churches, such persons as priests, or such situations as a personal crisis can serve to trigger TLTs. (Persinger 1987: 15.)

Most of the time the electrical activity of the temporal lobe is not exceptional, but there are moments when the threshold for a TLT is approached because of some external or internal factor, such as a personal crisis or intense concentration on some task during the early morning hours. When the threshold is crossed, TLTs follow in the form of mild "cosmic highs" or more intense experiences of conversion or rededication, that may actually completely change one's life. With a single burst in the temporal lobe, one may find truth and meaning that lasts for life. (Persinger 1987: 15-17.)

Extreme forms of TLTs are connected with temporal lobe epilepsy, characterized by psychic seizures without convulsions. Thus there may be a link to introvertive mystical experience. During these seizures, however, one may also experience vivid landscapes or perceive strange forms of living things, such as for instance small human figures or glowing forms, etc. Among other characteristics are déjà vu experiences, feelings of unreality, forced thinking and terror – or, alternatively, euphoria, "silly smiles," periods of amnesia with accompanying speaking in tongues, jumping or hopping, lip smacking and head jerking. Individuals become addicted to these experiences, because they are accompanied by an elevation of brainstem levels of norepinephrine that can elevate one's mood for days. Thus one needs to have the experience again and again in order to feel equally good. Such conditions as starvation, birth trauma, certain diseases, stress and hypoxia can produce the experience involuntarily, but fasting, breathing exercises, drugs and loud or monotonous music can also be deliberately used to help initiate the experience. (Persinger 1984c; 1987: 17-18, 30-32, 123.)

What Persinger calls a "God Experience," is a normal and more organized pattern of temporal lobe activity, which actually is not like a typical religious *experience*. "God Experience" has been found to typify the behavior of temporal lobe epileptics *between seizures*. These patients often show a remarkable interest in religion, even obsessively so, and have feelings of a unique personal destiny, see cosmic significance in everything and so on. (Persinger 1984c; 1987: 17-20, 129; Ramachandran and Blakeslee 1999: 175.) Moreover, people who report temporal lobe signs have also been shown to report paranormal experiences (Persinger 1984b).

The "God Experience" is characterized by the following features: even the most mundane situation can be felt as profoundly meaningful; there is a sense of understanding between the self and the cosmos; specific details of the experience cannot be reported; and the person feels that he or she has been allowed to see into another realm. Among the secondary characteristics are determined persistence on a topic, obsessive-compulsory behaviors, extreme sobriety and humorlessness, euphoria, and the interpretation of trivial everyday circumstances as part or proof of the "God Experience." (Persinger 1987: 23, 27-28.)

Although most TLTs occur as deep microseizures, some of them can apparently be recorded by such surface measures as EEG (Persinger 1984a: 127). Persinger (1984a) has published two such cases. The first subject was a 32-year-old woman, who had been practicing transcendental meditation for about ten years. Her EEG was recorded while she was meditating. At first alpha frequencies, typifying relaxation, were generated in the temporal, occipital, and frontal lobes. After 19 minutes, delta frequencies, with an aberrant spike and a slow-wave-like profile, emerged for about 15 to 20 seconds on the temporal lobes only. This TLT, with an amplitude about three times the pre- and post-occurrence activity, was followed by a silent period of a similar duration and then a return to the normal amplitude and frequency. After the session, the subject reported that this particular experience had been especially meaningful and that she had felt herself to be very close to "the cosmic whole." (Persinger 1984a: 128-130.)

The other subject was a 20-year-old woman, who claimed that she could speak in tongues. Her EEG was measured during a two-hour period which consisted of several speaking episodes of about 5 to 10 minutes. Spike events began to occur from the temporal lobe electrodes within 20 minutes from the beginning. Initially the spikes were related to speaking, but later they persisted even when the speaking episode was terminated. Afterwards the subject reported that the "closest contact with the Spirit" occurred during the latter periods. (Persinger 1984a: 131-132.)

These findings have recently served as a stimulus for Ramachandran and his colleagues. Their starting point is the concept of temporal lobe personality, persons who have temporal lobe seizures and therefore moving spiritual experiences of the divine presence and of cosmic significance. The limbic structures concerned with emotions create an aura of significance around everything and thus change the whole personality, even between seizures. We do not really know how this happens, but one explanation is that repeated electrical bursts within the limbic system permanently facilitate certain pathways or even open new channels, a process known as 'kindling.' It is this kindling that supposedly makes these people see cosmic significance in everything. (Ramachandran and Blakeslee 1999: 179-180, 185.)

Ramachandran and his colleagues devised an experiment with two patients with temporal lobe "symptoms." The subjects were shown words and images with ordinary, sexually arousing, violent or religious content, while their galvanic skin responses were measured. Although the kindling hypothesis would predict that the subjects would react with high galvanic skin responses to all stimuli, this was not what happened. The subjects were much more aroused by religious words and images than by anything else. While ordinary subjects would have reacted to the sexual and violent stimuli, these subjects showed diminished responses to all other than the religious stimuli. (Ramachandran et al. 1997; Ramachandran and Blakeslee 1999: 185-186.)

According to Ramachandran, this shows the kindling hypothesis to be wrong. People with temporal lobe symptoms do not see cosmic significance in *everything* around them. It was specifically the religious stimuli that aroused them. Thus one could try to explain that there are neural structures in the temporal lobes specialized for religion and enhanced by temporal lobe epilepsy. We cannot, however, be sure that the religious stimuli actually were processed in the temporal lobes. All we can safely conclude from this experiment is that there are circuits in the human brain that are involved in religious experience and that in some epileptics these are hyperactive. Ramachandran then poses the question whether these circuits have evolved for religion or whether they merely generate other emotions that are conducive to religious beliefs. (Ramachandran and Blakeslee 1999: 187-188.) Understandably, he has no answer. Here we leave behind purely experiential considerations and have to confront the question of the role played by religious concepts with regard to these temporal lobe experiences.

Neurophysiological processes and religion

Persinger (1987) has also tried to connect 'god' concepts with individual psychodynamics. The way whereby the "God Experience" becomes connected to specific concepts and behaviors is a kind of conditioning, which creates associations between the "God Experience" and various religious contents. This conditioning functions on four fronts: an emphasis on egocentric reference, a preference for particular kinds of space, the use of rituals and the use of specific verbal sequences (Persinger 1987: 102).

Of these four, the egocentric reference occupies a very central place in Persinger's account, although there seem to be some weak links in the argument. Persinger hypothesizes that some feature of the temporal lobe must be involved with the experience or even with the origin of the self-concept and the body image (which is later associated with the parietal lobe). This transient involvement of the temporal lobe with the early representation of the self then determines the themes of the "God Experience." As the infant matures, the temporal lobes assume other functions and early memories are forgotten. Only through TLTs is the adult able to reexperience the old sense of the infant self, in particular the relationship between the child and the parent. (Persinger 1987: 38-39.) The pattern of early relationships between the infant and the parents thus serves as an anticipation of the concept of 'god.'[27] A sudden coherence at lower frequencies among the temporal lobe structures can then allow access to and retrieval of mental functions that have been inaccessible since early childhood (Persinger 1984a: 127).

It is to be noted, however, that Persinger provides no references for his claims about the role of the temporal lobes with regard to the body image and the self. He merely says that there "must be" some such features. He also describes, as though echoing Freud, how the "semi-conscious" infant "floats in a dreamlike world . . . in confusion" (Persinger 1987: 44), without any discussion of the precise nature of infant cognition, which has recently been shown to be much more differentiated and realistic than has previously been thought (Stern 1985: Gallagher and Meltzoff 1996; Elman et al. 1998; Clark 1997: 35-51; Gopnik, Meltzoff, and Kuhl 2001). Be this as it may, for Persinger (1987: 42, 84), the "God Experience" is essentially an experience of the basic conception of self,[28] and "God words are symbolic extensions of these concrete childhood experiences into the adult world of words and abstract reasoning." In this way learning patterns and reinforcement history both complement and extend temporal lobe structure and function (Persinger 1987: 111, 137).

Egocentric reference is therefore of primary importance. By this concept Persinger does not mean egotism but egocentrism, in the sense that the individual places exaggerated emphasis on the validity of his or her own experiences. The most religious are also the most egocentric. They have a sense of being very special and of having special knowledge and a special mission in the world. They think they know best because they have had the experience, often answering criticism only by a condescending smile. Religions encourage this sense of

27   There have been many psychodynamic studies concerning the effect of a child's experiences and of the image of the parents on his or her later image of god (e.g. Erikson 1958; Dickie et al. 1997). I do here not discuss this issue, which is not directly relevant to my argument.

28   This view of Persinger's may receive additional support from the fact that the physiological characteristics of an ideal 'primal experience,' where one relives one's early childhood traumas or even birth, closely resemble those of a mystical experience (see Pyysiäinen 1992).

individual uniqueness; religious specialists try to convince people that their own experiences demonstrate the truth of the revelation they propagate. By creating associations between the individual's direct experience and a religious message, the message is made practically infallible. (Persinger 1987: 102-103, 114.)

There are two sources for this egocentrism. First, as also Damasio (1999: 142-143) notes, one mind always corresponds to one and only one body. We respond directly only to those stimuli that impinge on our own body, serving as the basis for the self. Although we may infer for instance that another person is hungry, this inference is not the same as feeling hunger pangs oneself. Were we able to experience the pain of others directly, the world would certainly be a very different kind of place from what it is. Secondly, this fact easily makes us ignore, or explain superstitiously, those things of which we do not have direct experience. (Persinger 1987: 43-47.)

In addition to egocentric reference, specific spaces are used to facilitate "God Experience." Churches, mosques, cemeteries etc. create unique associations, feelings of inferiority and of belonging to a group. Sacred places are set apart from the profane (see Anttonen 1996; 2000) and thus help to create an atmosphere of something non-ordinary. In this way they become paired with the religious experience, so that merely being in a sacred place can induce the experience. These places are often large in size, and are structures of a kind to make the individual feel himself or herself small, helpless and dependent, in fact very much like a child. A sacred space also allows one to experience a unique sense of belonging to a group set apart from all others. (Persinger 1987: 103-105.)

Sacred spaces are also places for rituals. According to Persinger, rituals are maintained because of what does *not* happen, i.e. because adversities are less frequent than the iterations of various rituals (see above pp. 89-90). Human beings are prone to maintain behaviors that are irrelevant to the delivery of any clear rewards but which also do not seem to bring about any harm. Thus for example praying for one's relatives can be considered effective as long as the relatives face adverse events, including death, less often than they are prayed for. This in turn serves to strengthen the egocentric religious belief. (Persinger 1987: 105-107.)

Finally, religious conditioning functions through the use of verbal sequences and special words. The omnipotence which the child attributes to its parents is transferred onto god by the language of association. The word 'love' for example first becomes paired with the mother's presence; when the powerful associations of 'love' are passed on to 'god,' 'god' becomes associated with the security of early parental relationships. (Persinger 1987: 63-67, 107-109.)

Let us stop here for a moment and call to mind Sperber's view of symbolism. According to Sperber, the symbolic mechanism performs evocative searches in the memory to find words and phrases that fit the item of information that initiated the search. Thus when a believer is asked what god is, he or she might reply: "God is love." The reply is an example of symbolism, in the sense that the believer constructs the reply by swiftly associating 'god' with another positive concept, 'love,' which is important in Christian doctrine.

This situation is very different than for example when one is asked "what is a dog?" Here the correct answer is that a dog is an animal with four legs and a tail, together with certain additional characteristics that allow us to divide all beings into dogs and non-dogs without residue (see Boyer 1994b: 187-188). But in the case of god, love is not provided as one of the necessary or sufficient characteristics of god, the reply being precisely of the form "god *is* love." In other words, the reply equates these two concepts. Yet believers probably would not agree that the statement could be reversed to the form "love is god," or that we could systematically substitute 'love' for 'god' in all possible cases. There is only a symbolic (and, for Persinger, also experiential) association between the concepts. For the believer, god remains ultimately a mystery, and the symbolic exegesis an unending process.

God words do not have any observable empirical referent. Their meaning is the result of the nonspecific clustering of a variety of different and emotionally loaded associations. When 'god' is associated with 'love,' 'life,' 'good,' etc., the positive responses associated with these words are transferred to 'god.' Then 'god' can also be paired with words that represent the upper boundaries of space and time. God words become catchall terms for the conceptual limits of space and time, and the adult concepts of infinity and eternity are experienced with the emotions of the child. (Persinger 1987: 84-85, 113; Pyysiäinen 1997.)

Unlike Sperber, Persinger does not consider such associations mere symbolic computations. They have a deeply emotive basis, emotions becoming bound to words and phrases through learning. If for instance one has prayed every night for years, it is difficult even to consider that prayers may not be efficacious, as one would then have to question one's own most intimate emotions. Repeating certain words ten thousand times cannot but make those words personally important. For Persinger, holy books, such as the Bible or the Quran, are "absolute nonsense" (*sic*) and receive their importance and authority from the fact that they are associated with the temporal lobe experiences of believers. Without such pairing, organized religion would be regarded as mere fiction and entertainment. (Persinger 1987: 78, 81, 97-99.) In other words, the way in which experiences derived from temporal lobe activity are actually conceptualized is determined by simple associations. The believer is conditioned to associate for example 'god' with an experience based on temporal lobe activity. This conditioning takes place in such a way that one learns to transfer infantile feelings towards parents or caregivers, neurally represented in the temporal lobes, to 'god' or other religious concepts. These concepts are then later able to trigger the temporal lobe experience.

To sum up somewhat: although the empirical evidence is still fragmentary, it seems probable that there is a quite specific neural mechanism involved in what has come to be known as "religious belief," "religious experience," and "mysticism." This mechanism produces an experience in which one feels that everything in the world has a meaning and that one is invested with knowledge of some great cosmic plan, of which one is also oneself a part. Persinger's theory of infantile associations, however, needs more evidence and theoretical foundation for its support. It may equally well be that religious concepts are used to express and interpret temporal lobe experiences because their counter-intuitive nature makes them consistent with the experience of cosmic oneness and significance. No infantile regression would thus be involved (see also Boyer 1996c: 87-89).

One important question is, why evolution has produced such a capacity in humans, and why human beings deliberately strive for such strange experiences. Persinger considers TLTs as providing a balancing effect for the experience of a separate and mortal self, and a way of coping with existential anxiety. While the development of the frontal lobes made it possible to inhibit one's personal desires, to anticipate the behavior of others, and to anticipate one's own future, including death, the temporal lobes provided a mechanism for experiencing a here-and-now unity with the universe, a cosmic harmony of sorts. Although the evidence for this still is very anecdotal, Ramachandran too mentions the possibility that evolution has provided us with special neural circuitry that allows for religious experience; however, he does not consider it very probable. Moreover, "existential anxiety," fear of death, etc. have not been shown to be a necessary part of religion. There are religious traditions in which they are in no way central (e.g. ancient Judaism and Vedic religion).

For Patrick McNamara (2001), the *raison d'être* of religious practices is that they activate the frontal lobes and thus contribute to the development of a free and mature individual who can feel empathy and identify with his or her fellow human beings. This is based on the fact that the prefrontal lobes, in addition to emotion, also mediate executive cognitive functions, i.e. the planning, initiation, maintenance and adjustment of non-routine and goal-directed behaviors. McNamara sees especially the ability to treat others as rational agents (see Leslie 1994; 1996 and p. 14-15 above) as based on frontal lobe activity. Feelings of empathy for example help one to understand and predict the behavior of others, and thus contribute to pro-social behavior. To the extent that religion involves interaction with superhuman agents, it serves as good practice in social and moral skills. The hyperreligiosity of temporal lobe epileptics, McNamara explains by the supposed fact that these individuals develop overactive frontal lobes as a response to the excessive electrical discharges in their temporal lobes. In other words, their frontal lobe activity tries to inhibit the chronic temporal lobe activation. This is an interesting (but seemingly unintended) reversal of Persinger's view. For McNamara, the frontal lobe inhibits the temporal lobe, whereas for Persinger it is the other way around.

The crucial question in speculations as to why we have religion is what we mean by 'religion.' We certainly cannot argue that evolution has produced any particular religious concepts and doctrines. All that evolution may have provided is a neurophysiological structure that allows for certain kinds of experiences. It may well be that we are dealing with a "runaway process," a genetically determined process which is extended beyond its initial domain (see Boyer 1994b: 289-294), not with any specific adaptation. We have religious experiences simply because our neural machinery makes this possible. The factuality of these experiences has then prompted us to develop conceptual labels and interpretations for them. These in turn may have enhanced the experiences and given them a highly esteemed status. Religious concepts are used because of their counter-intuitiveness, which allows for a certain fit between the odd experience and its conceptualization. For example the experience of cosmic unity can be interpreted as perception of an underlying unifying principle which may be referred to as "brahman," "god," etc.

As to the question of why various individuals strive for religious or mystical experiences, the answer may not be as simple as Persinger suggests. I think this question is in some sense rather similar to asking why people drink alcohol or use other drugs. They crave special kinds of experiences; different people, however, may have different reasons for doing so. Yet in each case the experience of being drunk, for example, is determined by exactly the same kinds of physiological facts and has the same psychophysiological characteristics. The mechanisms of addiction are the same, although the meaning of these experiences may be different for different people. There may in fact be much more in common between religious experiences and a state of intoxication than has yet been realized. James (1971: 373) for example likened drunkenness to a mystical state of consciousness and said that while "(s)obriety diminishes, discriminates, and says no; drunkenness expands, unites, and says yes." Some "mystics," such as the *sufis*, also have used drunkenness as a metaphor for "mystical" experience. We do not know all the psychological mechanisms related to addiction to religious experiences, or (I suspect) to being drunk. In both, however, feelings of deep significance, unity with everything, and a fading away of the boundaries of the self are characteristic, self-control being diminished and emotions strengthened. (See Barnard 1997: 25-29.)

In the next section, I attempt to construct a more subtle account of the relationship between religious experience/belief and religious concepts by focusing on the way emotions are related to counter-intuitive representations.

Emotions, religious belief, and religious experience

We began with the observation that in many different accounts of religion people are said to take religious beliefs seriously because they have learned them in ritual contexts dominated by all kinds of sensory pageantry and emotional stimulation. However, only Whitehouse and Lawson and McCauley have also tried to explain the mechanisms whereby this outcome is achieved. My own account differs from theirs in that I do not restrict emotions and religious experience to rituals only. In this sense it is closer to Boyer's account (in press: Ch 9), in which belief is viewed as a consequence, or concomitant, of use: if a belief is useful, i.e. one can make important inferences from it, it is by the same token "believed." There is thus no need to restrict the discussion belief solely in theories of ritual. (See also Hinde 1999: 65, 157.) Boyer, however, does not pay attention to emotions and religious experience. In what follows, I try to conceptualize religious belief and experience as strong emotional reactions to counter-intuitive representations.

Let us imagine that John believes in god. Does he believe because he can make many important inferences from 'god,' or can these inferences be made because John really believes in god? Which way is it? This is an important question if we want to explain why some counter-intuitive concepts and beliefs are taken seriously, or believed, and others are not. As Atran (1998: 602) says, it seems to be the emotional commitment that makes religious representations such powerful "invaders of minds," thus distinguishing them from mere fantasy like Mickey Mouse cartoons (also Pyysiäinen 2001b). For Boyer, belief follows from usefulness. But why are some representations (such as 'god') more useful than others (such as 'Mickey Mouse')? The reason why we cannot make vital social inferences from 'Mickey Mouse' is that no sane person considers Mickey Mouse to be real. That is why his representation does not have the same causal power as 'god.' (See Boyer and Walker 2000.) The crucial realization is that belief does not simply follow from usefulness and usefulness does not simply follow from belief. We are rather dealing with an interactional process. I do not think we can explain it without the notions of 'religious belief' and 'religious experience.'

If we claim that Persinger's description of the "God Experience" looks more like a description of religious belief, a way of distinguishing between belief and experience must be found. Both, after all, are defined by the emotional component. Here Whitehouse's theory of the two modes provides the right tools. Although both religious belief and experience involve strong emotions, belief does not contain the element of surprise that is so characteristic of the imagistic mode. Belief belongs to the doctrinal mode; it is the specific psychological modus, defined by emotions, that a believer assumes towards the doctrinal schemata he or she accepts as valid. Belief thus pertains to semantic memory.

Experience, for its part, is a conscious mental event (feeling, perception, thought, etc.) that does not quite fit the cognitive schemata that exist in a subject's mental databases (and which involves strong emotions). It is a *sudden* event which is encoded in episodic memory and is

felt to be somehow very important. Therefore it has the potential to
lead to a total reorganization of one's beliefs. Now, according to Sperber and Wilson's (1988: 48) relevance theory, information that is
entirely unconnected with anything in an individual's representation
of reality can only be added to this representation in the form of isolated bits and pieces, which usually means too much processing cost for
too little benefit. Religious experiences, however, often seem to have
such immediate consequences for one's life that they cannot be
ignored, although they may seem to be at odds with one's prevailing
cognitive schemata. It is this that makes them so salient, fascinating
and emotion-arousing. This may also explain the repeated claims of
"mystics" that the Ultimate Truth is beyond all words and conceptualization. Religious experience, as here understood, is by definition at
odds with the prevailing cognitive schemata.

To quote Clark (1998: 117), it is a kind of "fast 'flash-of-insight'
-style conceptual change" which we might explain as the invoking of
prototypes originally developed in another domain. A believer does
not have to be a hostage to his or her own trained responses. When
one realizes that one's pattern-recognition-based religious or non-religious convictions are not enough for a good life, new, stored prototypes can be activated by a recontextualization of the relevant problems. The cognitive tension that thus may be created between the old
and new prototypes is often expressed in various kinds of baroque
paradoxes,[29] or, alternatively, leads to a complete reversal of ones previous values (cf. Sundén's [1966; 1990] attempts at a neurophysiological explanation).

Both religious belief and experience can be explained by Damasio's
somatic marker hypothesis. The emotions that characterize both
belief and experience are bodily states that mark religious representations, in the sense that associations are formed between religious representations and bodily reactions that are experienced as fear, sad-

---

29   Both the early Mahāyāna treatises and the Lutheran tradition, for instance,
emphasize that humans cannot do anything (or almost anything) to attain their ultimate goal, which is a kind of free gift. Thus the distinction between the factual and
ideal condition of humans is expressed in highly paradoxical language. For Luther,
Christians are at once righteous and sinners: "*Simul ergo iustus, simul peccator*" (WA 2, p.
497, l. 13); "*Ideo simul sum peccator et iustus*" (WA 56, p. 70, l. 9); "*Vide nunc, quod supra
dixi, quod simul sancti, dum sunt iusti, sunt peccatores*" (WA 56, p. 347, l. 8); "*Ergo et hic simul
iustus et simul peccator*" (WA 57, p. 165, l. 12). Zen Buddhism, for its part, is famous of its
kôans ('riddles'), paradoxical stories consisting mostly of episodic scenes with no doctrinal interpretation (see the collections *Mumonkan* and *Hekiganroku*).

ness, happiness, anger or disgust. These somatic markers force particular attention on the negative outcome of the possible rejection of religious belief. As a rational cost-benefit analysis concerning the rejection or acceptance of counter-intuitive concepts far exceeds the capacity of human working memory, we have to decide by a "gut feeling," as Damasio puts it.

It is in no way necessary that one is conscious of one's somatic markers or remembers how they have been formed. Calling LeDoux's explicit and implicit memory systems to mind, we are in a position to explain how the somatic markers are formed and how they work in cases of fear. Let us imagine that a religious representation, for example the word 'god,' has become a conditioned fear stimulus for someone, due to the fact that as a child the person in question was frequently punished in the name of god for all kinds of trivial reasons. When this person later hears the word 'god,' its neural representation is transmitted from the auditory system to the amygdala and immediately elicits an emotion of fear, whose actual origins remain unconscious. If the sound also passes through the cortex to the temporal lobe memory system, the person consequently remembers the childhood punishments and feels bad.

These markers are established either slowly and gradually as one adopts religious belief, or suddenly in a religious experience. Once established, however, somatic markers are permanent, although depending on contextual factors they can be given new interpretations during the course of life. While thoughts can easily trigger emotions, it is extremely difficult if not outright impossible to turn off one's emotions by mere intellectual effort (LeDoux 1998: 303. Cf. however Ellis 1975). The markers relate religious beliefs so intimately to one's personality, and have such widespread repercussions, that they can be said to structure the whole self-system. Although I think Hinde misses the point when he says that religion can thus provide a coherent outlook on life, it is still true that religious beliefs can form a covering model for the interpretation of life. (Hinde 1999: 42.) It is not a question of coherence in a logical sense but of the fact that religious beliefs form a database, to be consulted in *abductive* reasoning. The wide applicability of religious beliefs is not a testimony to their coherence but to their evocativeness, complexity, counter-intuitiveness and non-empirical nature. As Rappaport (1999: 371) puts it, the Ultimate Sacred Postulates are "absolutely unfalsifiable and objectively unverifiable, but are nonetheless taken to be unquestionable." It is for this reason that they can occupy such a central position in the construction of the self-image.

As Hinde (1999: 38) puts it, for many belief is a basically emotional but intellectually supported part of the process of integration of the self-system. It may be, however, that *all* the basic schemata which structure our implicit, naïve theories of reality are derived from emotionally significant experiences (Epstein 1990: 170. See Ch. 7 below). This seems to have the slightly alarming implication that there is nothing specific about religion in this respect: we cling to all our mundane everyday beliefs just as emotionally as to religious beliefs. The reason why we do not usually realize this is that our naïve theories of reality are universally accepted and rarely contested. We think that we have them because they are true, not because there are some emotional reasons for believing them. Now, religious believers tend to have the same attitude towards their religious beliefs: they have them because they are true. What is different in this case is that there are always those who do not believe that these beliefs are true. Thus a controversy arises and the possible emotional basis of religious belief is revealed. This is possible because religious beliefs are counter-intuitive and thus cannot be justified by universal intuitions. And yet both religious and intuitive ontological beliefs seem to spring from emotionally significant experiences.

Ludwig Wittgenstein (1966: 57) once wrote that religious truths were more than indubitable, because "indubitability is not enough in this case . . . indubitability wouldn't be enough to make me change my whole life." But intuitive ontological beliefs too are "more than indubitable" in quite the same manner. Consider Antony Flew's (1972) argument for the nonsensical nature of religious belief. Flew summarizes John Wisdom's parable, illustrating the nature of religious belief, as follows. Two men walk in a jungle and find flowers growing in a clearing. One of them says he believes that a gardener tends the place, the other being skeptical about this. They do their best to find the gardener, but this quest proves increasingly difficult as they proceed. The believer little by little modifies his belief, saying that the gardener is invisible, intangible, etc., until the skeptic asks him how an invisible and eternally elusive gardener differs from an imaginary or non-existent gardener. (Flew 1972.)

By this means, Flew attempted to show that such statements as "God loves the world" are nonsensical because they are true for the believer in all possible worlds. No empirical fact can even in principle falsify them for the believer. They convey no information; we cannot say what difference it makes that god loves the world, all possible states of affairs being compatible with this belief. If there is nothing an assertion denies, then there is nothing it asserts either. (Flew 1972.) Clearly, however, for example the belief that the external reality exists is also regarded as true come what may, and yet it is hardly nonsensical. We obviously have many such basic beliefs which are impossible to refute, but which yet are "senseful" (See p. 32 above, and Hare 1963).

Religious belief thus is a phenomenon that relates to the doctrinal mode and semantic memory. It is the same kind of epistemic attitude we have towards all somatically marked basic beliefs, although religious belief has as its object counter-intuitive representations. This is an important difference between religion and common sense. It is possible that counter-intuitiveness has a specific, hard-wired capacity of arousing strong emotions in the same manner as large size, growling sounds etc. Emotions, after all, are an evolved mechanism that has enabled us to detect and avoid danger, and counter-intuitiveness is easily felt to be dangerous because we cannot deal with it on the basis of our intuitions. Counter-intuitive representations may both trigger emotions and be confirmed by such emotions, just as the representation of a snake triggers a fearful reaction and this fear in turn enhances cultural representations of the fear of snakes. Thus for example Guthrie's (1993) perceptual schema theory is based on the idea that belief in gods has emerged from a tendency to postulate the existence of humanlike beings to account for all kinds of threatening perceptual ambiguity (cf. Boyer 1996c; Barrett 1998: 617).

In this perspective, secondary religious emotions are specifically religious and occur when we automatically and involuntarily respond to signals arising from the conscious and deliberate manipulation of counter-intuitive mental images; in other words, when we are dealing with acquired rather than innate dispositional representations (although the acquired dispositions are obtained under the influence of innate dispositions). If there exists an innate tendency to react emotionally to counter-intuitiveness, then secondary religious emotions always also involve primary responses as one part (because religion always involves counter-intuitiveness). Thus, although Griffiths may be right in that not all secondary emotions involve primary responses, religious emotions may form an exception to this.

Primary religious emotions, if such there be, would be religious feelings corresponding to some preorganized bodily states in a Jamesian manner. On the input side this may not make sense (unless we take TLTs as somehow inherently religious), but on the output side the hypothesis that humans are hard-wired to respond with emotion to religious counterintuitiveness is an example.

But religious counter-intuitiveness is not only frightening. Gods, ancestors, etc. can equally well be comforting and a source of safety. This function is of course well known, and religion has often been judged to be something people have invented for their comfort. But religion obviously is not always comforting, as recognized by for example Guthrie (1993: 13-15). The old idea of religion as the product of fear can equally well be turned around: fear has grown out of religion. A belief in gods is not merely a wishful solace human being have invented for themselves but also a source of many kinds of fears.

This double nature of religious representations is understandable if we acknowledge that they have developed neither to lull us into a wishful sense of being taken care of by some superior beings, nor to account for various kinds of misfortunes. Rather, counter-intuitive representations exist only because they are possible (see Mithen 1998: 198-202), and because once they have emerged, as a by-product of intuitive ontologies, they have to be somehow incorporated into the human database and ascribed a meaningful role in it (see also Hinde 1999: 39). That they are used religiously for various kinds of comforting and explanatory purposes (see also Lawson and McCauley 1990: 155), is secondary to this. What may be hard-wired is the emotional reactions to counter-intuitiveness.

The fact that the same religious representations can be a source both of anxiety and of the greatest comfort may become understandable if we compare counter-intuitiveness for example to large size. A big man may appear threatening if he is a stranger, but is felt to be safe company if he happens to be one's friend. Otto's (1969) idea of a *mysterium tremendum et fascinans* thus well expresses the double nature of religious emotions.

Applying a modified principle of counter-intuitive immediacy, we may say that the strongest somatic markers relate to religious representations directly involving a counter-intuitive agent. Thus for example a representation of god tends to provoke more emotion than one of a priest. Representations of priesthood are emotion-provoking only because they necessitate the representation of a god. Following Lawson and McCauley, we could call representations that enable other representations to carry a religious meaning "enabling representations." In other words, such representations as "I want to talk to a priest," for example, receive their religious and emotion-provoking status only because of such enabling representations that connect them to representations of counter-intuitive agents such as gods.

This might explain Ramachandran's puzzling results: contrary to what was expected, the subjects did not ascribe emotional significance to everything. It may, however, be that those with a "temporal lobe personality" see deep cosmic significance in the smallest details of life only when they consciously represent the whole chain of connections that tie every fact of life to such counter-intuitive agents or forces as god. This, however, happens only momentarily. In Ramachandran's experiment the subjects may have failed to connect the sexual and violent stimuli presented to them to any counter-intuitive representations because the stimuli were presented as isolated bits without any meaningful context, and/or because the laboratory context did not allow for a religious experience to take place.

As we have seen, both Whitehouse and McCauley have emphasized that in certain rituals sensory pageantry is deliberately used to provoke emotions and thus to make the event memorable. I doubt, however, that this is always done consciously and on purpose. It is rather that those ritual forms and religious ideas that involve strong emotions (or are repeated sufficiently often) survive more efficiently. Being emotion-provoking and therefore memorable, religious counter-intuitive ideas thus are easily distributed even when they are not consciously taught. Emotional rituals are arranged because religious ideas are memorable and call for ritualized attention, but religious ideas are also memorable because of the emotional context of transmission provided by certain types of ritual.

Thus the persistence of religious representations both in individual minds and in cultures at large can be explained by the same mechanisms. Counter-intuitive representations emerge merely because they are possible, and religious thought and ritual behavior are ways of handling them in order to provide order both in mind and in society. Both the counter-intuitive nature of religious representations and the contexts in which they are transmitted contribute to the fact that religious representations tend to arouse primary as well as secondary emotions. This in turn forms the necessary basis for religious belief, and belief and experience enhance their recall and transmission.

This amounts to a new interpretation of the notions of 'religious

belief' and 'religious experience,' which thus cannot be regarded as
merely theological concepts with a Judeo-Christian bias. Defining religious belief and experience in terms of the somatic marker hypothesis
allows us to universalize the concept, so that – contrary to what many
an anthropologist would think – it can also be applied within non-literate, ethnic religions. Religious belief as a strong emotional attachment to certain religious representations obviously also forms part of
such religions as for instance native American religion, African tribal
religions or ancient Finnish folk religion, as it is based on the same
attitude we entertain towards our most basic intuitive beliefs. Religious experience, for its part, may be especially typical of non-literate
religions; imagistic religion is the oldest form of religion and is found
especially in religions with no general doctrinal schemata (Whitehouse
2000: 160-162).

The reason why this claim may sound suspect is that scholars of
religion have learned to associate the notions of 'religious belief' and
'experience' with the acceptance of theologically defined dogmas, and
to contrast them with scientific rationality. Belief is thus defined, misleadingly, in contrast to what is true. But religious belief may have as
its object any counter-intuitive representation, not only theological
doctrine. It is also not a necessary element in religious belief that it is
held against scientific evidence. The members of a non-literate ethnic
group practicing its own religion hold religious beliefs, in the sense
that they have somatically marked certain shared counter-intuitive
representations. In other words, they react with emotion to representations which play an important role in their lives, and persist in this
because these representations are felt to be important even though
they contradict intuitive expectations.

Only in the West, beginning from the 14th century (see Pyysiäinen
1999b: 111-114), has religion had to meet the challenge of science,
which has strongly shaped our view of religion (see Wiebe 1991). It is
important to realize that science is actually a unique rival to religion;
most scientific representations are also counter-intuitive (see Wolpert
1994), while yet being controlled by empirical evidence and rational
argumentation. Common sense cannot really compete with religion
because it cannot deal with counter-intuitive representations, which
common sense can only deny. Only science (and art) can claim to be
able to deal adequately with counter-intuitive representations and
thus also to make religion obsolete (cf. Durkheim). This controversy
has affected our thinking so greatly that we often tend to think that

religion can only be understood in contrast to science; it is anti-scientific by definition. This, however, is a serious mistake. In the evolution of religion science is a mere curiosity, although it has now become a very important factor shaping the development of religious thinking (see also McCauley 2000). Shifting the focus from science to intuitive ontologies allows us to understand religious belief and experience, much more fruitfully, as emotional attitudes and reactions to counter-intuitive representations.

It is this emotional mechanism that is responsible for what Durkheim and Geertz considered to be the effect of rituals, the "fusion of ethos and worldview" which gives rise to the conviction that religious conceptions are veridical. This effect, however, cannot be explained at all without psychological and neurophysiological considerations. Rituals by themselves cannot have any such effects independent of the mechanism by which rituals are mentally represented by individuals.

This opens up many vistas for future research. First, more neuroscientific research is needed on emotion and religion. This cannot take place either within the context of traditional comparative religion or of neuroscience alone; cross-disciplinary cooperation is needed. Second, the emotional effects of counter-intuitiveness need to be studied from a psychological perspective. Such studies could be carried out for example by presenting to both religious and non-religious subjects various kinds of counter-intuitive representations while measuring their galvanic skin responses, blood-pressure etc. An important part of such studies would be to explore the potential differences between religious and other kinds of counter-intuitive representations as emotional stimuli. Third, the persistence of religious somatic markers can be explored by longitudinal studies or by studying in depth the life-histories of a few people who have given up their faith after a hard personal struggle. Thus more accurate explanations could be developed of the ways in which religious ideas are adopted, sustained and transmitted. The persistence of religion as a "symbolic cultural" phenomenon cannot be explained without taking into account the emotional basis of religious belief and truth claims.

Summary

Counter-intuitive representations often seem to be at odds with the practicalities of ordinary life; it is difficult to rely on them alone in

everyday thought and decision-making. Rituals form an artificial reality of sorts, set apart from ordinary life, in which counter-intuitive representations acquire an aura of factuality; they can be used to guide
one's behavior and predict the behavior of others. Yet we do not confine the use of counter-intuitive representations to ritual contexts
alone. In non-ritual contexts as well there is much room for the application of counter-intuitive concepts and beliefs. It is not even possible
to draw a firm line between the ritual and the non-ritual.

The explanation of how and why certain counter-intuitive representations come to be regarded as true and of vital importance must
therefore be sought in something else than the mere ritual context as
such. Employing Whitehouse's theory of the two modes of religion,
the imagistic and the doctrinal, I argue that belief in the truth and
importance of religious beliefs is created in two ways: through repetition and through emotional stimulation.

Repetition not only guarantees a faithful transmission of religious
ideas but by the same token creates an attitude of belief and respect
towards the ideas and beliefs transmitted. In this mode, rituals are not
aimed at producing emotional stimulation. This, however, does not
mean that emotional reactions are missing from doctrinal religion.
Counter-intuitive representations can evoke emotions also within its
confines; often, however, these emotional experiences are soon interpreted according to the prevailing doctrinal schemata. They are then
encoded in semantic memory and lose their personal character. The
emotional commitment to schematized religious representations is
what is known as 'religious belief.'

The concept of 'religious experience' I have reserved for emotion-
laden thoughts and perceptions that come to be encoded in episodic
memory as unique events. Such experiences may be retained as such,
or be overwritten by doctrinal interpretations. On the other hand,
doctrines too may be enhanced by imagistic experiences. A specific
type of religious experience is what is known as "mystical" experience,
in which one undergoes a change in one's state of consciousness. A
specific form of "mystical" experience is what Forman calls a "pure
consciousness event" (PCE). Contrary to his claim that in a PCE one
is conscious but not conscious *of* anything, I have argued that a PCE is
an unconscious but wakeful state. In "mysticism" the tension between
personal experiences, encoded in episodic memory, and doctrinal
interpretations, stored in semantic memory, is especially salient.

Newberg and d'Aquili observe that "mystical" experience seems to be interpreted impersonally when it is accompanied by neutral affect, and personally when the affect is strongly positive or negative. Certain mystical experiences thus may be exceptional in that they do not involve emotional arousal, only an "altered state of consciousness." This, however, should be carefully studied before drawing any conclusions.

The way in which emotions contribute to religious truth claims is here explained by Damasio's "somatic marker hypothesis." The emotions that characterize both belief and experience are bodily states that mark religious representations, in the sense that associations are formed between religious representations and bodily reactions that are experienced as fear, sadness, happiness, anger or disgust. These somatic markers force particular attention on the negative outcome of the possible rejection of religious belief. As a rational cost-benefit analysis concerning the rejection or acceptance of counter-intuitive concepts far exceeds the capacity of human working memory, we have to decide by a "gut feeling," as Damasio puts it. Although this holds in most non-religious cases as well, religious thinking is special in that it involves counter-intuitive representations more difficult to process than representations merely confirming domain-specific intuitive ontology.

In the background is a neurophysiological theory of emotions on the one hand as phylogenetically ancient, informationally encapsulated, reflex-like responses that are insensitive to culture, on the other as conceptualized and conscious feelings, partly culturally determined. To the extent that we can speak of primary religious emotions, they are feelings corresponding to certain preorganized bodily states. Humans may be hard-wired for example to respond with emotion, especially fear, to religious counter-intuitiveness. Secondary religious emotions occur when we automatically and involuntarily respond to signals arising from the conscious and deliberate manipulation of counter-intuitive mental images; in other words, when we are dealing with acquired rather than innate dispositional representations. If there exists an innate tendency to react emotionally to counter-intuitiveness, then secondary religious emotions always also involve primary responses as one part.

Religious belief thus is a "gut feeling" that religious concepts and beliefs are in some sense true and important, whether one is consciously aware of having "religious beliefs" or not. Religious experience is a mental event in which religious belief is established in a sudden "fast 'flash-of-insight'-style conceptual change" (Clark), the invoking of prototypes originally developed in another domain. When one realizes that one's pattern-recognition-based convictions are not enough for a good life, new, stored prototypes are activated by a recontextualization of the relevant problems. Whereas belief can be established through the sheer repetition of the relevant beliefs, religious experience always involves emotion (with the possible exception of certain "mystical" states).

From the neuropsychological point of view, there seem to be certain specific types of experience that strengthen religious belief. Persinger uses the term "God Experience" for the deep microseizures in the brain that are known as "temporal lobe transients" (TLTs). These can be experienced as mild "cosmic highs," or as more intense experiences of conversion or rededication that may actually completely change one's life. In the more extreme forms of TLTs one may also experience vivid landscapes or perceive strange forms of living things, such as for instance small human figures or glowing forms. Among other characteristics are déjà vu experiences, feelings of unreality, forced thinking and terror (or euphoria), and periods of amnesia with accompanying speaking in tongues. Ramachandran's experiments offer further support for the hypothesis that abnormal functioning of temporal lobes correlates with hyperreligiosity.

This does not mean that religiosity can be explained as caused by brain dysfunction. All we can safely conclude is that what is commonly known as "religious experience" may be processed by special circuitry in the brain, and that abnormalities in this circuitry correlate with more extreme forms of religious thought and experience. The religiosity of an experience derives from its object: counter-intuitive representations, but the psychological and neural mechanism involved are in no way specifically "religious."

CHAPTER SIX

RELIGION, "WORLDVIEW," AND ETHICS

The work of Durkheim and Geertz has inspired some scholars of religion to view religion as essentially an expression of social categories, a specific orientation towards life, or a "worldview." The typical orientation of such views, like that of Geertz's, is towards the construction of macrolevel belief-systems which can be referred to as "worldviews," as well as by a general lack of interest in actual beliefs in counter-intuitive agents. Ultimately, however, religion cannot be thus conceptualized and explained, because it is counter-productive to see all kinds of worldviews as religious, and because only the counter-intuitive dimension can really help us to identify a specific kind of recurrent pattern.

One possibility might be to try to reduce religion in particular to the ethical dimension of worldview (in the sense of a *Weltanschauung*, not a *Weltbild*), i.e. to conceptions of good and evil, right and wrong. Although non-theological scholars of religion have rarely attempted thus to reduce religion to ethics alone, it seems to be a common idea among western laypersons that religion is above all a moral code. In fact, theologians as well often see a strong connection between religion and morality, although the more precise nature of such arguments varies.

In this chapter, I first review and critically assess views of religion as a "worldview;" I then discuss the relationship between religion and ethics in the light of Buddhist and Christian materials. My aim is to show that ethical principles spring from the practicalities of life and are given a religious justification by connecting views of right and wrong with the prevailing representations of counter-intuitive beings. Religion thus is not the source of ethics, nor is ethics the source of religion. Both reflect the natural conditions of life in social groups.

Religion as "Worldview"

The late Ninian Smart (1983: 1-2) wrote, as though echoing Geertz (to whom, however, he does not refer), that the "modern study of religions" is about "the systems of belief which, through symbols and actions, mobilize the feelings and wills of human beings." This "modern study" not only examines traditional faiths but also looks at secular symbols and ideologies, such as nationalism, Marxism, and democracy, which often rival religion "and yet in an important sense are themselves religious." According to Smart, the best expression to denote both traditional religions and ideologies is 'worldview,' a term which he says he uses in a general sense to refer to both religions and ideologies, but also to refer specifically to secular ideologies. (See below.)

According to this line of thought, religions exist because people have a need for a coherent outlook on life. Religions are regarded as bodies of systematized knowledge about the world, the self, and values and norms (i.e. ethics). The necessary background to this kind of thinking consists of epistemological assumptions that spring from Immanuel Kant's critical rationalism: objective reality is not directly mirrored in our minds but has to be reconstructed by ourselves and thus is always perceived from some particular point of view. We grasp the world through various "symbolic forms" (Cassirer) and can assume various kinds of perspectives on life, such as art and religion, as suggested by the Neo-Kantians. Edmund Husserl (1958) then attempted to create a phenomenological science, in order to study the structure of experience (*Erkenntnis*) of what is absolutely given in pure perception, without reference to empirical reality or to psychology (see Ryba 1991: 169-185, 203). Within sociology, Peter Berger and Thomas Luckmann (1966) presented their well-known thesis concerning the social construction of reality; finally, anthropologists have claimed that such world-construction is always culture-specific (e.g. Geertz 1973; Douglas 1970; 1984). Thus has emerged the question of the source of the (supposed) systematic structure of ideas concerning reality entertained in other cultures, and cognitive anthropology has developed as the systematic study of folk taxonomies and cognitive/cultural models and theories. (See Paden 1994: 52-53; 2000: 336-338; D'Andrade 1995.)

In 1975 Michael Kearney attempted to summarize the contemporary state of "world view theory." He admitted that worldviews did not constitute a well-established field of study, although there was plenty of anthropological literature dedicated to it. For Kearney, worldviews represented "culturally specific cognition" or "culturally organized systems of knowledge," and he distinguished their study from ethnosemantics in the sense that worldview research also studied nonverbal behavior, was not solely interested in folk taxonomies, and was interested also in underlying implicit assumptions. (Kearney 1975: 247-248.)

Some early worldview theorists took worldviews as consciously expressible by reflective informants,[30] although already with the studies by Robert Redfield in the 50's the existence of certain implicit structuring elements came to be recognized. Kearney himself presents a minimal set of "universal cognitive categories" which form the necessary dimensions of any functional worldview: self, other, relationship, classification, space, time and causality. He then points out that although many researchers had not been interested in the mutual interaction of the various dimensions of a worldview, there was an emerging trend towards the employment of the principles of formal logic for determining whether worldviews consisted of consistent and non-contradictory sets of "existential propositions." (Kearney 1975: 248-249.)

This highly questionable view of logical coherence in worldviews has produced one especially salient topic of discussion: the question of rationality and its relationship with cultural variability. Are members of other cultures irrational in believing and doing things that we (more often than not educated middle-aged western males) know to be untrue, ineffective, and based on mistaken assumptions and premises? In the background there strongly figures the old and often tacit assumption that there is such a thing as universal rationality and that the human mind is some kind of "logic-machine." There is assumed to be an objective reality, existing independently of the individual, and human beings are considered to be capable of perceiving this reality more or less accurately. In perceiving this reality, furthermore, the human mind is thought to operate according to the principles of logic. The more one's reasoning contradicts empirical observations and the principles of logic, the more irrational one is. But with anthropologists now arguing that all reality is culturally constructed, obviously there can be no cross-culturally valid knowledge or rationality. So how can

---

30   Juha Pentikäinen (1987: 38, 267) defines worldview as a "holistic view on nature, society, and man;" he comments that there seems to be – at least in the repertoire of his informant, Marina Takalo – a specific folk-tale category, the worldview tale, which has some "*weltanschaulich* elements." On the one hand, Pentikäinen (1987: 14, 20) interestingly criticizes the view of transmission of folklore as a mechanical process in which the human subjects are reduced to mere "talking automats," not contributing to the tradition they transmit (see also Honko 2000); on the other hand he accepts the Geertzian view that culture "develops humans," not the other way around. (Cf. Tooby and Cosmides 1995.)

we even understand, let alone criticize, the thought and behavior of members of other cultures? Does this not lead to the counter-intuitive idea that cultures (whatever they may ontologically be) are closed systems determining the behavior of individuals? And do we not know for sure that some things after all are everywhere rational and some irrational? (See Kearney 1975: 260-266; Wilson 1970; Sandbacka 1987; Stanovich and West 2000.)

Discussions of rationality have often centered upon what is almost notoriously known as "magic." It is immediately necessary to point out that underlying these discussions has often been the implicit assumption that "magic" is what others have; what we have is religion, science, or commonsense. Yet it is highly improbable that the concept of 'magic' identifies a consistent set of behaviors, i.e. that it is an analytically useful research tool. At least we cannot meaningfully differentiate between magic and religion, as was believed by the early anthropologists, Durkheim included. (See J.Z. Smith 1978: 190-207.) All of W.J. Goode's (1949) eleven oppositions characterizing the differences between magic and religion, for example, fail, because they are in fact mere illustrations of an implicit a priori conviction. We cannot distinguish between magic and religion by saying for example that religion focuses on collective issues of society while magic is employed to achieve concrete individual goals, because it is not clear what exactly this is supposed to distinguish: different kinds of organizations, modes of thought, actions, or what? In principle, we first need to have a theory of magic (if such is possible); only then can we try to define its relationship to religion. But it is doubtful that such a theory is possible, because 'magic' is such an elusive concept. In the end, all definitions of magic boil down to the assumption that people who do not belong to us (however the 'us' is defined) have certain irrational beliefs about the efficacy of certain practices. 'Irrational' here usually means 'contradicting scientific or commonsense knowledge about the world.' (See Versnel 1991: 175-179; Wiebe 1991: 4-6.)

But the class of such behaviors and beliefs is so heterogeneous that it cannot be explained by any one theory. Still less can we distinguish it from the class of religious beliefs and behaviors. From the scientific and commonsense points of view, believing for example that swallowing the oblate equals swallowing the body of Jesus is just as irrational as believing that sticking pins in a doll equals sticking them in your enemy. Yet such beliefs cannot be explained by postulating some "magical" mechanisms of thought, or principles of "magical causation." It is merely a question of transferring properties from one domain to another. The ground, for instance, has the property that it supports you when you stand on it, and this property can be counter-intuitively transferred to water (e.g. Jesus walking upon the water), using quite ordinary mechanisms of thought. (Boyer 1996a.)

Nor is it true that "magical" practices have not been tested; the testing is merely different from scientific testing. Practitioners of "magic" surely say that they know the efficacy of their practices from experience. As we have seen, however, in everyday thinking it counts as evidence of a causal relationship that two things are correlated: I prayed for grandma every night for 25 years and she did not die, so the prayer must have been efficacious. That one day she did die is nothing compared to those nearly ten thousand days that she did not. And everyone has to die sometime, right? For a believer, there is no contradiction between these ideas. Some writers, such as E.E. Evans-Pritchard (1937), have noted that science cannot be the criterion of rationality in such cases where people have no knowledge of science. Their behavior may be logical in relation to their own worldview, although that worldview itself is erroneous. Therefore the people in question are not irrational. What Evans-Pritchard fails to appreciate is that scientific rationality is not part of everyday thinking even in those cultures where science is practiced. (Cf. Winch 1970; see Horton 1993: 138-160.)

But from this it follows that it is extremely difficult to point to any specific category of "magical" beliefs and behaviors, and that the concept of 'rationality' is also very slippery. There is no absolute rationality, and one and the same action can be rational in some sense while simultaneously irrational in another. Praying for a sick child may be seen as irrational from the scientific point of view; yet it is psychologically rational if it helps one to endure the situation (I do not mean this as an exhaustive explanation of prayer). Thus 'rationality' is a very value-laden concept and expressive of one's subjective preferences. One's own religion is felt to be rational while that of others is all too often irrational – or not even religion at all but "magic."

An attempt to rescue religion from being swallowed by the categories of 'irrational' and 'magical' behaviors was apparent in Durkheim's work, and the same may be said to be the case with certain more recent attempts to downplay the supernatural element in religion and to see religion merely as a "worldview" or a means of creating, expressing, and sustaining social order. A prime example of this way of thinking is Douglas' (1984: 101) Durkheim-inspired conviction that "Religious beliefs express society's awareness of itself."

Douglas (1970: viii-xiv, 22-28, 57) distinguishes between the "experience of a bounded unit" (*group*) and the rules that bind a person to others (*grid*). As a bounded unit, the family, for example, is a group, while the ideas concerning the roles of the members of the family form a grid. Religion springs from the group, and secularization results in a situation where rules (the grid) tend to replace loyalty to the group. In the background is Basil Bernstein's (also Durkheim-inspired) theory of language as containing a worldview and linguistic codes as transforming speakers' experience. In small-scale societies speech strengthens social organization and maintains solidarity, while in more complex societies speech is expressive of individual thought (cf. Durkheim's mechanical and organic solidarity). Bernstein for example sees a correspondence between types of linguistic codes ("elaborate" vs. "restricted") and types of family. The distinction between elaborate and restricted speech corresponds to the distinction between independence from and dependence on social structure. Douglas then adopted Bernstein's idea that certain religious attitudes correspond to certain types of family, and generalized these attitudes into more comprehensive cosmologies. In other words, Douglas wants to integrate cognitive categories with social forms. (See Kearney 1975: 251-252.)

Distinguishing between weak and strong group/grid, Douglas (1970: 13-14, 57-60, 103-105, 158) arrives at four ideal types, presented below in Fig. 3. Social cohesion increases from left to right: at the far left are only loosely associated groups, while closed and strict groups are placed at the far right. Likewise, social rules and categories (grid) are stronger at the upper fields and weaker at the lower ones. Thus we obtain four cosmological ideal types, in which religion plays a role. The fact that ritualism appears in three of the four spaces is explained by the supposition that ritual, like speech, can be either elaborate or restricted, although Douglas admits that it is difficult to distinguish between these forms. In general, the more importance is ascribed to rituals, the less important are doctrines and ethics.

An important underlying idea here is that attitudes toward mind and matter are governed by the symbolism of the body. "The social body constrains the way the physical body is perceived." Thus the higher the value placed on social obligations, the more we find symbols of bodily control. Control of the body is an expression of social control; weakening of group and grid leads to weakened bodily con-

	Weak group	**Strong group**
Strong grid	Success cosmology, syncretism, ritualism, private magic, potential millennialism.	Complex regulative cosmos, a combination of dangerous and benign elements, ritualism.
Weak grid	Benign, unstructured cosmos, no magic, personal religion.	Ethical dualism, irrationalism, magical witchcraft, rituals for counter-witchcraft.

Fig. 3. Group and grid according to Douglas.

trol and by the same token to the kind of religiosity found in revivalist movements. (Douglas 1970: xiii, 64-84.)

According to Kearney (1975: 251-252), we can just as well substitute 'worldview' for 'cosmology' in Douglas' work, and take her work as the most "exciting, stimulating, creative, [and] inconsistent item concerning world view that has appeared recently." Kearney, however, warns us that in his opinion social structure should be seen as a cognitive structure. This bring us to the very important question of the mutual relationship between worldview/cosmology and social structure. Does the social structure determine the worldview or the other way around? Or is there some kind of interplay between the two?

In tackling this issue, we first of all have to recognize that whatever social organizations there are, they can only affect our behavior if they are somehow perceived and understood by human minds. In this sense social categories are necessarily also cognitive categories. On the other hand, cognition is not independent of the social environment in which it takes place. We are thus not dealing with two independent variables. All elements of a worldview must be mentally represented by individuals, but – as we have already seen in Chapter three – they are never all at once co-present in the mind of any one individual. A worldview – whether that of an individual, a culture, or an epoch – is always a scholarly construct. It is the scholar who gathers evidence and then constructs from these bits and pieces a more or less coherent whole. But we should not pretend that this whole, put together by the scholar, exists as such in the mind(s) of the individual(s) studied. It is therefore extremely problematic to look for coherence in worldviews, and to ponder how it can be that there are contradictions in people's worldviews. In everyday life it is of vital importance for us to be able to solve problems, especially those related to survival and reproduction, as we encounter them; it is less important for our varying solutions to form a conceptually coherent system.

Therefore, when a scholar tries to reconstruct the religion (in the sense of worldview) of such and such a people, it is important to realize that this is a quasi-theological enterprise of sorts, based on symbolic exegesis. This is not to say that such abstractions are illegitimate or useless. Like such concepts as 'Enlightenment' (the historical period), or 'Romanticism,' they have heuristic value, but we should not assume that they are shared by large groups of people as monolithic structures. Nor do they exercise any straightforward causal effect on our behavior. It would be an all too vague generalization to say for example that Christians go to the church because they have a Christian worldview.

This also means that the possible links connecting social forms and cosmologies/worldviews are abstract. When we go beyond these abstractions, we have to ask what makes individual people entertain certain kinds of ideas of the cosmos *and* of society. What for example makes some people participate in elaborate rituals with a minimum of doctrine? As we have seen, Whitehouse for example differentiated between two modes of religiosity and the corresponding types ritual by referring to certain cognitive principles which help to explain the social and religious forms in question.

This is not to deny that religions are characterized by cosmological ideas which can be summarized in a "worldview." I merely want to emphasize that in reality these "worldviews" are abstract summaries, not actually existing structures in people's minds, and that as such they cannot be causal factors in social development. More importantly, we cannot *define* religion as a "worldview," because "worldviews" by necessity also contain many other elements besides religious ones. A "worldview" that contained religious representations alone (if we can even imagine such a thing) would be strange indeed. If religions are just one type of worldview, then it cannot be merely being a "worldview" that characterizes religion. Furthermore, rejecting counter-intuitive agents as the defining characteristic of religion and equating religion and "worldview"/cosmological ideas gives us a concept of religion which is so broad that it no longer possesses any analytical value or explanatory power. If all cosmological ideas, or "worldviews," are religious, then we actually no longer need a separate concept of 'religion.' On the other hand, as we have seen in Chapter four, defining religion as essentially an expression of social order is a questionable practice.

Yet some scholars of religion have suggested something like this. Jacques Waardenburg (1978: 83, 103; 1986) for example argues that religion is "orientation" and that religions can be understood as "systems of orientation." Such systems make it possible for us to "find our way in life as well as in the world," to orient ourselves with the help of a frame of reference that provides meaning. There are many kinds of such systems, of which religious systems are one particular type. They involve conceptions of "spiritual beings," values and norms, and experiences and behaviors connected with cosmologically foundational forces. Religious systems of orientation only function when the meaning they provide is understood as objective and unconditional. It is the task of the scholar to reconstruct the mental universe that reflects the existential questions of the person or culture studied, and to interpret it in the light of its religious dimension.

Although this may be a good general characterization of the nature of religion, it does not really provide an answer to the question of what religion is. Since there are also other systems of orientation, religion is not *specifically* a system of orientation. Once again, we need the additional criterion of beliefs about counter-intuitive agents in order to be able to differentiate between religious and other kinds of systems of orientation; once we have this criterion, the notion of a 'system of orientation' becomes relatively inconsequential. It may even be misleading, in suggesting that the religious beliefs of an individual always form a coherent system. Such systematicity is only the property of the abstraction which is constructed out of individual beliefs by the theologian or scholar.

Another attempt to view religion as essentially an orienting worldview has been put forward by Smart (1983: 3-5, 11), who argues that the "heart of the modern study of religion is the analysis and comparison of worldviews." He claims, rather boldly, that religion is an aspect of life, and that *all* humans are "religious beings" because "orientation to life is itself a fact of life; and we are all in one way or another so oriented." We all have a worldview, and in the "modern study of religion" the main focus is on the description and understanding of worldviews; especially the more widely held, traditional belief-systems that have had widespread influence, such as Christianity, Islam, Marxism, Platonism, Confucianism etc. Yet Smart also argues for the breaking down of traditional compartmentalization, and for analyzing all worldviews and symbols together, whether traditional or not. His argument for this is that if a visitor from another planet were to visit Earth, he/she/it would not carve up the world as we do, and could not for example distinguish a temple from the Olympic stadium. Therefore, Smart argues, such distinctions are arbitrary and should not be regarded as of value in the study of religion, which "presents a perspective on the whole of human life." (Cf. also Smart 1985.)

I find this a strange argument; we know that humans *can* tell the difference between a temple and a stadium, between a priest and a psychiatrist, and that they regard the difference as very important indeed. It needs to be explained why this is so, and this can be considered the task of the study of religion (or, comparative religion). Smart (1984: 15), however, has a different conception of the study of religion, and his arguments become all the more unconvincing when he proceeds to ask rhetorically: "Why shouldn't the view that religion is our illusion itself be an illusion?" In like manner, he asks: "And isn't Marxism itself possibly a sort of projection...? Doesn't Freudianism itself become a sort of religion, with psychoanalyst as priest?" But, given Smart's own view of what religion is, the answer is obvious, and certainly no big news in any sense: Freudianism is (or presupposes) a worldview and orientation to life. Moreover, we can of course in like manner ask: why shouldn't Smart's own view be an illusion? Although such rhetorical questions may look like arguments, in fact they are not such and cannot establish anything.

Smart (1983: 15), however, goes on to argue that the first task facing the scholar is to describe religions and secular worldviews "as they actually are." I agree that we have to make clear what our data are, and describe them as accurately as possible, but that does not necessitate a naïve view of pure description uncontaminated by theory. Treating religions "on their own terms" cannot be the ideal of the study of religion, because scientific study of whatever kind simply is not part of the terms of religions (modern Christian theology perhaps partly excluded), and such an ideal would necessarily amount to the mere repetition of religious beliefs and doctrines. Even the translation of a religious text is already affected by scientific ideas concerning language, truth, history, etc., and thus cannot be carried out with absolute fidelity to the intrinsic terms of the tradition in question.

Nor can "structured empathy" be a scientific method, for the simple reason that no knowledge can be gained merely by being empathetic. No matter how much empathy I have for you, I will not know anything about you unless I draw some inferences. Knowledge can only be inferred, not transmitted by feelings. The ideal of empathy relates to Smart's (1973a: 49-50) opinion that the study of religion should be "more" than science but "less" than theology. The scholar of religion struggles on two fronts: to the right are "traditional believers" who are afraid of a dispassionate judgment of the world's religions, to the left "humanists and (*sic*) Marxists" who want to "explain away" religion. For Smart, the study of religion should also set the scene for a personal quest for spiritual truth. He asks how far we can account for religious ideas by considering them projections whose origins lie in ourselves; as though this were a meaningful question within a scientific context. (Smart 1983: 16-17, 22, 162; 1973b: 160. For a thoughtful critique, see Wiebe 1999: 53-67.) Beyond the description and classification of materials, Smart has little to offer for a methodology and theory of the study of religion. Saying that "It is also a good idea, in developing a feel for religions and worldviews, to think about symbolism" (Smart 1983: 176), is not much of a methodological program. (See Wiebe 1999: 284-286.)

It thus seems that Smart's idea of religion as worldview reflects on the one hand his unwillingness to restrict religious truth to any one tradition, on the other his unwillingness to consider religion as a set of purely human thoughts and behaviors. He therefore sacralizes the entire cosmos, and predicts that in the future some kind of religious humanism may emerge in which the numinous character of the cosmos is recognized (Smart 1983: 166). It is not the ultimate truth of some source of revelation that Smart is defending, but the binding nature of an individual's strong conviction, i.e. religious belief, whatever its object. Smart (1973a: 62) argues that although the scholar should not make judgments concerning the *existence* of gods, etc., he or she nevertheless should accept the *reality* of the objects of belief. But, as Wiebe (1999: 64) has argued, this reality, according to Smart's own analysis, springs from the believer's belief. Consequently, the description of the believer's relationship to the object(s) of belief is no more than a description of a human condition, no matter what phenomenological or hermeneutical sleight-of-hand one resorts to. It is the believer's belief that can make any kind of worldview religious; the only important thing being that the worldview fulfils the same function as the traditional religions. This is why Smart can say that all humans are religious because we all must orient ourselves to life; and this is why he can say that Freudianism is a sort of religion because it too presupposes a view about the world. Much like Waardenburg, he seems to think that basically non-religious systems can function religiously when their meaning is experienced as absolute and binding. But then we are defining religion according to the type of religious belief we discussed in the previous chapter; and it is obvious that such belief is most often found within the confines of religions in the traditional sense of the word because only they involve beliefs about counter-intuitive agents.

A more refined version of what is basically the same argument has been put forward by Paden (1994; 1999; 2000), according to whom "(r)eligions do not all inhabit the same world, but actually posit, structure, and dwell within a universe that is their own" (Paden 1994: 51). This view springs from the very sensible observation that the world of various traditions is not something that is just given to us, the natural context of our being, the context of all contexts, but the basic concept that makes all conceptualization possible (cf. Heidegger 1987). As 'world' thus is a basic, undefined concept in all folk theories of reality, the scientific idea that the world or universe is finite but without boundaries, and has emerged out of nothingness, appears as counter-intuitive from the common sense point of view (see Pyysiäinen 1998: 164).

Paden, however, has not analyzed in detail any specific world concepts or the cognitive processes involved in the representation of reality. He merely presents this concept as a heuristic tool with which to characterize the supposed function of religion in "worldmaking." A religious world is "an inhabited place," not reducible to doctrine or belief alone. In Paden's view, the idea of plural worlds "gives intelligibility to the subject matter of comparative religion" in a dozen ways. Religions create, maintain and oppose worlds by their mythic symbols; "understanding others" can be conceptualized as seeing things from the perspective of a different world; differing religious worlds have in common certain general forms of mythic and ritual behavior. The concept of 'world,' which Paden considers value-free and philosophically neutral, helps to understand the social boundaries of religion; it calls attention to the cultural diversity and social differences among and within religious systems; and it underscores how language organizes reality. The concept of 'world' also provides a unifying conceptual framework for integrating the otherwise disparate contributions of the various social science disciplines. (Paden 1994: 53-58; 2000: 335.) A world is religious to the extent that it involves "transhuman" agencies that legitimate a moral order which is part of a cosmic order (Paden 2000: 340-342).

Paden (2000: 334-336) stresses that in his view we cannot first posit what the world "really" is and then describe how it is represented in various religions. Rather, religious systems create their own worlds. 'World' is not just a term for "the totality of things," but rather draws attention to the ways totalities are constructed. Thus it serves the goal of understanding the other, which, according to Paden, cannot be achieved by imposing a foreign classification onto other peoples' representations. In this way he seems to subscribe to the kind of hermeneutical relativism that values experience (*Erlebnis*) and empathy as means of gaining knowledge, and sees cultures as closed systems. Yet he also argues that in addition to *emic* understanding the scholar has to ask what specific religious concepts refer to in the scholarly horizon of explanation, and thus to "account for them within the broader conceptual resources of the outside scholar." The comparativist interprets any single world in the light of "a general understanding of world formation."

What such general understanding might be Paden does not say, but it would be quite natural to take cognitive science as one particular field that contributes to our scientific knowledge about how people construct 'worlds.' The social sciences are another such field. But then what Paden is actually saying is that we can and should scientifically explain how and why people have the representations of the world they do. This, however, is quite at odds with the hermeneutical goal of empathetic understanding, and Paden has done nothing to indicate what kind of methodology he is actually after. One way out of this dilemma is to say that the emphasis on an *emic* approach is only meant to underscore that we should first be clear about what kinds of beliefs we wish to explain, and not to take our own implicit or explicit beliefs as the explicit beliefs of the people studied. Good description must precede explanation.

Whether this is what Paden means I do not know, but it seems to me that ultimately his program only amounts to the description and classification of materials, using the concept of 'world' as a convenient label. Although Paden (1996b) underlines the importance of comparison, without a theory we do not know what to compare, what similarities and differences are important, and in what sense. Paden's program for comparing religious worlds thus still hangs very much in the air, and does not provide a new or a fruitful way of conceptualizing religion. (Lawson 1996. See Murphy and Medin 1985; Rips 1995; Pyysiäinen 2001a.)

Horton's "neo-Tylorianism" is a philosophically more sophisticated version of the idea of religion as worldview. Horton (1993) has defended the view that there is a "deep-seated similarity between much of the world's religious thought, past and present, and the theoretical thought of the modern sciences" (Horton 1993: 347). Both religious and scientific thought try to "make up for the explanatory, predictive and practical deficiencies of everyday, common-sense reasoning." Both take the phenomena of the everyday world to be manifestations of a hidden, underlying reality. Both also try to depict this underlying reality by employing analogies with various aspects of everyday experience. Religion merely uses more personalistic language than science. The meaning of religious statements thus should be taken at their face value. If the informant says for example that god has created the world, this should be taken literally: that person believes that the world has been created by god. His or her statement is not a symbolic expression of social categories, psychological traumas or anything similar. It is an attempt at explaining how the world has come into being, by postulating an invisible agent behind it. In other words, religious thinking participates in creating a worldview.

I agree with Horton that interpretations of religious statements as "symbolic" of this or that tend to be high-handed speculations, based on a symbolic exegesis which participates in the very symbolic discourse it purportedly explains. Such theorizing does not explain the religious beliefs in question, but merely creates a new version of them. That much is true. As we have already seen, however, there is the serious problem with Horton's own view that religious explanations are compatible with all possible states of affairs, and thus are immune to evidence and argument. This entails that they are explanatory, predictive, and practical in a much more complicated way than Horton thinks. Religious beliefs cannot serve as the basis for the practical explanations and predictions which normally control our behavior, because it is impossible to deduce anything definite from them. If for example one has the religious belief that it is the ancestral spirits which make the crops grow, all we can predict on this basis is that one is likely to perform certain rites *in addition* to all the practicalities one has to do to make the crops grow. But the belief does not in any other way change the way crops are in fact grown. If one for example stops working, believing that the ancestors will do everything necessary, one will soon starve to death. Religious beliefs merely seem to explain how various entities in the world behave; however, as they lack any indication of the specific mechanisms through which counter-intuitive agents supposedly control the world, they can only be used to create behaviors that do not directly interfere with the practical manipulation of reality.

Thus the underlying reality to which religious explanations make reference is very different from that postulated by scientific explanations. It is believed to be – at least to some extent – beyond the reach of our reasoning powers even in principle, and it thus forms in some sense an ontologically separate reality, which nevertheless is somehow intertwined with the known reality. Scientific theories, for their part, simply presuppose one reality, which is believed to be explainable in principle. We cannot perceive all its dimensions accurately without special equipment, such as microscopes or particle accelerators, although the behavior of matter and energy are predictable within the limits of the statistical theory of causality in a quite different sense than is the case in religion. There are of course different opinions among scholars as to whether we should call 'real' only that aspect of reality which is revealed to us by particle physics, or whether we should accept that there are different aspects or levels or reality, so that the tables, animals, headaches, etc. of intuitive ontologies are also real. If the reductionist views of nuclear physicists occupy one end of a continuum, then the other end can be said to be occupied by those who consider that the cultural level (Popper's world-3) is also real. As I see it, these disputes boil down to how we want to define the word 'real(ity),' and I leave the question open. For my purposes it is sufficient to claim that the explanatory power of our concepts and theories increases if we take culture to be in a way 'hovering over' the microprocesses of cognition on which it is dependent.

In sum, the various versions of the view of religion as worldview fail to establish what is specific about religion because they try to define religion as essentially a system of knowledge, treating counter-intuitive agents as merely an accidental part of such a system. In the background is an unarticulated tendency to belittle what is considered "irrational" and to reinterpret other people's beliefs so that they begin to look rational from the scholar's point of view, regardless of Paden's warnings against not taking seriously people's self-reports about their explicit beliefs. Horton's view is a welcome exception to this, but he overstates his case, over-emphasizing the similarity between religion and science. What is important is that foregrounding such macro-level structures as "worldviews" has prevented scholars from realizing that ultimately all views, religious and otherwise, must be mentally represented by individual humans, and that human cognitive capacities thus set important constraints on all forms of religion.

In the next section, I turn to ethics as one important aspect of a *Weltanschauung*, attempting to show that we need on the one hand to explore ideas about good and bad, right and wrong, in a historical and evolutionary perspective; on the other, we have to look seriously at the constraints set for all ethics by moral psychology.

An Outline of Ethics as a Field of Study

Theories of ethics

It seems to be a very widespread idea – at least in the West – that there is a close link between religion and ethics. In everyday thought they are sometimes taken to be almost synonymous concepts, and religion is thought to be above all a code of right conduct. Religion is regarded as the source of our knowledge that some things are good and right, others bad and wrong. Lay persons accept this simply as given, while philosophers and theologians have sought an absolute, non-relative basis for ethics by means of rational inquiry. They have thus tried to find reasons for regarding ethics as founded on something transcending human biology, cultural ideals, and psychological facts. This attitude is in a sense shared for example by Buddhist philosophers, who have considered the goodness and badness of actions to be based on the extent to which they advance the attainment of "liberation" or "enlightenment," i.e. a counter-intuitive ultimate goal. They differ from western philosophers, however, in that their approach is much more practical (and naturally does not include 'God'). In what follows, I first try to provide a naturalistic account of ethics and morality, and then to show how, and why, ethical principles and religious counter-intuitive representations have co-evolved so that neither one can be reduced to the other.

People must have had ideas about right and wrong kinds of behaviors from very early times (see Mithen 1998; Katz 2000). In oral traditions, however, abstract logical arguments are rare; ideas are presented in the form of narratives, a patterned story of a hero's adventures being one particularly typical example. (Burkert 1996: 56-79; Rubin 1997: 15-20, 60-61; Pyysiäinen 1999a; 2000). Many early formulations of ideals about good and evil have been presented in mythological form. The texts of the Bible mainly consist of mythical and mytho-historical narratives, although in particular the letters of St. Paul also contain more abstract arguments. Exegetes have written both Old and New Testament theologies, trying to show that these two collections of texts contain more or less coherent theological systems. The enterprise, however, is based on symbolic thinking, not on a historically sound treatment of the nature of the respective texts (see also Corless 1978). As Heikki Räisänen (1990) has shown, the heterogeneity of the biblical materials is such that no single coherent "theology" can be explicated on their basis. Still less is a coherent ethical theory presented in the Bible. In their search for a central theme in the Bible, theologians have thus usually ended up selectively emphasizing Jesus' teaching of love of one's neighbor. Anders Nygren (1966) for example claims that this altruistic Christian love (*agápe*) is distinct from the merely human love (*eros*) which characterizes all other religions. The systematic treatment of religious ethics has emerged only in those cases where religious traditions have been written down and theologies have been subsequently established (see Pyysiäinen 1999a; Goody 2000). To the extent that ethical ideals are expressed and justified through stories about agents with counter-intuitive properties, however, they can be said to be expressed religiously, even though we are not dealing with a systematic presentation of religious ethical principles.

The first analytical arguments about ethical issues that we know of in the western tradition are found in Socrates' dialogues with the Sophists. Plato, and especially Aristotle, then created the tradition of philosophical ethics that has so greatly influenced Christian theology. Ethics thus understood is the philosophical, conceptual study of what is good and evil, right and wrong. Morality in turn is ethics in practice. Descriptive ethics studies the actual ethical ideals of different people(s). Normative ethics tries to establish a theoretical framework within which decisions as to what is good and right can be made on rational grounds. Metaethics, finally, studies the meaning of such concepts as 'good' and 'evil.' (See Frankena 1973: 1-9, 95-96; von Wright 1963: 1-8.)

Various theories of ethics have been presented, all of which share one feature: they are based on the view that people rely on certain abstract rules in deciding what is to be considered good and evil, right and wrong. Axiological theories say that what should be done depends on what is good in a moral sense. Deontological theories merely present certain norms of behavior, without basing them on axiological concepts (value concepts). G.E. Moore (1922), for example, considered that moral norms are always based on moral values, whereas Kant insisted that moral duties are primary. (Frankena 1973; Bayles and Henley 1989: 12-14, 58-81.)

Among normative ethical theories are contractarian theories, natural law theories, utilitarian theories and the so-called "divine command theories." Contractarian theories, such as that of Kant or that of John Rawls, exclude self-interest as a component of the rationality determining right conduct. Morality is based on an imagined ethical contract (cf. Rousseau, Locke, etc.) made behind a "veil of ignorance" – to use Rawls' counter-intuitive simile – at a time when no one yet knows under what specific conditions he or she will be thrown into the world. (Frankena 1973: 30-33; Bayles and Henley 1989: 65-67, 90-98; Johnson 1997: 22-29, 65-76, 110-125.)

Natural law theories, such as that of St. Thomas Aquinas, are based on the assumption that the physical laws of nature are supplemented by an ethical law; this directs humans toward their highest goal, which is determined by the specific essence of humanity. Thus all people all over the world supposedly know that good should be done and bad avoided, and the things that immediately follow from this. Only the most difficult ethical problems are such that only the wise understand them. (See Bayles and Henley 1989: 29-57; Johnson 1997: 72-74.)

Utilitarianism (e.g. Jeremy Bentham) in turn is based on the principle of beneficence, which says that moral conduct must always aim at producing as great a balance of good over bad as possible. Happiness is the only intrinsic good, and each person's happiness is as important as anyone's else's. Utilitarianism can be divided into act utilitarianism and rule utilitarianism, according to whether one wants to decide which acts or which rules are such that they produce the most goodness. (Frankena 1973: 34-48; Bayles and Henley 1989: 99-130.)

Divine command theories say that right conduct is obedience to the commands of god. Such theories thus steer a middle course between ethical relativism and reason-giving ethical theories. We simply need to find out what is god's will, i.e. which are the right beliefs about god's will, and then try to follow god's will as well as we can. (Quinn 1978.) Neither the Catholic Church nor for example Luther, however, have accepted this view. Their theory is one of natural law, which yet is based on the conviction that all natural laws are ultimately the creation of god. But humans can rationally understand what is good, without needing to rely on god's command alone. (Bayles and Henley 1989: 8; Gustafson 1982.)

Moore's intuitionism (1922: 10-14 *et passim*), for its part, is based on the claim that 'ought' cannot be derived from 'is;' this would be a "naturalistic fallacy." According to Moore, such derivation is not possible because morality is a nonnatural characteristic. It cannot be derived from any natural conditions, but only realized by moral intuition. Morality cannot be derived from anything else by a practical syllogism, or what Kant called a "hypothetical imperative." In other words, a morally good choice cannot be based on reasoning such as this: if, for instance, I want A, and know that A cannot occur without C, I understand that I must strive for C. Therefore C is a good choice. For Moore, moral facts are different from psychological ones, and therefore this reasoning cannot establish that C is morally good. Naturalism would deprive morality of its binding nature and would lead to ultimate relativism. Moore's own solution was to take moral knowledge as part of our intuitive knowledge. He argued that we simply *know* certain things to be *morally* good and others bad, without any need to find justification for this knowledge. In fact, such knowledge *cannot* be justified by referring to something else. It is foundational, and morality is thus an independent property of our actions.

All these theories involve well-known problems. Utilitarianism, for example, does not say how we should distribute goodness in a society, and natural law theories must face the fact that people do not always agree on moral issues and do not always do what they know to be good. The most important problem, however, has been raised by Alasdair MacIntyre (1982): since there are at present numerous competing ethical theories, ethical problems seem to be impossible to solve. We are always forced to start by considering within which theoretical framework we wish to solve a given ethical problem, which means that a given solution can be accepted as binding only if it can be shown to be exclusively superior to all others. (See Johnson 1997: 185-187, 232-236.)

Naturalist criticism of philosophical ethics

In practice we naturally have to make many kinds of choices which have ethical significance, but this does not necessarily entail that any ethical problems are solved in a philosophical sense. On some specific occasion, for instance, I either steal or do not, without basing my action on a conscious choice to do good (or bad). Naturally we also ponder what would be the right course of action in a given situation, and in not being able to accept any single authority as fundamental we may end up bewildered. But an unresolved theoretical problem does not necessarily mean that no action is therefore taken.

This reveals a very important metaethical question, which has recently been discussed: perhaps we do not rely at all on any abstract rules in our moral perception, cognition, deliberation, and action? Such authors as Paul Churchland (1989: 197-303; 1995: 143-150, 286-294), Andy Clark (1998), Owen Flanagan (1998) and Mark Johnson (1997; 1998) have argued that classical ethical theories lean on a mistaken conception of the nature of human cognition, and that taking moral psychology seriously will lead to important reconsiderations in moral theory. Various moral naturalists have reacted to the classical view in slightly differing ways. In the view of some, the impact of naturalism is primarily on metaethics and moral psychology, but not on normative ethics. Others, such as Churchland, do not accept Moore's distinction at all, and extend naturalism to normative ethics as well. (See May, Friedman, and Clark 1998: 1-4.)

According to Flanagan (1998: 19), the rational moral 'ought' of the classical theories is a secular repeat of religious transcendentalism. Likewise Johnson (1997: 12, 19-22) claims that the "Moral Law folk theory" is grounded in the Judeo-Christian moral tradition that underlies almost all western morality. With the rejection of the idea of simple divine commands, philosophers have started to look for some non-religious and yet absolute foundation for ethics. If there is no necessary reason for people to be compelled to act according to their nature, even if there were agreement as to what this nature is, how can we logically derive value judgements from factual statements? And how can one consistently choose only some aspects of human nature as the basis for ethics? (See e.g. Bayles and Henley 1989: 22-23.)

Johnson (1998: 46-47) observes that the first six decades of twentieth-century moral philosophy were dominated by metaethical questions, and yet philosophers also wanted moral philosophy to offer them moral guidance for their lives. It is as though philosophers had tried to find concrete and absolutely binding moral rules by analyzing the nature of such concepts as 'good,' 'ought,' etc., irrespective of all psychological and cultural questions. Afraid of the possibility that psychological considerations might make a truly normative moral philosophy impossible, such moral purists have sought the moral imperative in abstract concepts detached from everything that is specifically human. It is as though these philosophers were after a divine command theory without a divine being; a moral imperative which does not spring in any way from our own human constitution but rather comes from outside, as something that is just given.

In searching for the really good, philosophers thus have sought absolute normativity, grounded in some metaphysical origin which cannot be explained with reference to anything else. Philosophical systems in general have been anchored in such varying axiomatic concepts as 'essence' (Aristotle's *ousia*), 'clear and distinct ideas' (Descartes), 'sense impressions' (Hume), 'logical simples' (Russell), and 'being' (Heidegger). (See Hart 1989: 32, 39, 83; Pihlström 1996: 174-197.) In ethics the ultimate foundation can be for example a categorical imperative (Kant), moral intuition (Moore), happiness (utilitarianism), or god (divine command theories). Normative ethical systems derived from such ultimate principles supposedly cannot be naturalized (see Flanagan 1996: 193-194).

Moore's distinction between 'is' and 'ought' may well correctly describe our intuitive attitude toward moral beliefs, but these intuitions are never timeless ideas bestowed upon us from the heavens. They have their basis in the conditions in which humanity has evolved, in the cumulative experience of humankind. In that sense moral goodness is not absolute but historically conditioned. It is not a *sui generis* property but a way of saying that something is good *for us*. But Moore, like so many other philosophers, was not satisfied with this. That people regard some things as good is one thing; that some things really are good is another. There is supposed to be an "Absolute Good," which nevertheless may be completely beyond our reach (Moore 1922: 182-186).

It is this obsession to find an ultimate ground that "deconstructionists" like Jacques Derrida have criticized, on the basis that all such grounds are actually mere conceptual representations which are derived from other representations; in other words, they are not grounds in any absolute sense. (See Hart 1989: xi, 5-8, 14, 20-28, 37-39, 67, 114-117, 185.) Although "postmodernism" and cognitive science are two completely different systems of thought, they here converge, in the sense that cognitive scientists such as Varela, Rosch and Thompson (1996: 198-217, 231-233), and (with some reservations) Clark (1997: 83-102), have for example emphasized the relational, i.e. non-absolute nature of such concepts as 'self' and 'world.' Neither concept can provide an ultimate ground for ethics or for anything else, both of them being conditioned by the natural drift of evolution. The difference between postmodernism and cognitive science is that cognitive scientists accept the process of evolution as a truly explanatory factor. Neither the external world nor cognition is taken as a fixed given, both being viewed as co-evolving systems without any ultimate ground. The human cognitive system is an emergent outcome of the self-organization of matter; external reality is perceived in the way it is because evolution has shaped the human perceptual system to be such as it is. Organisms and environment enfold into each other and unfold from one another.

The human mind has not evolved to provide a coherent picture of the world, or to solve metaphysical problems, but to solve quite practical problems, related for the most part to survival and reproduction. It thus deals with practical, not logical, necessities. (Boyer 1999: 53; Barkow, Cosmides, and Tooby 1995.) We therefore have to distinguish between practical and theoretical reasoning in dealing with ethics. Theoretical reasoning employs rules of argument that are not necessarily rules for revising one's view in practice (Harman 1986: 2-4; Churchland 1996b; Stanovich and West 2000). Bearing this in mind, we may regard ethical theories as attempts at capturing people's *de facto* intuitions in systems of abstract rules, much as an anthropologist tries to summarize in a "worldview" the beliefs entertained by a given tribe. What is the *de facto* basis of ethical behavior and whether this behavior can be philosophically justified are two different questions. At the root of worries about deriving values from facts is a mistaken view of human cognition as operating according to logical principles. If this really were the case, then and only then would it be legitimate to demand that all rational behavior should always be compatible with logic, and thus that truly moral behavior should always be capable of logically sound justification. (See also Harman 1986.)

But if connectionism is right, as critics of the classical view insist, then our reasoning does not operate by abstract rules and symbols, not even in ethical problem solving. Just as our knowledge of a language for example is embodied in a hierarchy of prototypes for verbal sequences, which admit of varied instances and indefinitely many combinations, so also our moral knowledge consists of prototypes and their applications in various situations, not of abstract rules-to-be-followed. Moral learning thus consists of slowly generating a hierarchy of moral prototypes from a large number of relevant examples. In this perspective, moral disagreements are not about which rules to follow in moral reasoning, but about which moral prototype best characterizes a given situation. (Churchland 1989: 298-300; 1995: 143-147; 1996a: 305; Johnson 1997: 1-12, 78-107, 189-192; Flanagan 1996: 193.) Different people(s) also have partly different prototypes of moral decision-making situations. Interestingly, such a view is well in line with Aristotle's view of moral virtue as something acquired and refined over a lifetime of social experience (Churchland 1995: 150).

Towards naturalist ethics

According to Churchland, from the connectionist perspective we can explain how such concepts as 'good' and 'bad' emerge, how they are mentally represented as kinds of neural vector spaces, and how they guide our moral behavior. (Churchland 1996a: 302.) Moral knowledge is genuine knowledge about objective reality because it results from the continual readjustment of our convictions and practices in the light of our unfolding experience of the real world. It is more a matter of "knowing how" than "knowing that," to use Ryle's (1990: 28-32) famous distinction. Thus the authority of moral knowledge is the authority of our collective social experience. (Churchland 1989: 297-303; 1995: 286-292.) The 'ought' is not mysteriously absolute, but relatively objective.

This view of the moral person as one who has acquired a set of moral skills is very different from the traditional view of the moral person as one who has agreed to follow certain rules, such as "Always keep your promises," or who has certain overriding desires, such as maximizing the general happiness. It is simply not possible to capture all of a person's moral knowledge in a set of explicit rules, just as it is impossible to capture all of a person's athletic or artistic skills in a set of imperative sentences. Nor can appropriate desires serve as the real basis of morality; one must also have a complex understanding of what kinds of things serve lasting human happiness, be able to recognize other people's emotions, aspirations and purposes, and be able to cooperate with others in practice. (Churchland 1995: 292-293.)

A small refinement, however, may be needed, and it is offered by Clark (1998: 109-120). He emphasizes that the connectionist view of cognition does not require that we completely exclude linguistically formulated abstract rules from moral theory, or give them a place only in the initial, novice stage of learning. On the contrary, linguistic reflection and exchange are a necessary part of moral knowledge when it comes to modifying or altering acquired moral knowledge. After all, connectionist-style learning cannot account for fast "flash-of-insight"-style conceptual change, except in the sense that prototypes developed in one domain are suddenly invoked in another, where they provide the required additional resources for problem-solving. According to Clark, moral rules expressed in linguistic form may serve as context-fixing descriptions that activate new, stored prototypes. Yet the linguistic expressions do not aim at embodying the reasoning underlying moral judgement. Moral rules and principles are merely catalysts for context-fixing when we realize that our pattern-recognition-based responses are not serving well. In this way we are not hostages to our own trained responses.

In addition, linguistic exchange is also a medium in collaborative problem-solving. This is based on the commonsensical but empirically tested idea that a group of people often solve problems more efficiently than single individuals. The communal effort to achieve a consensus leads to discussion, joint planning, critiquing of each other's ideas, and requests for clarification, which helps to formulate solutions that an individual alone would not have reached. Such a capacity is an essential component of moral cognition. Language is thus used to convey to others what they need to know to facilitate the taking of a mutual perspective. Summary moral rules are flexible and negotiable constraints on collaborative action, without exhaustively reflecting our moral knowledge. (Clark 1998: 120-124.)

Johnson (1997: 109; 1998: 45-49) has tried to solve the problem of the naturalistic fallacy by suggesting that, as moral psychology tells us what is involved in making moral judgments, it thereby cultivates in us a certain wisdom that comes from knowledge concerning the nature and limits of human understanding. The purpose of moral theory should be the enrichment and cultivation of moral understanding. Moral psychology occupies a central place in this, as it provides us with moral insight into complex situations and personalities. There cannot be good moral theory without a knowledge of human motivation, of the nature of the self, of the nature of concept formation, reasoning etc. Moral theory thus understood does not provide us with rules of behavior, but with tools for judgment.

Ignoring this leads to the morality of either a fool or a tyrant. A fool's morality is characterized by "stupid mistakes," based on lack of knowledge of mind, motivation, communication etc. A tyrant's morality imposes on us absolute standards, regardless of whether as human beings we are capable of living up to such standards. Johnson argues against moral purism that 'ought' takes its content from its role in metaphorically defined moral networks. He lists nine such metaphors: moral accounting (what people owe to each other), morality as health, morality as uprightness, morality as strength or balance, morality as being in the normal place (e.g. staying on the right path), morality as obedience, morality as order, morality as light, and morality as seeing things from the right perspective. All these metaphors are based on the use of a few concrete domains as source domains in the conceptual mapping that creates the moral discourse. These source domains relate to our physical bodies and our bodily interactions with the environment we inhabit, and to physical well-being and growth. (Johnson 1997: 32-77, 193-196; 1998; see also Johnson 1987.)

Thus even the philosopher who claims that normative ethics cannot and should not be naturalized does not make his or her claim outside the space of human nature and conduct and their natural constraints. The argument according to which taking all moral behavior as natural would be dangerous and morally naïve cannot establish the falsity of ethical naturalism. Naturalist ethics can also be normative, in the sense that moral reasoning is regarded as a natural capacity of the socially-situated mind/brain, but some methods and norms of achieving moral knowledge are considered superior to others. Ethical naturalism implies no position on the question of whether there really are moral properties in the world as distinct from all other types of things, and it does not involve an attempt to define 'good' in some unitary way. It merely postulates that moral claims can be rationally supported and that they are based on facts that the sciences and humanities (including the arts) can help us understand. Naturalists, however, sometimes seem to take the refinement and growth of moral knowledge over time too much for granted. There is no intrinsic necessity for moral knowledge to grow. (Flanagan 1996: 194-195, 207-208; 1998: 22-24, 33.)

Flanagan argues that although moral knowledge is not entirely different from scientific knowledge, it is local in nature; scientific knowledge, in contrast, is universal, in the sense that for example gravity is everywhere the same. Moral knowledge is ecological, in that in different natural and cultural environments different kinds of things are good or bad for humans. What we consider moral or ethical goodness is a reflection of this (cf. von Wright 1963). Thus there are inherent tensions in ethics of a kind that are lacking in science. Yet moral knowledge is objective, in the sense that under certain circumstances things really are good, bad or neutral from the point of view of human well-being. This also entails, as Churchland has argued, that growing up as a morally good individual is not merely socialization in the sense of a passive internalization of prevailing values and norms (which would be quite at odds with the cognitive view of learning and maturation). There are constraints that govern the assessment and adjustment of moral learning, and we are capable of assuming a critical attitude towards the surrounding cultural environment. Morality does not consist of sets of fixed beliefs but rather is the quality of one's continuing performance in solving moral problems. (Churchland 1989: 298-302; 1996a: 302-303; Flanagan 1996: 205-210; 1998.) Churchland (1996a) also takes a more modest view than Flanagan (who applies a more restricted concept of science) on the difference between ethics and science as regards their local nature. For Churchland, much of scientific knowledge is also local in nature (e.g. biological knowledge about specific natural environments); conversely, within ethics there is also a tendency to try to universalize moral knowledge. (See Johnson 1997: 217-228; cf. Flanagan 1998: 24.)

A good example of a universal (or near universal) moral principle is the much discussed case of incest avoidance, which is known among all cultures. Besides humans, inbreeding is also destructive in (other) animals and even plants. Today we can say with some confidence that the most probable explanation of incest avoidance is the fact that the offspring born of incestuous relationships do not survive as efficiently as children from non-incestuous relationships. If a woman for example is impregnated by her brother (and if their own parents are unrelated), the child has one chance out of eight of dying as a fetus or infant. The early mortality of children born of incest is about twice that of outbred children. Those that survive are ten times more likely to suffer from such genetic defects as dwarfism, mental retardation or deaf-mutism. Wilson (1998: 173) thus suggests that we unconsciously follow a simple rule of thumb: "If a boy and girl are brought together before one or the other is thirty months of age and then raised in close domestic proximity ... they are devoid of later sexual interest in each other, and the very thought of it arouses an acute aversion." There is evidence that various cultures all over the world have been aware of this, although the knowledge has often been expressed in mythological form. Thus it is most probable that incest avoidance originated through genetic evolution by natural selection, although we do not as yet know the psychological mechanisms involved. (Westermarck 1921: II 82-161; 1906/1926 II 364-378, 747-752; Wilson 1998: 173-180; Hinde 1999: 178-180.) The reason why we regard incestuous relationships as immoral is that they are detrimental to the species.

Edward Westermarck, an early defender of the biological basis of incest avoidance, was not without critics during his day. His view that moral concepts are ultimately based on emotions of indignation or approval (Westermarck 1906/1926: I 4) was not favorably met in its time, although modern primatologists consider it insightful and accurate (Flack and De Waal 2000a: 20-24). This should not come as a surprise now that we have already seen how emotions are essential in all sane reasoning. James Frazer, however, argued that no "taboos" would be required if humans had a natural inclination to evade incest, thus presupposing that "taboos" cannot be expressive of moral thinking. Instincts need not be reinforced by law. Frazer's thinking reflects the contractarian view of society and morality: Humans are immoral by nature, and only commitment to a shared code of obligations and duties can tame the "savage" in us. In other words, the source of morality is considered to be in "the social" (see pp. 56-57 above). Westermarck's view, on the contrary, was that morality is based on individual judgment. Westermarck's other renowned critic was Sigmund Freud, who naturally realized that Westermarck's theory of incest avoidance was at odds with his own "theory" of the "Oedipus complex." (See Westermarck 1921: 203; 1906/1921: 747-750; Wilson 1998: 178-179.)

Westermarck's sober reply was that, while there is no law when there is no transgression (even in principle), not all laws can be taken as meant to suppress tendencies that are actually shared by people. The most obvious example is parricide, which is severely treated in many law books. Does Sir James really believe that we all have a general propensity to kill our fathers, Westermarck ironically asked. Laws should be regarded as expressive of moral feelings, not as their substitutes. (Westermarck 1921: II 203-204.)

This view of ethics is not very far from the one outlined here. Ethical statements, although influenced by emotional responses, yet represent objective knowledge about what is good (or bad) for us either locally or universally, depending on which kind of problems we are dealing with. Such goodness and badness are natural properties of things, although we have developed strong ideologies (see Bloch 1989: 120-136) to express and justify our moral judgments, and often fail to perceive their natural origins (see Hinde 1999: 174). In the statement "He is a good human being," for example, the word 'good' is often thought to express moral goodness, not technical, beneficial, hedonic, or any other variety of goodness (see von Wright 1963). But from the naturalist point of view the statement can be explained as meaning that the person in question has developed a good capacity to critically assess moral problems and arrive at the best possible solutions. This is due to the fact that the person has had a chance to learn a vast number of prototypical solutions and is sufficiently intelligent (see Churchland 1995: 227-236, 253-257) to be able to use them in an insightful manner.

From the naturalist point of view, such capacities are based on evolved mechanisms of the mind; it is hard to see how anybody could deny this. Even though the development of morality must be seen as gradual, it is nevertheless true that at some point in evolution human beings manifest the property of morality, while at an earlier point they did not. And, even if we interpreted this new capacity as a divine gift, we would have to admit that it had to have been somehow implemented in the human mind, i.e. it cannot be independent of the natural features of the mind. When and how morality has appeared or developed, however, and whether it is on a continuum with certain primate behaviors, is a matter of dispute. (See Katz 2000.)

It has been argued that all social animals, not only humans, have developed certain kinds of tools that make living together possible. These include such sympathy-related traits as attachment, helping, emotional contagion and learned adjustment, together with a system of reciprocity and punishment; the ability to internalize social rules; and the capacity to work out conflicts and repair relationships damaged by aggression. Human morality is a development of these faculties in the sense that we have an innate capacity for morality, although we are not born with a moral code in place. We humans are also invested with such unique features as for example rule internalization. What is common to us and certain other species are moral sentiments; what distinguishes us from other species is that they do not seem to have the same capacity for moral *judgement and reasoning*. (Flack and De Waal 2000a,b.)

It is, however, impossible to derive human morality from the behavioral traits of other species, without considering the psychological mechanisms that make these behaviors possible. In other words, it is not possible to combine the insights of "Hume and Kant" (Flack and De Waal 2000a: 21) without detailed psychological arguments; we need to combine Darwin and Churchland/Flanagan/Johnson, etc. to be able to trace those non-moral capacities that make moral judgements possible (see Flack and De Waal 2000b: 68).

The critics of Flack and De Waal have claimed, for example, that non-human primates (and other animals) do not have an understanding of morality, even though they have expectations concerning the immediate consequences of their behavior, and thus even achieve certain ends they have been striving for (I.S. Bernstein); that these animals do not apply the concepts of 'good' and 'bad' and that primate behavior thus does not lie on the same continuum with human morality (Jerome Kagan); that animals have not been shown to be able to identify their own acts with those of other group members (Hans Kummer); that only humans are capable of adjusting the boundaries of the social network to which prosocial behavior and a normative imperative apply (Jim Moore); that the Darwinian significance of the pro-social abilities of non-human primates should not be explained with reference to their possible functions in humans; and that in the absence of communication about mental representations animals cannot transmit learned social rules (B. Thierry). (See the respective papers in Katz 2000: 31-62.)

However, Flack and De Waal do not claim that animals are moral beings; they merely want to point out that they have those same sentiments that in us make our morality possible. Thus for example the *capacities underlying* human food sharing, not food sharing itself, are building blocks of morality. Some critics seem to think at least implicitly that, although we may recognize the existence of such building blocks, human morality is something more than a sum of all its natural building blocks (cf. also above). Like religion, it is considered to be an entity-like something that supposedly cannot be reduced to its components. It is not a graded category but something we either possess or do not. (See Flack and De Waal 2000b.) This, however, is misleading. 'Morality,' like 'culture' and 'religion,' is an abstraction based on various behaviors; it does not single out any specific entity.

The distinction between a capacity or mechanism, and the work it performs, however, may not be altogether clear in Flack and De Waal's account. We should here understand these capacities as cognitive processes that make it possible for us to represent knowledge about social relationships and also to regulate behaviors related to these relationships. Thus it is not mere abstract capacities that have evolved, but also certain moral principles as such. This, however, is not to deny that there are also non-universal moral principles that relate to specific cultural circumstances. In other words, we have both intuitive and implicit moral knowledge, and non-intuitive explicit moral knowledge.

It is also not always clear whether a particular issue is a moral issue or not. We may for example distinguish between moral principles and mere conventional rules. Experimental data from both the United States and North Korea suggest that humans have an innate capacity to recognize moral issues. That one should not for example hit other people is recognized as a moral principle, while such things as wedding etiquette are understood as mere custom. Children as young as three years old, and even children that have themselves been treated quite immorally, seem to be able to make and understand this distinction. (Turiel 1983: 75-99, 130-160; Boyer in press: Chapter Five.) There are also such problematic moral issues as abortion, pornography, and homosexuality. These are atypical moral issues in the sense that people disagree on them because of differences in the relevant background information they possess ("When does life begin?"; "What is sexuality?" etc.) The disagreement extends even to the question of whether these are moral issues at all. According to the study by Turiel, Hildebrandt and Wainryb (1991), those who took a negative perspective towards these issues employed contradictory reasoning to support their view, while those who had a positive attitude claimed that these were merely matters of personal choice.

But if basic moral issues are such that we recognize and judge them employing an innate emotional mechanism, then various religious commandments and principles cannot be the ultimate source of ethics and morality. Although religious teachings seem to contain principles and commandments that are not universal, and often may even seem to outsiders to be trivial or just plain wrong, the most important ethical doctrines often are such that they recur in most other religions as well. Therefore they have to be based on some common underlying prototypes. The various religious formulations are mere *post hoc* expressions and justifications of these principles. In the following section, I compare the ethical teachings of two different religious traditions, Christianity and Buddhism, to see what kinds of differences and similarities they possess.

It must be borne in mind that 'Christianity' and 'Buddhism' are abstractions, not coherent bodies of ideas shared by all Christians and Buddhists. When I speak of Christian and Buddhist ethics, I am talking about "theologically correct" (Barrett 1999) doctrinal formulations that are not necessarily used as such in online reasoning either by lay persons or by specialists. Yet the basic elements of these formulations can often be traced back by means of conceptual analysis to elements of various folk conceptions, which they serve to systematize, explicate and elaborate further. Thus it is often possible to show that theologically correct doctrines to some extent also reflect the ecological and socio-cultural circumstances in which they have been elaborated. When we accept that moral knowledge is genuine knowledge about objective reality, because it results from the continual readjustment of our convictions and practices in the light of our unfolding experience of the real world, the door is opened for an analysis that takes into consideration both psychological and environmental factors.

Religious Ethics

Christian and Buddhist ethics

In this section, I want to highlight the nature of religious ethics by briefly comparing Christian and Buddhist ethical doctrines as context-dependent formulations and elaborations of basic human insights. In popular writing, Christianity and Buddhism are sometimes contrasted by claiming that in Christianity various deeds and even thoughts are deemed "sinful," whereas Buddhism speaks of bad and wrong only with respect to what is and is not good for oneself in a natural sense. In Buddhism, unlike Christianity, there is no divine legislator. This view, as we will soon see, is misleading.

The concept of 'sin' is actually quite interesting. It has been specifically worked out by theologians, using a few concrete domains as source domains in the conceptual mapping that has created the concept. In the Old Testament, we find such concepts as *peša'* ('rebellion, revolt'), *het* ('misdeed, misconduct'), and *ʿavon* ('offence, misdemeanor'), which reflect the idea of a covenant between Yahweh and the

Israelites. The Israelites were supposed to keep the commands of their god. (Pöhlman 1973: Ch. VIII.) In other words, what is good and what is bad is expressed through what in a sense are legal metaphors.

In the New Testament, 'sin' is *hamartía*, a word form which in *koine* Greek means 'error, fault' (Chantraîne 1968: 71). For St. Paul, sin is 'disobedience' (*parakoe*, e.g. Romans 5:19) and 'lust' (*epithymía*, Romans 7:7), and is always directed against god, sinners being god's enemies (Romans 5:10). For Paul, sin thus is not just a name for evil deeds and bad things, but an actually existing force that inhabits humans (Romans 7:17). St. Augustine and St. Thomas subsequently developed their well-known classifications of various kinds of sins. Aquinas for example reasserted the list of "seven deadly sins," first created by Pope Gregory the Great (590-604): sloth, greed, gluttony, anger, lust, envy, and pride. These are supposed to lead one to lose god's grace, unless one repents. (See Bloomfield 1952: 43-104; Solomon 1999.) Luther in turn regarded sin as a radically personal matter, equating it with the unbelief of an individual. (See Pöhlmann 1973: Ch. VIII.)

An important distinction is made between actual individual sins and original sin (*vitium originis, peccatum originale*). St. Augustine argued that the cause of evil was sexual desire (*concupiscentia, epithymía*), and that Adam's original sin was transferred to all subsequent generations through the act of sexual intercourse (see Wolfson 1965: 158-167). The Lutheran *Confessio Augustana* (Ch. II) for example then insists that, after Adam's fall, all naturally born humans are born in sin (*cum peccato*), i.e. "without fear of God, without trust in God, and with lust (*cum concupiscentia*)."

Sin thus seems to be conceived of as a contagious entity, or even a counter-intuitive force or agent of sorts, as though folk-biological reasoning mechanisms have been transferred to the social realm (see Boyer 1993b). Thousands of pages have been written on this concept and its relation to other theological concepts, just as predicted by Sperber's theory of symbolism: an endless symbolic exegesis consisting of the search for encyclopaedic entries consistent with the concept that initiated the search. In the major theological traditions the concept of 'sin' has been detached from its moral dimension, so obvious in folk religion, and given an ontological interpretation as something that separates humans from god. 'Sin' does not seem to be a concept that might serve as a basis for a social ethics in a complex and pluralistic society. Only small-scale societies, such as the various revivalist movements, whose relationship with the surrounding mainstream society is more or less tense, have tried to build their ethics strictly on the concept of 'sin.'

It may well be that, just as personal religious experience is considered much more important in small-scale religious groups than in institutionalized religions (see above p. 95), so also a specific religious ethics needs to be supplemented, if not replaced, by a secular ethics when a religious movement grows into an organized state religion. This is usually accompanied by a development in which notions about counter-intuitive being(s) assume an increasingly subtle form, so that it becomes extremely difficult to employ them in online ethical reasoning (see Barrett 1999; Pyysiäinen 1999a); thus religious ethics and practical morality become separated. As Horton (1993: 58) observes, a lack of concern with the religious explanation of this-worldly events is a peculiar characteristic of modern Western Christianity.

Catholic moral theology (see Mausbach 1936-1938) is based on the great Aristotelian-Catholic synthesis created by St. Thomas in the 12th century. According to Thomas, ethics is based on the idea of a natural law (*lex naturalis ethica*). This law is a collection of ethical norms, which we can derive from the nature of things and which we can perceive by our reason as ethically binding. Yet it is based on the *lex aeterna* existing in god's mind. It is in the moral teachings of Christianity that the natural law is most clearly expressed. The Ten Commandments, for example, roughly correspond to the immediate conclusions (*principia secundaria*) all humans can draw by their reason from the first principle (*primum principium*) that good should be done and evil avoided (*bonum agendum, malum vitandum*). The immediate conclusions thus exist in the conscience (*synteresis*) on an innate basis. A good life can only be achieved by following the immediate conclusions. For Thomas the natural desire to realize one's essence as a rational being also includes the desire to "see God" (*visio Dei*), which, however, cannot be fully realized in this world. The worldly happiness (*beatitudo*) of humans thus is only imperfect. (See Mausbach 1936-1938: I 86-115; Gustafson 1982; Bayles and Henley 1989: 29-33.)

Continental Protestantism,[31] for its part, has produced responses to

---

31   Catholic theology has been more conservative; the most important renewals within it took place in the Second Vatican Council in 1962-1965. A few years later, Gustavo Gutierrez helped to create what is known as the "theology of liberation," with his book *Teología de la liberacion*, published in 1972. The movement subsequently spread to North America and Africa. The theology of liberation emphasizes practice over thought, substitutes the social sciences for philosophy as the servant of theology, and emphasizes that righteousness is not merely a spiritual concept but also something we have to try to realize in the sphere of economics, politics, and other secular institutions. (Ferm 1986.)

Kant's epistemological revolution and his justification of religion as a postulate of practical reason. Kant argued that we cannot know reality as it is in itself (*Ding an sich, noumena*), but only as mediated by human categories of thought and forms of perception, and that it is only our practical reason that demands that we believe that god exists. Thus the foundations of religion were no longer ontological but ethical. (Putnam 1981: 56-61; Byrne 1998.)

Kant has influenced such eminent thinkers as Schleiermacher, Albrecht Ritschl, Wilhelm Herrmann, and Adolf von Harnack, all of whom have attempted to exclude metaphysical speculations from religion, because religion was thought to belong only to the domain of value. Thus religion is reduced to mere ethics, and traditional counter-intuitive representations are interpreted as figurative ways of expressing values. (Macquarrie 1988: 73-77, 84.-89; Gustafson 1982: 74-75.)

The historical roots of the tendency of Lutheran theologians to deny the possibility of a specifically Christian ethics may be in Luther's distinction between the "worldly" and the "spiritual" kingdoms or governments. According to this teaching, god creates faith through his law and gospel. When humans realize that they can never fulfill the divine law, they can only seek refuge in Christ and god's mercy. The human world thus cannot be governed either through the divine law or through the gospel, which concern only the relationship between human beings and god. The sociopolitical order that protects human life is governed by human laws and civil authority. These, however, should be in accordance with natural law, which is not essentially different from divine law, because it reflects the essence of god's good creation. Thus Luther wanted to distinguish his teaching from what he took to be the Catholic tradition more with regard to the religious question of "salvation" than to that of ethics. (See Gustafson 1982: 12-14; Mannermaa 1998; Peura 1998; Raunio 1998.)

Thus, ironically, when certain Lutheran theologians have attempted to reduce Christianity/religion to ethics, they have also had to argue that there is no specifically Christian/religious ethics. This is because reducing religion to ethics means that the existence of counter-intuitive beings is no longer considered to be essential to religion. Representations of these beings are merely a figurative means of saying that something is good and something else bad. But, if counter-intuitive beings are not believed to exist (because they are mere metaphors), then the question arises: why should their supposed commands be binding on us? Since the specifically religious element consists precisely of counter-intuitive beings, eliminating them also entails the disappearance of the distinction between religious and other kinds of ethics. Even when the existence of counter-intuitive beings is not directly denied, their role is restricted to the purely "spiritual" realm, distinct from ethics. (See also. Wiebe 1991: 7.) Consequently religion loses its legitimating power, becoming merely a source of inspiration and of useful ethical metaphors and similes. In this way a sociocultural situation such as that described by Luhmann (above p. 73) gradually arises: religion, reduced to ethics, is no longer the backbone of the society, but instead becomes just one social sub-system among others, trying to compensate for deficiencies in them.

Reformed theologians such as Calvin, however, have favored a different solution from the Lutherans: for them the divine law has an exhortative and instructional use to those who have received grace. According to the radical Anabaptists, furthermore, Christ and his teachings were a "new law" for Christians. In the light of this law judgments were made about the rectitude of the lives of persons, leading to the disciplinary practice of "banning" offenders from full fellowship (as later within some Protestant revivalist movements). (Gustafson 1982: 13-20.)

It has thus been typical of the Christian theological tradition that god as a counter-intuitive agent is thought to have laid down certain principles of conduct which are to be obeyed and from which new principles can also be deduced. This is most clearly the case in the Anabaptist and revivalist movements, more recent "divine command theories" and Barth's dialectical theology. Catholic and Lutheran theologies, on the other hand, have placed human reason between god and morality: ethical decisions can be made in the light of human reason, but this reason has been given to us by god.

In the Catholic and Lutheran traditions the *raison d'être* of ethical behavior is that human social relations are thought to be best arranged on a moral basis. It is thus for our own worldly good that we should follow god's will or the right reason given to us by god. In the Reformed tradition, as well as in various Protestant revivalist movements, this is also thought to affect the relationship between god and humans, in the sense that believing Christians are considered both constrained to and capable of a more ethical behavior than sinners. In other words, in reformed theology questions of salvation (what happens to us in counter-intuitive reality) and ethics become merged, whereas in the Catholic and Lutheran traditions these are by and large separate issues: humans are saved by grace alone, and ethics is a worldly matter.[32]

Only in small-scale religious groups, such as revivalist movements, can a strict religious ethics be accepted as a binding ideal. As soon as a religious movement is institutionalized and develops into what is often called a 'church' (in contrast to 'sect'), the strict other-worldly ethics must be compromised in favor of a more mundane view, the religious group now being an essential part of the profane society. One good example is the way in which the radical ethical demands of the Sermon on the Mount (Matthew 5-7) have been reinterpreted as either meant only for the small group of the perfect or as an "interim ethics," meant to be valid only during the very short time before the Kingdom of God came about. Yet exegetes nowadays assume that at the time when Jesus supposedly proclaimed his teachings, they were meant and understood literally. (See Berner 1979; Syreeni 1987.) Similarly, in the Buddhist tradition, the legendary first converts of the Buddha are said to have attained enlightenment very easily, whereas at present many Buddhists say that enlightenment is now impossible and they will have to wait until a new buddha comes into the world (e.g. Bunnag 1973: 19-23; Spiro 1972: 67, 77). Thus nirvāna cannot be the guiding ideal in practice.

Religious groups with a rigorously "other-worldly" ethics thus can never develop into dominant forces in a society. Cultural selection favors those religions which compromise their strict ethics. Moreover, various extreme forms of religious ethics may be so destructive that the whole movement is placed in peril, as is the case with the various small groups that have committed collective suicide for religious reasons. If for no other reason, such ideals can never become widespread.

Whatever the interpretation of the possibility and necessity of a specifically Christian ethics, it is the Ten Commandments (Exodus 20: 1-17), the "double commandment of love," and the "golden rule" that are generally regarded as the core of Christian ethics. The double commandment tells us to love god with all our heart and our neighbor as ourselves (Matthew 22:37-40); the golden rule says that we should

---

32 This of course is a gross simplification of the many theological subtleties involved, which could only be properly discussed in a separate monograph. This brief presentation, however, outlines the main tenets. For a more detailed comparison, see e.g. Pöhlmann 1973.

do to others what we wish them to do to us (Matthew 7:12). The Ten Commandments prohibit seven kinds of things: drudgery without holiday, disrespect for one's parents, killing, adultery, stealing, false testimony against another, and aspiring to another's house, wife, servants, cattle etc. In addition, the first three items listed in verses 1-7 relate to one's duties towards god: one is not to keep any other god, make an image of god, or take god's name in vain.

* * *

We now come to the ethics of Buddhism. Although the term 'Buddhist ethics' is occasionally used by both western and non-western authors (e.g. Thomas 1975: 180; Johansson 1985; 147; Keown 1995: 6; de Silva 1998. See Jamgön Kongtrul Lodrö Tayé 1998), there is no systematic exposition of a theoretical ethical framework in the canonical or commentarial sources of the Buddhist tradition (see also Rājavaramuni 1990). Instead, we only find straightforward precepts for "right conduct" or "morality" (*śīla*).[33]

As in the case of Christianity, similarly in the Buddhist case it is not always clear how we should draw the line between ethics/morality and soteriology. On the one hand, there are five explicit precepts for lay persons (eight for very devoted ones), over 200 for monks (227 in the Theravāda tradition), and 350 for nuns. On the other hand, these precepts are considered to have the same function as the whole doctrine: helping one to attain liberation. Thus the Buddhist doctrine as a whole can be considered to be co-extensive with ethics, or, alternatively, there can be said to be no specific ethics in Buddhism.

The five precepts are expressed in the following formula: "I take upon myself the precept of abstaining from killing, from taking what is not given, from sensuous misconduct, from lying, and from intoxicants that cloud the mind" (*Papañcasudani* 9. 7-10). Very devoted laypersons may adopt three additional precepts: not to eat at the wrong time, not to watch dancing and shows or wear garlands, perfumes etc., and not to sleep in high and big beds. These eight principles were known in the old "Hīnayāna" schools, and appear in the texts in various forms and in various contexts, but are systematically

---

33   The Pāli word *sīla* (skt. *śīla*) means 1) 'nature,' 'character,' 'habit;' specifically 2) "moral practice, good character, Buddhist ethics, code of morality." (*Pali-English Dictionary* 1972: 712.)

presented and commented only in the writings of the 5th century CE commentator, Buddhaghosa (see Thomas 1975: 176-180; Hirakawa 1990: 55, 61-66).

The precepts for monks and nuns are grouped in seven sections, according to the gravity of the offences they deal with and how the offender is to be treated. The four most serious offences, leading to exclusion from the monastic community, are sexual misconduct, stealing, killing, and lying. Other precepts deal mostly with the monks' (or nuns') proper behavior in general, and with their relationships with nuns (or monks) and laypersons and with private property. Many of the precepts seem to us rather trivial, such as for example the prohibition against tickling another monk with one's fingers. (*Vinayapitakam.*)

A new emphasis as regards the ideal of the good life was first put forward by the Mahāyānists at the beginning of the common era. They criticized the "Hīnayāna" ideal of enlightenment as selfish, and also disapproved of the cold intellectualism and the strict dichotomy between monks and laymen that typified the *Abhidharma* tradition explicating the teachings of the *sūtras*. In their stead they offered the ideal of the *bodhisattva*, one who strives for buddhahood but remains in the world for the benefit of others. This ideal was now considered to be within the reach of everyone, and the striving was conceived of as taking place through the ten mythological phases (*bhūmis*) and the six or ten "perfections" formerly regarded as the Buddha's properties before his buddhahood, the lists of which vary in various sources. In certain Mahāyāna sources they consist of giving, right conduct (*śīla*), patience, vigor, meditation and wisdom; in some cases also skill in means, vows, power, and knowledge. Right conduct is divided into the ten precepts of the *bodhisattva*: abstention from killing, stealing, sensuous misconduct, four kinds of wrong speech, lust, anger, and wrong views. (Hirakawa 1990: 299-303.)

The precepts are said to be not only meant as a basis for a worldly social ethics, with the merely instrumental value of facilitating social organization, but rather to be intimately related to the Buddhist idea of the ultimate, counter-intuitive goal of human beings. As John Holt (1981) has argued, the *vinaya* is meant to help the monk or nun to eradicate all delusions and craving and to attain *nirvāna* (see also Rājavaramuni 1990: 30). Although the "Hīnayāna" and Mahāyāna schools are much in agreement as to the contents of the five precepts and the *vinaya*, they differ in their interpretation of the ultimate goal.

The "Hīnayānists" regard *nirvāna* as an "exit" (*nihsarana*) from the world, with 'world' here meaning what is variously referred to as *samsāra*, the 'three levels of reality' (*lokas*, *vacararas*, or *dhātus*), and 'compounded dharmas.' (Pyysiäinen 1993: 91-94.) Says the *Udāna* (pp. 80-81):

> There is, o monks, a supranormal (*abhūtam*) an unborn, a not made and an uncompounded (*asankhata*), because, o monks, if there were not this supranormal, unborn, not made and uncompounded one would not know an exit (*nissarana*) from what is born, produced (*bhūta*), made and compounded.

Whether this exit was understood literally or metaphorically, the idea itself has the structure of an opposition between *samsāra* and *nirvāna*, or world and a counter-intuitive reality/condition. In the Mahāyāna *samsāra* and *nirvāna* were paradoxically claimed to be identical in the final analysis, and all sentient beings were declared to be already enlightened, whether they knew it or not. This teaching is also accompanied by a greater emphasis on compassion toward all beings. (Pyysiäinen 1993: 104-120.)

It thus seems that while there is basic agreement between "Hīnayāna" and Mahāyāna as to what kinds of things are to be avoided and what kinds cultivated, the significance of these things with regard to attaining the ultimate goal is different in the two branches of Buddhism. In Mahāyāna right conduct cannot be a means to attain enlightenment because everybody is already enlightened. It is said for example that the bodhisattva "neither discriminates Samsara as Samsara, nor Nirvana as Nirvana. When he thus does not discriminate, they, i.e. Samsara and Nirvana, become exactly the same." (*Astadasasāhasrikāprajñāpāramitāsūtra* in a Gilgit manuscript, p. 650.) And, "... from the highest view-point ... the Phenomenal Life itself is Nirvāna ..." (*Ratnagotravibhāga* p. 219.)

Thus the whole of Buddhist teaching is only a "skillful means" (see Pye 1978) by which the Buddha instructs beings, without necessarily corresponding to anything in reality. Nirvāna is "like a dream, like an illusion," a "mere word and sign" (*Pañcavimsatisāhasrikāprajñāpāramitāsūtra* p. 211; *Astadasasāhasrikāprajñāpāramitāsūtra* in a Gilgit manuscript p. 531). And, "(n)irvāna is like a dream; nothing is seen to be in transmigration, nor does anything ever enter into Nirvāna" (*Lankāvatārasūtra* p. 77). The precepts of right conduct are likewise "mere words and signs" and an illusion, which must be taken seriously only in so far as we participate in the mock show called the 'world.' But when *this* teaching itself is taken as merely a skilful means, what follows is an infinite regression (see Pyysiäinen 1996b).

Thus both Buddhism and Christianity are characterized by the fact that moral knowledge is expressed in linguistically formulated abstract rules which seem to function along the lines suggested by Clark. This has led Churchland (1995: 291-292) to observe that although morality emerges from our ability to learn from mistakes, the Judaic, Christian and Islamic views of moral truths are supposed to be based on divine revelation and command, which seems to make such learning impossible: revealed truths are eternal and do not change. This is an oversimplification which yet contains an important truth. The major Christian churches do not consider morality simply as based on divine commandments, that much is true. But what individual preachers proclaim in their sermons is another and practically more important matter. At the level of the mental representations actually held by the majority of believers, the relationship between ethics and god may thus be much more straightforward (to infer from Barrett and Keil 1996 and Barrett 1998 *mutatis mutandis*). Churchland is also right in that from the churchly point of view the Christian dogma is considered immutable, and all theological changes are attributed to reinterpretations that are supposed merely to restore the 'original' meaning of the revealed texts (see Pyysiäinen 1999a).

The reason why religious beliefs, ethical and otherwise, are considered to be immune to all change is that, as we have seen in the previous chapter, they have been somatically marked. In not being inductive generalizations from observations or deductions from some general principles, but rather abductions from emotion-provoking mythical prototypes, they cannot lend themselves to rational criticism. It is only in practice that they may gradually change (somewhat contrary to Clark's argument). Such change, however, is usually interpreted as merely restoring the lost original meaning. Due to the evocative nature of religious ethical sanctions, they cannot change because of purely rational argumentation. One can never empirically establish, for example, that saints and martyrs are after all not rewarded in heaven, and evil persons not punished in hell.

If we now compare the basic ethical principles of Buddhism and Christianity, it is apparent that they contain both common items that may be said to derive from the common human experience in evolution, and also items that reflect specific sociocultural situations. Lying, stealing, killing, and adultery appear in both religions as the gravest offences. They are also such that it is easy to see their import for negotiating social relationships and maintaining equilibrium. Jesus' reinterpretations in Matthew are also in accord with this, despite their rather radical formulation: we should treat our neighbor as our equal. The only difference between Christianity and Buddhism in this respect is that while the Old Testament commandment specifically prohibits adultery as such, Buddhist monks are expected to abstain from all expressions of their sexuality; only lay persons can interpret "sexual misconduct" as meaning adultery only. In addition to the above, the Decalogue also mentions disrespect for one's parents and aspiring to another's house, wife, servants, cattle etc. These too clearly belong to the class of principles that relate to social behavior. Thus the two religions obviously give expression to moral views their followers would have anyway (with the exception of the ideal of celibacy), irrespective of their religion.

But the Decalogue also prohibits drudgery without holiday, and warns against keeping any other god, making an image of god, and taking god's name in vain. The first of these commandments may also have some important social consequences, but the latter three can clearly be considered specific to monotheistic religion. They do not have a direct bearing on social relationships. Thus the commandments about the importance of keeping a holiday and about the proper worship of god, and the warning against coveting one's neighbor's property, are lacking in the Buddhist list. They are exclusively Judaic. In their stead we find in Buddhism such things as precepts prohibiting the wearing of garlands etc., sleeping in luxurious beds, using intoxicants, and watching shows. Whereas the language of the Decalogue reflects the problems of an agrarian society, certain of the Buddhist precepts are expressive of urban life. As we shall soon see, Buddhism arose in a rapidly urbanizing context.

Mind and society in interaction

In this section, I give an overview of the most important factors in the sociocultural development that has led to the emergence of organized societies and the related ethical norms and values. Thus I want to illustrate how the social mind has coevolved together with the development of society. It is neither the mind alone that has shaped society, nor society alone that has shaped the mind; both have shaped each other in a process of interaction. (See Varela, Rosch, and Thompson 1996; Clark 1997.)

Jared Diamond (1999) has put forward an interesting theory concerning the factors that have determined the course of world history during the last 13 000 years. According to him (Diamond 1999: 86, 103), the single most important factor in world history, affecting all subsequent economic and cultural development, was the transition from a hunter-gatherer life-style to one based on agrarian food production. Food production, which according to Margaret Ehrenberg was a female invention, first arose in the Fertile Crescent in Southwest Asia in *c.* 8500 – 8000 BC; in China a thousand years later; in Meso-America and the Andes in 3500 BC; possibly in the Sahel zone in Africa (by 5000 BC), West Africa (by 3000 BC), and Ethiopia (?), as well as in New Guinea (7000 BC?); and in the Eastern United States in 2500 BC. In Western Europe, food production arose between 6000 and 3500 BC as an imported invention. (Diamond 1999: 94-101; Ehrenberg 1995: 77-80, 99.)

The adoption of agriculture gave a headstart to those who took this decisive step first. In agriculture and cattle breeding, one acre of land can feed ten to a hundred times more people than in hunter-gatherer societies. As a result of agriculture people adopt fixed abodes; this in turn makes a shorter birth interval possible, thus contributing to population density. As a food surplus can now be stored, a class of non-food-producing specialists (kings, bureaucrats, priests etc.) can emerge. A political elite, protected by soldiers, now gains control over the food produced by others, and some form of a system of taxation develops. (Diamond 1999: 88-90. See also Gellner 1990; Ehrenberg 1990: 85-90; Sahlins 1968: 5, 15.)

There are five reasons why people gradually change their hunting and gathering life style in favor of agriculture: 1) a decline in the availability of wild foods; 2) an increased availability of domesticable wild plants makes steps leading to plant domestication more rewarding; 3) the cumulative development of technologies on which food production eventually depends; 4) the two-way link between the rise in population density and in food production (the causal chain operates in both directions); and 5) the higher density of food producer populations enables them to kill hunter-gatherers by their sheer numbers. (Diamond 1999: 107-113.)

Diamond distinguishes between bands, tribes, chiefdoms and states. Probably all humans lived in *bands* until at least 40 000 years ago; most until 11 000 years ago. The New Guinea Fayu people have until quite recently lived as single families scattered throughout the swamp, only coming together once or twice a year to exchange brides. These comings together of a few dozen Fayu have been rare and frightening events for the participants. Murder for instance being the leading cause of death in bands, similarly these Fayu gatherings have been characterized by the fact that in them murderers must face the relatives of the people they have killed, and the possibility of a violent outburst is constantly present. *Tribal organization*, consisting of more than one formally recognized kinship group, began to emerge around 13 000 years ago in the Fertile Crescent and later in certain other areas. *Chiefdoms* had arisen by around 5500 BC in the Fertile Crescent and by around 1000 in Meso-America and the Andes. According to Diamond, it was only now, for the first time in history, that people had to learn to encounter strangers regularly without attempting to kill them, the monopoly on the right to use violence having been handed over to the chief. *States* in turn arose around 3700 in Mesopotamia, in *c.* 300 BC in Mesoamerica, over 2000 years ago in the Andes, China, and Southeast Asia, and over 1000 years ago in West Africa. (Diamond 1999: 265-281.)

Proceeding from bands towards states the size of the group increases, and so do bureaucracy and class differences. The strongest single predictor of societal complexity seems to be the size of the regional population. An increase in population brings about an increase in conflict between unrelated strangers; the impossibility of communal decisions increases; a means of transferring goods between members of society is needed; and the higher population density requires some arrangement for determining the rights and obligations of individuals sharing the same territory. All these factors contribute to the development of chiefdoms and finally states. Part of the solution to these problems was to give a monopoly over the use of force to a single person, the chief. This is related to the newly arisen elite's fourfold solution to the problem of how to gain popular support while maintaining a more comfortable lifestyle: 1) arming the elite and disarming the populace; 2) making the masses happy by redistributing in popular ways much of the tribute received; 3) using the monopoly of force to promote happiness by maintaining public order; and 4) constructing an ideology or religion justifying the existing order. While the supernatural beliefs of bands and tribes did not serve to justify central authority or to maintain peace between unrelated individuals, the emergence of chiefdoms introduced a change in this respect. Counter-intuitive beliefs became institutionalized. (Diamond 1999: 265-292; Gellner

1990: 27. Cf. Sahlins 1968.) Douglas (1984: 112) argues that although beliefs about spiritual powers always have a relation to social order, this naturally is not possible when there is no such order.[34] Precisely this seems to be Diamond's point. Whitehouse (2000: 3, 160-2, 170), for his part (and apparently independent from Diamond), dates the first emergence of the doctrinal mode of religion to c. 6000-3000; during that period it arouse in Mesopotamia and also in North China, the Nile and Indus valley, Mesoamerica, and the Andes.

In western Eurasia, from 8500 BC until the rise of Greece and then Italy after 500 BC, almost all major innovations arose in or near the Fertile Crescent. Even between 1000 and 1450 CE the flow of science and technology was for the most part from the Islamic societies into Europe, and China was much ahead of Europe in technology and culture. Soon after that, however, things started to change. The Fertile Crescent had no other geographical advantages than the concentration of domesticable wild plants and animals. With the Greek conquest of all advanced societies from Greece eastward to India, power for the first time started to shift westward. This development was continued by Rome's conquest of Greece in the second century BC. After the Fall of Rome, power shifted to western and northern Europe. The reason is obvious: the Fertile Crescent and eastern Mediterranean societies had arisen in an ecologically fragile environment. Large areas of the former glory are now desert, semidesert, steppe, or heavily eroded, because the large forests have been destroyed. Because of the low rainfall, the regrowth of vegetation was unable to keep pace with its destruction. In Europe west and north of the Alps things were different, making possible the development of such things as capitalism, a merchant class, patent protection for inventions, and democracy. (Diamond 1999: 409-417.)

In India food production seems to have begun in the seventh millennium BC, when wheat, barley, and other crops that had been domesticated in the Fertile Crescent spread through Iran to the Indus Valley. Domesticates derived from the indigenous species of the Indian subcontinent, such as humped cattle and sesame, appeared later. Rice cultivation began in the valleys of the Indus

---

34   Douglas (1984: 133-136) argues that various kinds of purity regulations do not belong to ethics, but that they can yet maintain morality. Moral transgressions are transformed into transgressions of the purity regulations to make them easier to handle ritually. This, however, seems to mask an implicit conception of ethics as something non-natural and unrelated to psychological and social conditions.

and the Ganges around 1800 BC (see Parpola 1988: 207). (Diamond 1999: 101. Cf. Parpola 1988: 196.) There is also evidence of cultural changes that resulted from contacts between India and Mesopotamia. In the late fourth millennium an urbanization process had begun in Mesopotamia and had spread to Elam, Baluchistan and India, which in the third millennium formed a common, more or less uniform cultural and commercial area. The famous Indus civilization flourished in northwestern India and what is now Pakistan in 2500 – 1900 BC. After its destruction, a process of reurbanization, resulting from advances in paddy cultivation, began in the Ganges Valley in the 6th century, reaching its peak around 300 BC. This is also the background of the rise of Buddhism. (A. Parpola 1993; S. Parpola 1993; Erdosy 1985: 94-98; Gombrich 1988: 50-53; Collins 1993: 307.)

The shift from a hunter-gatherer lifestyle to one based on agriculture is interestingly reflected in the Buddhist cosmogonical myth which is found in such works as the *Aggaññasutta* in the *Tipitaka*, the *Mahāvastu*, the *Abhidharmakośa*, and the *Mūlasarvāstivāda Vinaya*. The *Aggaññasutta* relates how the first people, who had bodies formed of mind and were nourished by joy, for the first time tasted the "earthessence" and thus acquired corporeal bodies. Then, after the invention of rice cultivation, the storing of food, and private ownership, some began to steal rice from their neighbors, which in turn led to violence. Therefore people had to elect the best from among themselves as a king, with the exclusive right to punish and reward. (Dīghanikāya III 84-93; Collins 1993: 341-346.)

There is also another myth about the "wheel-turning" king, which is related in the *Cakkavattisīhanādasutta* in the *Tipitaka* (*Dīghanikāya* III 58-79). According to this narrative, once upon a time there was a "wheel-turning" king who ruled according to the *Dharma*, not with the sword, and who later became a recluse. After his death, his son, grandson, etc. likewise ruled with the *Dharma*, until a successor came who could not understand the *Dharma*, and thus soon brought the whole kingdom into peril. Thus, whereas the *Aggaññasutta* (*Dīghanikāya* III 84-93) sees kingship as a necessary restraint people have set for themselves because of their evil tendencies, the *Cakkavattisīhanādasutta* describes "a fantasy world in which royal rule is possible without violence" (Collins 1993: 442). But, as Steven Collins (1993: 387) has observed, there is no evidence that the story of the first king has ever been used in practice to legitimate kingship, although in the long run world-renunciatory asceticism has been supportive of kingship rather than subversive of it (Collins 1996: 443). It seems, however, that King Aśoka (reigned *c.* 268-232 BC), who favored Buddhism, has been regarded as an embodiment of this idea of the good ruler, in whose figure the king and the holy man (*sādhu*) are combined. On the other hand, the myth may actually have been formed according to the model provided by Aśoka's rule. (See Strong 1983.).

Thus it is apparent that ideas about good and bad, right and wrong, have developed and grown increasingly organized together with the development of society. The complexity of social organization increasing as we move on from bands to tribes, from tribes to chiefdoms, and from chiefdoms to states, likewise the ethical problem of the organization of relationships between individuals become more complicated. In bands, ideas concerning good and bad behaviors may be as unconnected as are the individual members of the band.

The most important shift seems to have been the adoption of agriculture and the concomitant way of life with fixed dwellings, the storage of food, and the subsequent division of labor (see Gellner 1990: 17-18). Just as the Buddhist *Aggaññasutta* relates how the institution of kingship arose following food production and the violence that it helped to unleash, the biblical myth of Cain and Abel (Genesis 4) shows Abel as a peaceful herder, Cain as a violent farmer. If, however, Diamond (1999: 277) is right about violence as the leading cause of death in bands, then the cultural change related to the emergence of agriculture marks not so much the onset of violent behavior but *inequality* as the specific cause of violence. On the other hand, some have argued that hunter-gatherers live a very peaceful and harmonious life, with more pleasure, humanity and social equality than in agriculturalist societies, and that the emergence of agriculture was a moral and also a material catastrophe (e.g. Sahlins 1972: 11-17; Ehrenberg 1995: 38,42, 52. See Gellner 1990: 31-33). Likewise Diamond (1999: 104-105) recognizes that the onset of agriculture did not make people's life easier than in hunter-gatherer societies.

Speculating along these lines, we may say that here, as in so many other cases, specific problems and their specific solutions have coevolved. If counter-intuitive representations had not been used (because of their simplicity) to organize social relations in bands, then there would have been no organized religion and no systematic ethics. These two then evolved together with more advanced forms of society, counter-intuitive ideas having become more organized concurrently with social relationships. Thus social forms are created by religious and ethical ideas as much as they are reflected by them.

What may be taken as moral precepts are thus closely interwoven with religious duties. Religious representations are used to express and to sanction certain natural moral duties related to everyday life, and no sharp distinction can be made between the ethical and the religious. From the naturalist point of view, it is apparent that just as individuals acquire moral knowledge by learning a vast number of prototypes, abstract religious moral precepts too have developed in social practice to function as a kind of control mechanism. Theoretically we could of course imagine religious commandments that for example exhorted people to parricide, promiscuity, systematic lying etc., yet nothing like this is anywhere found. The reason is simple: such a society would not survive for long. Suicide cults do not last for centuries. Religious ethical principles thus are not random speculations but relate firmly to social reality. It is here also that the question of power sets in; religious representations being highly evocative and involving inferential gaps, they underdetermine their own interpretation, and judging some interpretations as heretical means exercising power. Although individuals may entertain any religious ethical ideas whatsoever, only a restricted number of such ideas tend to be dominant in a given culture at a given time. Yet religious representations do not always legitimate the *status quo* but may also be used to criticize the existing order (see e.g. Alho 1976).

Differences in the sociocultural backgrounds of Buddhism and Christianity

If we now compare Buddhism and Christianity, it is notable that the development of Buddhism has not taken place continuously in any one cultural sphere dominated by Buddhism alone. Instead, it has always had to adapt itself (if such a figure of speech may be allowed) to new environments, and has approached monopoly status only in Tibet (absorbing the local shamanic *Bon-po* into itself), Myanmar (Burma), and Cambodia. In Sri Lanka there has been a bitter war between the Sinhalese Buddhists and the Tamil minority, who are Hindus, the history of this struggle going back to the 4th century CE. (B.L. Smith 1978; Tambiah 1986; Lopez 1990: 11.) These countries, however, have been too small, too poor, and too isolated to acquire such power as to give rise to a need for a secularized universal ethics (as in Catholic Europe). It is imported western secular views on ethical issues (see Gombrich 1988: 181-197) that now form the most relevant challenge for Buddhist ethics, due to the economical and technological supremacy of western civilizations.[35]

The development of Christianity has followed a different path. If we accept Diamond's vision, the key to understanding this is that Europe has taken the lead in technology and economics partly due to geographical reasons. European geography has been ideal for the development of technology and the concomitant modern way of life because of the indented coastline and the five peninsulas, together with the lack of any major geographical barriers within the European continent. Eurasia also spans a much greater distance east – west than north – south, quite unlike the Americas and Africa; this means a larger area with similar climatic conditions, over which innovations related to food production can spread rapidly. These geographical characteristics have stimulated competition between various parts of the continent and thus innovation, at the same time keeping Europe internally connected. Europe has never been politically unified (the present development of the European Union notwithstanding); dozens or hundreds of independent statelets have competed with each other, thus stimulating economic growth and all kinds of innovation. When for instance Columbus was turned down by the first three rulers to whom he turned for funding for his voyage, he could go to the fourth, the king and queen of Spain, who finally consented – with well-known consequences. In unified countries such as China such competition was not possible, and technological and economic development might stop completely because of a single wrong decision. Despite the dispersed political power, however, ideas and innovations were able to travel in Europe, where there was no geographical boundaries of the kind that split the continents of Africa and the Americas. (Diamond 1999: 176-191, 412-416.) In not being united under a single despot, Europe was an ideal place for innovative competition. Tolerance of heretical views had already helped to produce science in ancient Greece, and now it continued to foster innovation. This explains why Europe has been the leading force in the industrial and technological revolution. (Diamond 1999: 92, 250.)

---

35   This relates to so-called "globalization," a process whereby all the countries of the world have gradually become subsumed under a single global economic system. This supposedly has a unifying effect also on such non-material aspects of culture as religion, although Peter Beyer has argued that no such global community exists which would allow the emergence of a single global religion. (See Beyer 1984.)

All this means that Christian theology could develop over centuries without serious rivals in an optimally unified Europe, whereas Buddhism never gained such a monopoly in India, and was finally destroyed there by Muslim invaders by the 13th century. Western Europe was characterized by Catholic cultural unity from the creation of Charlemagne's empire in the 8th century until the Reformation. Thus the Graeco-Roman tradition in philosophical thinking could continue in theology, even though Aristotle was first forgotten and then rediscovered in the 11th century due to the preservation of his writings in the Arabic world. (See Copleston 1950.) The Reformation, which finally broke this cultural unity, was made possible by the fact that Europe was divided into different nation states in which there was growing dissatisfaction with papal supremacy. There was thus competition between various churches and views; yet this competition occurred within what can be regarded as the same religion.

An important difference between the Buddhist and Christian cultures is that in the former philosophical thinking has always been closely tied to religion, whereas in the West these two split apart in the 17th century. (See Lopez 1990: 11-12.) Buddhist ethics too is closely tied to "the broader philosophy of leading a meaningful life," as Padmasiri de Silva (1998: 65) puts it (see e.g. Jamgön Kongtrul Lodrö Tayé 1998). Likewise the myth of the ideal king testifies to a very different attitude than that for instance of Luther, who argued that although it was possible for a ruler to be a Christian, such a combination was rare and difficult (WA 11, pp. 273-274). In Buddhist cultures there has been no indigenous tradition of purely mundane ethics, i.e. ethics as not related to the counter-intuitive goal of humans and not expressed in religious terms. Nor is there a systematic theory of ethics, or meta-ethics, in the Buddhist scriptures.

During modern times, however, new ethical issues have arisen, necessitating the creation of new moral guidelines. Some Theravādins, for example, have reacted in a conservative manner, emphasizing the religious aspect of Buddhism, while others have opted for reform, in the sense that they want Buddhism to contribute to the development of the secular society and in this way contribute to the "welfare of the many," as the traditional formula has it. (Reynolds 1990). In Sri Lanka for example a sort of Buddhist "social gospel," emphasizing mundane social reform, has emerged (Bond 1988: 241-294). Certain modern authors have also tried to systematize Buddhist ideas about right and wrong behaviors into some kind of ethical sys-

tem. Keown (1995: xiv-xv) for example writes that he will appeal to
textual sources "as authoritative evidence for the 'Buddhist view' on
ethical issues and seek to apply them in a modern context." He
believes that if the problems of scriptural interpretation can be over-
come, and "the meaning of scripture established beyond reasonable
doubt," we will have discovered moral truths which are as valid now
as they were in the 4th century BC, and thus can be used to solve such
modern ethical problems as those related for instance to embryo
research. De Silva (1998), for his part, has extensively discussed environmental ethics from a Buddhist point of view.

It seems, however, that *nirvāna* and the buddha ideal (see Griffiths
1994), as they have been understood and developed by specialists, are
too abstract to be used in online reasoning about ethical issues. Buddhist practice has therefore been influenced by various popular elements, such as Hindu devotionalism, which in a way complement it
(see Ames 1966; Obeyesekere 1966; Tambiah 1970; Spiro 1972;
Evers 1977; Collins 1982: 147-153). The same, of course, is true of
Christian theology and its relation to popular religion. (See Barret and
Keil 1996; Barrett 1999).

Only within the Christian tradition has ethics been divorced from the
religious realm proper and become a matter of natural reason alone.
Yet in this case too natural reason has ultimately been regarded as given
to humans by god. It is true that the Ten Commandments are to be
found in the holy book, the Bible; nevertheless, they have been interpreted in the major churches as only expressing natural morality (e.g. as
corresponding to the *principia secundaria* of the Catholic tradition). It is
my hypothesis that such a naturalization of revealed truths is only possible when the religion in question has acquired such a monopoly that its
doctrines can really be believed to give expression to "what everybody
knows to be true." This is precisely the formula St. Thomas uses in his
proofs of god's existence: "(e)verybody understands" (*omnes intelligunt*)
that the first mover has to be god, and "everybody speaks of this as
God" (*quod omnes dicunt Deum*) (*Summa Theologiæ* I, Q II art 3). Such thinking and parlance is only possible when there are no serious competing
ideologies against which it is necessary to argue. It was the voyages of
discovery and the Reformation that eventually broke this cultural unity.
At that time, however, Europe was gaining the lead in technology and
economics, and Europeans were thus soon able to subsume the newly
discovered cultures. Consequently, what was considered natural in the
way of ethics could still be dictated by Europeans.

We can therefore speculate that religion and ethics tend to part when a sharp dichotomy emerges between the unique worldly lives of unique individuals and an eternal life in a counter-intuitive reality (presided over by a counter-intuitive agent), while at the same time the religion in question has a monopoly in an aggressively expansive society. It is then possible for religion to become "otherworldly" and not directly involved in ethics (although it serves as a kind of background condition). In the case of Buddhism for instance, the ideas of eternal life and a counter-intuitive agent as well as a religious monopoly in an expansive culture are both missing.

It is not possible here to go beyond these vague speculations. What would be needed is detailed historical work on the religious, social and ethical development of particular societies, together with empirical work in moral psychology, to determine how people actually reason in ethical judgments. On the social level, we need for example systematic studies of how strict religious morality correlates with the size of the religious group in question, as well as with its openness vs. closedness vis-à-vis the society. On the level of the individual, exploration is needed as to how actual moral reasoning is guided by religious proto-types or micro theories. My hypothesis is that for example what looks like inconsistent thinking and behavior in ethical issues, such as killing physicians who perform abortions, can be explained by the fact that we do not rely on abstract rules in moral judgment even in religion. Explaining the mechanisms involved in such reasoning is of vital importance in creating a just society, although moral conclusions never follow from scientific explanations as neat logical inferences.

Summary

It is counter-productive to equate between 'religion' and 'worldview.' "Worldviews" are mere abstract summaries constructed by scholars and thus are not such identifiable wholes that could be empirically explored. The microprocesses of cognition must be taken into consideration if we want to explain how individuals build and organize their cognitive environments. Moreover, serious beliefs about counter-intuitive agents and forces clearly form an identifiable recurrent pattern across cognitive environments; it is this pattern that I consider the primary object of the cognitive study of religion.

Ethics and morality are often considered an important aspect of a

"worldview." Laypersons and theologians even sometimes see religion
as nothing more than ethics. This is incorrect because morality is partly an evolved property of our social reasoning mechanisms (or, the
social mind module); most religious ethical teachings thus are expressive of moral feelings, not their substitutes. They are parasitic on
moral intuitions people have irrespective of any religious education.

Unlike Moore, I consider these intuitions purely natural. They are
the outcome of continual readjustment of our convictions and practices in the light of our unfolding experience of the real world. Morality is the quality of one's continuing performance in solving moral
problems; it is something acquired and refined over a lifetime of social
experience. It consists of slowly generating a hierarchy of moral prototypes and their applications from a large number of relevant examples, not of sets of fixed beliefs and abstract rules and symbols. In this
perspective, moral disagreements are not about which rules to follow
in moral reasoning, but about which moral prototype best characterizes a given situation. It is simply not possible to capture all of a person's moral knowledge in a set of explicit rules, just as it is impossible
to capture all of a person's athletic or artistic skills in a set of imperative sentences. This view of the moral person as one who has acquired
a set of moral skills is very different from the traditional view of the
moral person as one who has agreed to follow certain rules, such as
"Always keep your promises," or who has certain overriding desires,
such as maximizing the general happiness.

Yet moral rules expressed in linguistic form may serve as context-
fixing descriptions that activate new, stored prototypes. They do not
aim at embodying the reasoning underlying moral judgement, but are
merely catalysts for context-fixing when we realize that our pattern-
recognition-based responses are not serving well. In this way we are
not hostages to our own trained responses. In addition, linguistic
exchange is also a medium in collaborative problem-solving. It is here
that the teachings of various religious traditions come into play. They
serve a context-fixing function and guide moral reasoning by helping
activate a pertinent prototype in any given situation. Besides, they also
serve as conscious explanations and justifications of our tacit intuitions.

Morality and ethics do not form a clearly demarcated domain,
however. Philosophical ethics, as distinct from theology and mere
practical moral commands, has only emerged in the modern West. In
Catholic and Lutheran theology ethics has been understood as a mat-

ter of natural reason; the idea of specifically Christian ethics has been maintained mostly in the Reformed tradition and in Protestant revivalist movements. In Buddhism, it is much more difficult to distinguish between ethics and soteriology; the eight precepts of a devoted layperson and the over 200 precepts of monks and nuns are understood as instrumental for a strive for liberation or a better rebirth. Yet in both religions the 8 or 10 most serious offences include lying, stealing, killing, and sexual misconduct, i.e. things that obviously are important in any attempts to regulate social relationships, quite irrespective of the doctrinal subtleties of a particular religion.

In addition to this, both Christian and Buddhist teachings also include precepts that do not seem to have a similar evolutionary basis. Three of the 10 commandments of the Judeo-Christian tradition for example emphasize monotheistic belief, while the 8 precepts of a devoted Buddhist layperson include such prohibitions as not to watch shows or wear perfumes and garlands. It may not be easy to draw the line between clearly ethical commands and commands that only relate to local custom. Yet there is experimental evidence that even children are capable of making such a distinction. This suggests that the ethical codes of various religious traditions include both evolution-based ethical intuitions and culture-specific customs. These customs do not relate to universal aspects of negotiating vital social relationships, but rather are subservient to some specific counter-intuitive goal of humans.

CHAPTER SEVEN

RELIGION AND COGNITION:
TOWARDS A NEW SCIENCE OF RELIGION

Domain Specificity

We have already come across the idea that human cognition is domain-specific. The human mind is not an all-purpose problem solver but a collection of enduring and independent subsystems performing specific tasks (Hirschfeld and Gelman 1994: 3-4). As Leda Cosmides and John Tooby (1994; Tooby and Cosmides 1995) have argued, our cognitive apparatus is the outcome of evolution, and natural selection tends to produce functionally distinct adaptive specializations. When two adaptive problems have different or even incompatible solutions, a single general solution will be inferior to two specialized solutions, and thus domain-specific solutions will be favored. All of the problems that our Pleistocene ancestors had to face simply could not have been solved by one and the same mechanism. A domain-general cognitive architecture just could not have consistently behaved adaptively, because what counts as fit behavior differs from one domain to another. Such a system would have collapsed due to a kind of combinatorial explosion. (See also Mithen 1998.)

It now becomes important to consider whether religion can be understood as a unique category in the sense of a specific cognitive domain. So far our evidence is somewhat contradictory. On the one hand, religion seems not to be a clear-cut category, while on the other hand the counter-intuitive representations that so well typify religion seem to constitute a separate domain.

In the following I first review the various theories concerning cognitive domains, in order to provide a coherent account of domain specificity for my own purposes. Secondly, I present empirical evidence to support the claim that people intuitively associate religion with counter-intuitiveness. I then explore the possibility of distinguishing between religious counter-intuitiveness and other kinds of counter-intuitiveness. Thus an answer is provided to the question whether religion is a separate cognitive domain. Finally, the rudiments for a program for the scientific study of religion are briefly outlined.

According to the classical view, represented for example by Piaget, we only employ certain general reasoning abilities in all kinds of cognitive tasks equally. Thus for example when a small child says that "the clouds wanted to go away," this utterance is not taken as testimony to the child's lack of empirical knowledge, but to the fact that a child of this age is unable to perform abstract cognitive operations at all. In what follows, instead of dwelling on the shortcomings of Piaget's methodology, I shall focus on the cognitive domains view as an alternative for the classical view of a general intelligence. (See Boyer 1994b: 135-140; Gopnik, Meltzoff, and Kuhl 2001.)

There are at least six research traditions which have contributed to the emergence of the cognitive domains view (Hirschfeld and Gelman 1994: 5):

1) Chomsky's ideas of a universal grammar and a 'language organ;'
2) Modular approaches to such cognitive skills as vision;
3) Research on constraints on inductive reasoning;
4) Philosophical theories concerning such knowledge structures as theories;
5) Research on expert performance in various task environments, such as chess;
6) Comparative studies of animal cognition, the evolution of cognitive skills, and cross-cultural differences/similarities in cognitive performance.

In these fields of study, it has been shown that such skills as language, vision, face recognition, numerical reasoning and reasoning about people are each acquired and represented in distinctive ways. Fodor (1983), for his part, has tried to show that perceptual processes are modular in the sense of being carried out by specialized mechanisms, although thought processes are not. Research concerning constraints on reasoning has suggested that there are some constraints on the form taken by conceptual development in various domains in ontogeny, but no agreement has been reached as to what is meant by a domain. As to knowledge structures, an important question is whether or not common sense (folk theories) is located in some sense on the same continuum with scientific theories. Expertise-driven skill domains such as chess (Saariluoma 1995) exemplify the fact that people can develop a skill as a result of extensive experience, thus giving the idea of domains a new meaning. With regard to comparative studies, mention must be made of cross-cultural studies of color vision and studies of folk biological classification (Atran 1990; 1998; Medin and

Atran 1999). (Hirschfeld and Gelman 1994: 5-20; Atran 1990: 47-52; Karmiloff-Smith 1992: 165-173.)

Thus the central idea in domain specificity is that the mechanisms for acquiring knowledge, knowledge structures and the related modes of reasoning are different in differing domains. There are three main types of argument for domain specificity: (1) the claim that there are certain innate cognitive modules; (2) claims concerning folk theories; and (3) expertise studies, which show that such specific skills as playing chess cannot be explained with reference to general intelligence. Superior performance in chess for example is strictly task-specific, in the sense that it cannot be explained by any other skill and does not affect the subject's other skills (Saariluoma 1995).

Cognitive Modules

Perhaps the strictest form of domain specificity is represented by modularity theories, such as those of Atran (1990; 1994; 1996; 1998) and Sperber (1994; 1996b: 119-150). The two most important questions related to modularity are whether the modules are innate, and whether it is only perceptual processes that are modular, or reasoning processes as well. Atran for example has forcefully argued for the existence of an innate folk biological module, which does not constitute a folk theory and is not due to accumulated experience. This argument is important both as one possible explanation of the domain of folk biology and as an example of the modularist view of the relationship between folk reasoning and scientific theories (Atran 1998: 548).

According to Atran, in every human society people think about plants and animals in the same special way, and classify them in taxonomies composed of a rigid hierarchy of inclusive classes of organisms, or taxa. Plants and animals are thought to form species-like groups, such as the groups *redwood, raccoon, and robin*, which Atran refers to as "generic species." A taxonomy is formed when these groups are in turn classified in groups within groups, like *white oak/ oak/ tree*. These groupings form absolutely distinct hierarchical levels or ranks. According to Brent Berlin's standard terminology, the folk-biological ranks are the following: folk-kingdom (e.g. *animal, plant*), life-form (e.g. *bug, fish, bird, tree, bush*), generic-species (e.g. *shark, robin, oak, holly*), folk-specific rank (e.g. *poodle, white oak*), and folk-varietal rank (e.g. *toy poodle, swamp white oak*). (Atran 1990: 5, 48; 1998: 547-549, 563.)

Each generic species is thought to have an underlying causal nature, an essence. The typical appearance and behavior of the species is due to this essence, which thus accounts for the identity of a given organism as a complex, self-preserving entity even when it grows and undergoes changes. Tigers for instance are thought to have stripes because of an underlying "tiger essence" which cannot be changed by making changes in the outward appearance of the animal. Yet the existence of this essence is presupposed because of such perceptual cues as stripes (in the case of tigers). Thus the representation of natural kind terms involves general assumptions about the typical features of the members of a group together with the presumption of an underlying trait or essence that is common to all members of the group. (Atran 1994: 321; 1998: 548, 563-564; Boyer 1993b; 1994b: 161, 173; Cosmides and Tooby 1994: 101; Gelman and Hirschfeld 1999.)

Atran's (1998: 554-555) empirical studies with Lowland Mayas and Midwest Americans seem to show that fundamental categorization processes in folk biology are rooted in domain-specific conceptual assumptions rather than in domain-general perceptual heuristics. Folk biology is a "core domain" in the manner of Kant's "synthetic a priori" knowledge; it is the extension of an innate cognitive module. In other words, it is an innately determined cognitive structure embodying the naturally selected ontological commitments of humans. It provides a domain-specific mode of causally construing the phenomena in its domain. Such a core domain, however, is not an encapsulated module, but rather has preferential – not proprietary – access to the domain-specific representations. The core modules for naïve physics, intuitive psychology and folk biology can make use of each other's inputs and outputs, yet preferring the processing of a different predetermined range of stimuli. (See also Sperber 1994.)

It is important that, according to Atran, such modularity means that humans are genetically predetermined to a certain kind of classification as well as a certain way of thinking about the entities classified. We do not gradually construct folk theories of different types of entities. This also implies that folk biology and the science of biology are not end points on a single continuum but are essentially different domains. This, however, is somewhat contrary to the notions held by many psychologists and philosophers of science. (Atran 1998: 565-566. Cf. Lawson and McCauley 1990: 26; Carey 1996a&b.)

Atran (1998: 563, 566) sees three differences between scientific and folk systems: integration, effectiveness and competition. As to *integration*, few, if any, folk-biological explanations seek causal accounts linking species and groups of species among one another. In other words, folk biology does not represent an attempt at a coherent and exhaustive system of explanations, covering all living kinds. Aristotle may have been the first person in history to attempt to integrate an entire taxonomic system. It is scientific biology that aims at explanations that are universally *effective* but not necessarily of any real value in the daily lives of ordinary people; folk biology is the exact opposite. Thirdly, scientific theories *compete* with each other as scientists try to approximate the final truth, which, however, they never expect to reach (see Niiniluoto 1987: 156-289). Folk biology, on the other hand, aims at cooperative subsistence behavior, in which there is no room for theoretical debate or development. Folk biology is conservative in nature.

All these three criteria seem to be centered around the fact that the human mind, as it has evolved, is not a "theory-building device," every operation of which is aimed at optimizing the overall representation of the world. Rather, the human mind is constantly trying to solve domain-specific problems with a minimum of cognitive fuss. (Boyer 1994b: 231-242; 1999: 53.) In this sense, all scientific attempts at coherent, theoretical explanations of phenomena, independent of time and place, have introduced new demands on the human mind.

For Atran, this means that science is not an inevitable outgrowth of common sense. The cumulative development of natural history, finally leading to scientific biology, has occurred only in Europe, and thus cannot be based on any universal cognitive mechanism. Moreover, it is a peculiar bias in cognitive psychology and analytic philosophy that intuitive "data-organizing principles" are called "theories," and that the emergence of scientific knowledge is used as the standard by which to evaluate the formation of ordinary knowledge about the everyday world. According to this line of thought, science, as a natural and more perfect extension of common sense, is ontologically and methodologically continuous with it. Consequently, people are supposed to refine their use of natural-kind terms as science improves, this being an inherent part of understanding what these terms "mean." (Atran 1994: 317, 335; 1998: 566.)

It is of course fairly obvious that the developing child learns folk biology spontaneously, while the acquisition of scientific biology is an arduous process (see Wolpert 1994). We have already discussed this in connection with Sperber's distinction between spontaneous and reflective beliefs. But, it is not clear to me what it actually means that common sense and science are not continuous with one another. As Susan Carey (1996a: 273; 1996b: 191) notes, it is not clear what Atran is denying when he denies that ordinary cognition relies upon theory-like representation. McCauley (2000) for example considers science "unnatural" and yet holds the view that common sense and science are on the same continuum (Lawson and McCauley 1990: 26). When and how does a quantitative difference become a qualitative one?

It is, first of all, important to be clear about whether we are speaking of an individual scientist's reasoning or of the collective enterprise that constitutes the history of science. As Keith Oatley (1996: 138-139) puts it, science is largely based on the fact that humans are capable of joining together to do things that are too difficult to do alone (cf. Clark, above p. 166). It seems that all three of Atran's criteria that differentiate science from common sense strongly relate to science *as a collective enterprise*: it is science as a collective project that strives for a coherent and exhaustive system, universal effectiveness, and competition between theories. These are not descriptions of the cognitive processes of individual scientists. Atran thus seems to be – misleadingly – contrasting science as an institution with common sense as certain kinds of cognitive processes.

The "theory theory" of conceptual change, criticized by Atran, views the development of scientific theories neither as a sociological nor as a logical problem. Rather, it is based on the view of theories as explanatory structures embedded in the cognitive process of individual scientists. In this sense, there are assumed to be some similarities in the ways scientists and children think. Scientists are seen as "big children," not children as little scientists. (Carey 1996a: 272; 1996b: 189-190; Gopnik and Wellman 1994: 258-259; Gopnik, Meltzoff, and Kuhl 2001: 9.) Thus, as Paul Harris points out, the parallelism between children's thinking and scientific thinking is between the ways children reason and individual scientists reason, not between children and science as a public enterprise (Harris 1994: 294-295).

Harris, however, rejects the theory theory of folk psychology, replacing it by a "simulation theory." According to this view, people understand the behavior of others by simulating their choices and decisions in their own minds. There is nothing theoretical in this. Children and scientists think alike because neither is guided in their thinking by theory. Theoretical change in science is a collective, sociological phenomenon, which should not be likened to psychological changes in the thinking of individuals. (Harris 1994: 302-308.)

The weakness in Harris' work is that he denies the domain specificity of thinking, although he accepts the domain specificity of perception. He backs his view by the claim that children "entertain the possibility that objects can be created out of thin air, that one object can turn into another, and that a representation such as a model or a picture can turn into what it represents." Clearly, children's thinking is not governed by domain-specific constraints. This then leads Harris to a quite implausible account of children's "magical thinking." We cannot, however, argue from the fact that people *can* entertain counter-intuitive representations to the conclusion that no intuitive constraints exist (Boyer 2000). This comes close to being self-contradictory. Harris himself, quite revealingly, adds that "although children acknowledge that the world typically obeys certain physical principles, they are not entirely skeptical about the possible violation of those principles...," thus turning his whole argument upside down. (Harris 1994: 308-312.)

This is precisely the point. Children and adults know that the physical world obeys certain constant principles, although they are not *entirely* skeptical about possible violations. Such violations, however, are always recognized for what they are: counter-intuitive, attention-demanding and exceptional, as I have been arguing throughout. Toward the end of this chapter I also provide empirical evidence for this argument. Even children are far more competent at discerning the difference between fantasy and reality than psychologists have believed. If the child really regarded just about anything as possible, his or her life would become quite impossible. (See Cosmides and Tooby 1994; Karmiloff-Smith 1992: 125-138; Elksnis and Szachara 1996; Barrett 2001). People can afford "magical," or religious, thinking only in specific contexts. You cannot grow crops, hunt or trade in the stock market merely by praying to gods. Even the most pious must also do many quite mundane things to earn their living, and this presupposes domain-specific cognition.

As to the nature of science, as a cultural institution it may be a rather unique phenomenon. It is usually ascribed only to the ancient Greeks and/or to modern western Europeans. In 6th century BC Greece, people are assumed for the first time to have begun to construct universal theories of the world as a whole. This was made possible by democracy, which allowed critical discussion of traditional ideas. (Harré 1986; Hussey 1986: 10-11; Wiebe 1991: 84-129; Wolpert 1994: 35-55; McCauley 2000: 68-69.) However, such people as the ancient Sanskrit grammarians (Staal 1989: 37-46) and the Buddhist logicians (Stcherbatsky 1930-32) for example also developed quite scientific systems, and Chinese traditions have a lot in common with European science, despite some important differences (Lloyd 1996). But, when it comes to individual men and women, it is obvious that modern European scientists do not have radically different kinds of minds from present-day laypeople or for instance the ancient Buddhists. They merely use their minds for different kinds of purposes. (See Rubin 1997: 196, 308-314 .)

Ordinary, everyday thinking has certain characteristics, which include at least the following. In contrast to scientific thinking, ordinary thought proceeds from the immediate experience of individuals; it aims at short-term, practical efficacy, not at creating general theories; it seeks evidence and not counter-evidence; it makes use of individual cases as evidence and personalizes values and ideals; it makes use of abductive inference; and its argumentation often takes a narrative form. (Epstein 1990; Kuhn 1996: 263; Oatley 1996; Rubin 1997.) What is meant by abductive reasoning in everyday thinking – as we saw in Chapter three – is a form of guessing based on observation and a database. It is reasoning toward the best explanation by putting forward conjectural assumptions such that, if they were true, would account for the data in question. A new empirical rule is invented to render predictable what would otherwise be mysterious. (Boyer 1994b: 146-147. Oatley 1996: 126-128. See Stanovich and West 2000.)

Adopting Seymour Epstein's vocabulary, we may thus contrast everyday experiential and rational thinking. According to Epstein, everyone has an implicit, experiential theory of reality, a hierarchically organized set of schemata and networks of schemata. The most basic schemata describe 1) the degree to which the world is regarded as benign versus malevolent; 2) the degree to which it is regarded as meaningful, predictable, controllable, etc.; 3) the degree to which others are regarded favorably rather than as a source of threat; and 4) the degree to which the self is regarded as worthy. These are the highest-level constructs in the hierarchy. As we descend in the hierarchy, the schemata become narrower in scope and more closely related to direct experience. The lowest ones are purely situation-specific and can change without affecting higher-order structures, whereas invali-

dation of some of the higher-order schemata can profoundly destabi-
lize the entire structure. (Epstein 1990: 165-166.)

Experiential theories of reality, like scientific theories, serve the purposes of organizing the data of experience and guiding behavior.
However, while the subject-matter of scientific theories consists of
data that are theoretically organized, the subject-matter of experiential theories emerges from experiences of everyday life. Whereas the
scientist merely pursues understanding and theoretical explanation,
experiential theories direct people trying to go about living their daily
lives in an emotionally satisfying way. Experiential theories of reality
thus have the following functions: 1) to assimilate the data of reality; 2)
to maintain a favorable pleasure-pain balance; 3) to maintain related-
ness to others; 4) to maintain a favorable level of self-esteem. (Epstein
1990: 166.)

In the context of science, as Peirce argued, abduction should only
be used in creating hypotheses from some observation. After this, a
fact not yet observed is deduced from the hypothesis; it is tested
repeatedly, and only then is a generalizing induction made by comb-
ing the original observation and the test results. (Oatley 1996: 134.)
Deanna Kuhn (1996: 261-262, 276-277) calls the reasoning processes
that lead to inductive inferences *theory-evidence coordination*, but she does
not want to distinguish sharply between scientific and ordinary thinking. According to her, good or sound thinking is very broadly based
rather than narrowly scientific.

What is essential in all good thinking is that people become aware
of their own thoughts and thinking habits. This is achieved by practice. Using Perner's (1993) vocabulary, we can say that one must
become aware of one's own knowledge as representational. Although
children in general achieve this ability around the age of five, it is
much more difficult to use it effectively in individual cases (see Perner
1993: 253). As Kuhn's experiments showed, the subjects did not
reflect on their theories as objects of cognition, but rather seemed to
take them as direct reflections of how things are. The counter-evidence offered was not regarded as a challenge but was dismissed as
not actually being counter-evidence. "This pretty much goes along
with my own view" was a common comment. Subjects not used to rig-
orous thinking did not differentiate between theories and evidence.
Those who had achieved control of the interaction of theory and evidence in their own thinking were able to distinguish what came from
their own thought and what from external sources. It is apparent that

such ability may be especially well developed in scientific work, but it
may be applied also in other contexts. (Kuhn 1996.) In terms of
Epstein's theory, this means that rational thought is employed as a
strategy for living.

It is science as a collective enterprise that helps people to achieve
these goals. The individual scientist in a concrete situation may have
difficulty in thinking according to the scientific ideal. This may be due
to the fact that the principles of ordinary thinking are so deeply encoded in our genome. (See e.g. Atran 1998: 562.) Moreover, the fact that
the attentional capacity and the capacity of the human working memory has certain absolute limits partly determines what kind of reasoning is possible. Except for highly automated tasks, attention, the selection of perceptual figures from the perceptual background, has a
capacity of a single unit. The capacity of working memory, for its part,
is limited to approximately four units. (Saariluoma 1995: 34-69. See
LeDoux 1998: 184-186.) All this supports the view that if science is
somehow unique, it is unique as a cultural institution. It affects how
people think, but it is still not easy to see in what sense this makes scientific theories completely different from folk theories. Science, after
all, grows out of everyday knowledge, and underneath the theoretical
presuppositions of science can always be found tacit common sense
assumptions (Saariluoma 1997: 11).

What Atran says may be true: placing common sense and science
on a single continuum means that scientific thinking becomes the ideal kind of thinking, with ordinary thinking losing its rightful place as
the best ideal in ordinary contexts. But this cannot answer the question whether scientific thinking really is something wholly different
from common sense. Moreover, we still have to explain what it means
to say that something is or is not a theory. Here the important issue
seems to be Atran's claim that folk biology is not only non-theoretical
but innate.

According to Atran (1996: 231, 233), the universal, a priori presumption that species constitute "natural kinds" by virtue of their tele-
ological natures, the spontaneous arrangement of living things into
taxonomies, constitutes "a prior set of constraints on *any and all possible
theories* about the causal relations between living kinds." It is logically
implausible that humans could generalize from limited experience
without some preexisting cognitive structures projecting finite and
fragmentary instances onto organized classes (Atran 1994: 317-318).

Atran's empirical study of the ways in which the Itzaj Maya and

Midwest Americans draw inferences about natural kinds shows that the generic-species rank was favored by both groups as an absolute level of reality in biological reasoning. At that level the biological world is understood to partition into non-overlapping kinds with unique causal essences which form the basis for inference. This finding cannot be accounted for in terms of domain-general notions of perceptual similarity or the structure of reality. People can classify a folk-biological category as a generic species even without much perceptual data. Certain kind of information about, say, an oak (how it looks, grows, etc.) can trigger the assumption that oaks comprise a generic species even when the person in question has not seen oaks and has no detailed prior knowledge about oaks. Such learning must therefore be motivated by cross-cultural cognitive mechanisms that do not depend primarily on experience. Input into the mind alone cannot cause an instance of experience to be generalized into a category that subsumes a rich and complex set of many instances. Nor can this be explained by appealing to a domain-general process, because people cannot generate the categories of any number of domains from the stimuli alone. Rather, categorization processes in folk biology are rooted in domain-specific conceptual assumptions. (Atran 1998: 552-554, 595.)

Thus the object domain consisting of generic species of biological organisms "is the extension of an innate cognitive module." Universal taxonomy is "an innately determined cognitive structure that embodies the naturally selected ontological commitments of human beings and provides a domain-specific mode of causally construing the phenomena in its domain." (Atran 1998: 555). This notion of innateness brings us back to the question of what cognitive domains really are.

Jeffrey Elman and his co-authors take innateness to mean putative aspects of brain structure, cognition or behavior that arise as the result of interactions occurring within the organism itself during ontogeny. There are, then, three levels on which things can be innate in this relative sense: representations, architectures of the brain, and timing. On the representational level, knowledge may be innate in the form of patterns of synaptic connectivity at the cortical level. This, however, is a relatively rare phenomenon. The architectural constraints of knowledge in turn may be properties of individual neurons, of local cortical architecture, or of the global architecture of the brain. Timing refers to constraints in the developmental schedule: a given solution may not be encoded from the start but is guaranteed to appear at some point as an inevitable result of brain development. (Elman et al. 1998: 22-35, 360-361.)

The boundaries between internal and external are not absolute, however. Developmental change is due neither to a mere triggering of innate knowledge nor to inductive learning alone. Rather, we are dealing with a genetically controlled interaction between maturational factors and environment. Elman et al. thus reject representational nativism but do not subscribe to the *tabula rasa* idea either. Rather, it is "interactions, all the way down." Thus modularization is an outcome rather than a cause. We need to be careful to distinguish between the mechanisms and the content of innateness. Domain-general cognitive architectures and learning algorithms can also give rise to domain-specific representations that then become modularized. (Elman et al. 1998: 1-3, 19-23, 167-170, 332, 359, 365. See also Clark 1997: 35-51.)

As Atran, for whom folk biology is based on a mere triggering of innate knowledge, has not explained what he means by innateness (see also Elman et al. 1998: 369), it is possible in principle that the view put forward by Elman et al. is compatible with Atran's empirical evidence. I naturally do not pretend to have solved the problem; I merely want to point out that Atran's strict opposition between common sense and science seems to necessitate a strict opposition between nativism and empiricism, between nature and nurture. But if learning and development really are "interactions, all the way down," then common sense and such acquired skills as scientific thinking must also lie on a continuum. They both depend on innate potentials that are actualized in practice. Consequently, the competing views of 'innate modules' and 'acquired theories' do not form a strict opposition either. They merely emphasize different aspects of the same thing.

Intuitive Theories and Cognitive Domains

In Chapter One, the "theory theory" of categorization was introduced. According to this theory, people categorize things as belonging or not belonging to a class or category by relying on intuitive theories about the phenomena to be classified. This is necessary because there is no similarity without a theory of what counts in comparison. Any two things can be similar in numerous ways, and only some of these are relevant in a given classificatory task.

A similar idea of folk theories, or intuitive theories, has also been employed in studies concerning the development of domain-specific knowledge in children by those who reject the idea of innate modules and favor accumulated experience as an explanation. According to Susan Carey (1996a: 268, 272-273; 1996b: 189-191), who leans on Wesley Salmon's (1984; 1989) views of scientific theories, 'theory' here refers to an explanatory cognitive structure. A theory character-izes the causal mechanisms that make explanation in a given situation possible. Such a psychological approach to theories should be differ-entiated from the logical analyses of scientific explanation put forward by philosophers of science. Psychologists are more interested in rea-soning and explanation as psychological processes. i.e. in how they are actually mentally represented. (See also Gopnik and Wellman 1994: 258.)

Thus for the psychologist an intuitive theory is a cognitive structure that embodies a person's ontological commitments and provides modes of explanation for the phenomena in its domain. Such a theory indicates what basic kinds of things there are in the world and in what ways their behavior should be explained, i.e. certain kinds of causal mechanisms. In saying that a domain is "a domain of phenomena involving entities recognized by the theory," Carey – unlike Atran and Sperber – leaves room for other than a purely extensional understand-ing of domains (cf. Lawson and McCauley's holistic semantics). In other words, we are not dealing with a domain of things, objects, or entities, but with a domain of *phenomena*, of things *as they appear to us*. Domains are not simply out there in external reality, but are estab-lished in the interaction between external reality and the human cog-nitive system. As Gopnik and Wellman (1994: 287) put it, "theories not only reflect domains but also actually constitute them." Percep-tion and reasoning are guided by a single knowledge system, identify-ing perceived objects as belonging to a certain domain and therefore only allowing certain kinds of explanations.[36] Cognitive domains, like folk biology and folk psychology, thus are theoretical constructs. (Carey 1996a: 273, 278-279; 1996b: 190. See Murphy and Medin 1985.)

Alison Gopnik and others have applied theory theory to the

---

36 I do not deal here with Carey's (1996a: 280- 299; 1996b: 196-204) attempt to explain folk biology as emerging from folk psychology around the age of six or seven at the earliest, as this is not directly relevant to my argument.

everyday understanding of the mind, which they think develops as a succession of implicit, naïve theories. According to Gopnik and Wellman, the progress of science reflects processes of conceptual change of a kind first seen in very young children. Some differences notwithstanding, scientists and children employ essentially the same learning mechanisms, neither of them starts from scratch, both make predictions, perform experiments, and revise their theories in the light of what they have found out. Among differences are that kids make up theories mostly about close, middle-sized, common objects (including people), that scientists co-operate in an organized and institutionalized manner, and that they also invent some new cognitive procedures. (Gopnik and Wellman 1994: 257-259; Gopnik, Meltzoff, and Kuhl 2001: 155-162; cf. Brewer, Chin, and Samarapungavan 2000.)

Gopnik and Wellman (1994: 259-261) first differentiate between empirical typologies and generalizations on the one hand and theories on the other. Empirical typologies and generalizations order evidence but share the same vocabulary as the evidence used, and thus operate on the same level of abstraction. Theories, in contrast, propose abstract entities, events and processes as theoretical constructs that explain things. Thus the vocabulary of theories is of a higher logical type than the vocabulary in which the evidence is expressed. Besides being abstract, theories also form coherent, lawlike structures. Theoretical entities and processes are interrelated in such a way that changes in one part of a theory have consequences for other parts. Unlike empirical typologies and generalizations, theories have explanatory force and allow prediction. As Lawson and McCauley (1990: 26-27) have emphasized, a scientific theory must apply to a larger set of phenomena than just those with regard to which it was initially constructed. Unlike typologies, theories make predictions about entities and processes far removed from the initial evidence.

Gopnik and Wellman (1994: 264-275) insist that there is no one single "child's theory of mind," but rather a succession of theories. The child is never a "behaviorist." Between the ages of two and a half and four there is a gradual shift from one mentalistic theory to another, as the child comes to understand that people's *representation* of the world determines their actions. For Gopnik and Wellman, this is a theory change. (Gopnik, Meltzoff, and Kuhl 2001: 23-59.) There is, however, no single type of evidence that speaks against such alternative accounts as the innate modules view or Harris' (1994) simulation theory. At closer glance the innate modules view as well as Harris' view seem to fail however.

The simulation theory depends on the questionable view that we have direct access to our own mental states, without any inference, interpretation or conceptual mediation. One cannot misconceive one's own mental state. This, however, is highly unlikely (see e.g. Churchland 1995: 205-206; LeDoux 1998: 29-34, 306-307; Saariluoma 1997: 104-106, 122), and the theory theory predicts that erroneous self-interpretations are in fact to be expected. As has often been shown in experiments, children for example misinterpret their own experience when it conflicts with their theories. (Gopnik and Wellman 1994: 275-280. See Perner 1993: 257-268.) The child does not come to understand the relevant aspects of its own mind any earlier than it understands those of other people (Perner 1993: 270).

Although a naïve theory of mind may begin from an innate starting state, there is no innate theory of mind module, contrary to the argument of Leslie (1994; 1996). Gopnik and Wellman admit that it is not always easy to tell whether a given piece of evidence supports the modular view or the theory theory, but they consider that especially the dynamic features of theories, particularly their defeasibility, makes such discrimination possible. The theory theory thus provides a satisfactory account of the interaction between a cognitive system and the external reality. Theories both reflect domains and constitute them. A domain is what one's framework theory says it is. (Gopnik and Wellman 1994: 280-288. See also Karmiloff-Smith 1992: 117-138.)

As we have already seen, Perner's (1993) account follows the same lines. For Perner, the critical feature of a theory is that it provides a deeper explanation of how something works. It is not enough that there are certain kinds of ontological commitments in a coherent body of knowledge together with an explanatory framework. To have a theory of mind for example the child must have knowledge of a mechanism explaining the workings of the mind. A rudimentary form of such knowledge, or theory, appears around the age of four. (Perner 1993: 240-247.) The theory of mind is an important example of the theory theory because – if it is correct – it also explains how knowledge in other domains, such as biology and physics, is constructed by the human mind. A theory of mind is also a theory of theories about mind.

According to Perner, during the first year of life the child operates by primary representations and has a "single updating model of reality." The infant can only understand real situations, and for example regards pictures as objects resembling the depicted, not as representations. Pictures are merely objects, "boring pieces of paper," not a way of presenting something else. During the second year the child becomes a "situation theorist," capable of using secondary representations "decoupled" from reality, as well as multiple models. He or she now understands his or her own mirror image and can interpret pictures as pictures of a depicted situation but not as representations. A picture of Daddy on skis for example is understood as depicting Daddy in a certain situation, but not as a physical object representing Daddy. Without a proper concept of representation, the child cannot understand that a picture can be given different interpretations, that it has a sense and a reference, and that pictures can also misrepresent. (1993: 7-9, 70-75.)

Only around four does the developing child become capable of metarepresentation, i.e. of using models of models and of understanding that human knowledge consists of properly caused mental representations of the facts known. He or she is now a "representation theorist." This is supposed to be a genuine theory change. At this age children start to talk and ask about reasons for knowing something, whereas a three-year-old cannot answer such simple questions as "How is it that the boy knows what's in the box?" even if he or she knows that the boy has looked in the box. Only around four do children begin to understand the causal relationship between looking in the box and *therefore* knowing what is in it. Now they also become capable of understanding that for example seeing yields knowledge about such things as color but not about such things as weight. Knowledge is always aspectual. (Perner 1993: 9, 107-109, 124, 145-163.)

However, the shift from a situation theory, or mentalistic theory of behavior, to a representational theory of mind does not mean replacement but extension. The representational view does not supplant the situation theory but merely amends it for certain problems. Even adults tend to be situation theorists whenever it is possible, and only adopt the representational view when necessary. Consider for example that you have agreed with someone to meet at a certain corner. This requires that you know what has been agreed and that you also know that the other person has the same knowledge. Furthermore, you also have to be sure that the other person knows that you know. In principle, a genuine mutual awareness of what has been agreed upon can only be established by an infinite series of knowings: I know that you know that I know that you know .... Yet in real life we do not engage in such reasonings but are satisfied with being situation theorists and assuming that everyone part of an interactive situation is directly linked to that situation, i.e. knows everything he or she has to know. A problem only arises when knowledge is conceived of as a representation of a situation that is not itself part of the situation. (Perner 1993: 231-239, 249-255.)

The concept of representation is ambiguous, however. Although it can be defined as something that stands for something else, it may not be clear what this 'something' should be taken to refer to: the representational medium or the content. For Perner, it is the picture (the medium) of a scene for example that is a representation, not the scene depicted. This is obvious in those cases where the depicted object falls within an intuitive ontology and can be ostensively singled out, independently of the initial representation. However, when, say, a picture depicts something whose real existence we have reasons to doubt, things get more complicated. A picture of a unicorn can be said to represent a unicorn only in the sense that it is a picture of something that only exists as an idea in the mind. But what is the idea, the mental representation, of a unicorn a representation of? To account for this, we must differentiate between a mental representation (the medium) and a proposition that is represented (content). (Perner 1993: 15-41, 280-282.)

Thus our knowledge of the world consists of mentally represented theories in the sense that the child's conceptual system is geared to explanation from the start, major changes do not consist of a mere accumulation of facts, our concepts form networks of interrelated concepts, and the notion of mind itself is a theoretical construct (see Dennett 1987). Our intuitive theories tell us what kinds of entities exist, group them into distinct domains, and provide us with explanatory frameworks and also with more detailed explanations of how things happen in reality. (Perner 1993: 240-241.)

Atran (1998: 599), however, has argued that the theory theorists have not put forward a single principle that would allow us to test whether something is or is not a theory, and that the theory theory is either false or too vague (he refers however neither to Gopnik and Welman nor to Perner). He himself offers the three principles of integration, effectiveness, and competition as discriminating between everyday and scientific thinking. But, as we have seen, Atran's own view of innateness is rather vague, and the three principles describe science as a collective institution, not as certain kinds of cognitive processes.

The important thing here is not in what ways everyday thinking and science resemble each other, or how to define, 'theory,' but what is the nature of cognitive domains. What is the contribution of experience to the formation of categories and how do modules – if such there be – emerge? As suggested by Atran's (1998: 555) claim that folk biology resembles Kant's synthetic a priori knowledge, we are dealing with the same kind of problem as in traditional philosophical epistemology: how our knowledge is mediated by our "categories of understanding." But now the question is approached empirically and not only conceptually. And the inescapable answer seems to be interactionism: experience shapes cognition and cognition mediates reality to us in a certain form.

These important disagreements notwithstanding, the notion of a cognitive domain can be quite generally characterized as follows:

> A domain is a body of knowledge that identifies and interprets a class of phenomena assumed to share certain properties and to be of a distinct and general type. A domain functions as a stable response to a set of recurring and complex problems faced by the organism. This response involves difficult-to-access perceptual, encoding, retrieval, and inferential processes dedicated to that solution. (Hirschfeld and Gelman 1994: 21.)

This however overlooks the fact that domain specificity can occur on at least five levels: tasks, behaviors, representations, processing mechanisms and genes. The most important question is whether domain-specific representations are handled by domain-specific processors. If for example the mechanisms that store linguistic representations are broadly distributed in the brain, then those mechanisms are likely to be responsible for other types of cognitive functions as well. It is therefore no wonder that those who argue for domain-specificity usually reject connectionism and favor local processing models. Yet there is no reason in principle why connectionist systems could not be modular and involve some innate constraints. In fact, Elman et al. try to show how domain-specific representations can emerge from domain-general architectures and learning algorithms, and how these can then result in modularization. (Elman et al. 1998: 38-41, 115, 392.)

From a truly interactionist, or "enactive" (Varela, Rosch, and

Thompson 1996), point of view, we must conclude that it is in vain to try to determine whether the modularity of the mind reflects real domains of the external reality, or whether we project innate domains on reality. The human mind is as much part of the world and of evolution as various natural kinds in the "external" world. Therefore neither has causal priority over the other. The human mind has co-evolved with the world it reflects, and cognitive domains should be understood as the outcome of this interaction. (See Clark 1997.) It is essential, as we shall see in the next section, that we humans can also form cross-domain concepts that do not correspond to any natural domain. A black cat for example can be thought of not only as a natural kind but also as a sign of bad luck, and a weapon can also be a work of art (see Mithen 1998: 195-198). Such distinctions cannot be anything but theoretical constructs, i.e. they are not merely empirical typologies.

Is Religion a Cognitive Domain?

Violating the boundaries between domains

The archeologist Steven Mithen (1998) has proposed a theory of the evolution of the human mind, in which changes in domain-specificity play an important role. Briefly, his idea is that what first appeared in evolutionary terms was a general intelligence, which was then divided up into various encapsulated domains. However, culture as we know it, especially art, science and religion, became possible only after *homo sapiens sapiens* had learned to transfer knowledge between domains some 60,000 – 40,000 years ago. This is the third phase in the development of the mind.

Mithen (1998: 31-64) begins his psychological considerations by discarding Piaget's notion of a general intelligence. He then presents Fodor's (1983) idea of perceptual modularity, Howard Gardner's (1983) idea of multiple intelligences, Cosmides and Tooby's (1994) evolutionary psychological argument for domain-specificity, and such developmental studies as for example Karmiloff-Smith (1992). Whereas for Fodor only perception is modular, not the thinking mind, Gardner considers that intelligence itself consists of seven aspects (cf. Sperber 1994). Cosmides and Tooby, for their part, have argued that our minds still reflect the specific problems our Pleistocene ancestors had to meet. The mind is divided into different modules according to the kinds of problems it has had to solve. Evolution being a rather slow process, we cannot claim that our minds have adapted to the circumstances in which humans have lived for the past five thousand years or so. Our minds still reflect the conditions of the Pleistocene, some 2.5 million – 10,000 years ago.

But how then, asks Mithen (1998: 46-52), is it possible that we have such abilities as for instance doing higher mathematics. And how is it possible that we often think and act as though animals were like humans (Donald Duck), physical objects were like persons (the Holy Cross), and things existed which do not actually exist (unicorns)? On what kinds of modules are such abilities based? Surely the human mind cannot consist of encapsulated modules that were formed hundreds of thousands of years ago.

Mithen (1998: 52-61) answers these questions by referring to the work of those developmental psychologists who believe that strict domain-specificity cannot be the whole story. Patricia Greenfield (1991) for example argues that until the age of two, the child's mind is not domain-specific, but a general-purpose learning program (cf. Perner's single updating model). Only after that age does modularity begin to take place. Karmiloff-Smith (1992; 1994) agrees with this. According to her, the intuitive ontologies merely provide a starting point for development in which new micro-domains evolve. These are sensitive to cultural context and can be explained by the plasticity of early brain development (see also Elman et al. 1998: xii, 3). Learning mathematics for example may involve using the intuitive physics module for a new kind of task. In this way, it is possible to learn skills which do not derive from Pleistocene conditions, although with much more difficulty than those skills, such as speech, which seem to be based on a special module dedicated to one particular task.

Karmiloff-Smith (1992; 1994) suggests that soon after modularization has occurred, the modules begin to work together, a phenomenon she calls "representational redescription." This leads to multiple representations of similar knowledge and to the use of modules for tasks for which they have not initially evolved. Thus, links, or mappings (Carey and Spelke 1994), across domains are formed. Mithen also compares this to Sperber's (1994: 46-49, 60-62) idea of a specific metarepresentational module, whose only input consists of the conceptual output of other modules. It solves problems that do not belong to any natural domain and only emerge due to the workings of the mind itself. For instance, we not only have all kinds of intuitive beliefs about cats, handled by the folk biological module, but also reflective beliefs about the concept of 'cat', handled by the metarepresentational module. This capacity for cross-domain formations is the basis of human creativity, and we are usually able to recognize conceptual metaphors, metonymies, analogies, similes, etc. for what they are, i.e. as not being literal descriptions of reality. (Mithen 1998: 61-64.)

Distinguishing between religion and other forms of counter-intuitiveness

But how about religion? As we have seen, religious thinking is based on counter-intuitive representations, where domain boundaries are crossed and which are often taken quite literally because of the emotional reactions associated with them. This is also Mithen's (1998: 198-202) answer to the problem of religion. He merely recapitulates Boyer's (1994b) basic idea of intuitive ontologies and their violations as the characteristic mark of religion (cf. Boyer 2000).

Mithen's standards thus do not permit a differentiation between fiction and religion. Inspired by the idea that the child's cognitive development also reflects the phylogenetic development of the human species, Mithen has developed a three-phase model of the evolution of our cognitive capacities: originally there was only a general intelligence, then the special capacities of social, psychological, and technical intelligences, and finally the capacity for cross-domain mapping (Mithen 1998: 65-78). On subsequent pages, Mithen (1998: 79-170) gives these bones some flesh, based on what we know about the development of the human species ever since the missing common link between us and the chimpanzee some six million years ago.

The origins of art, for example, are to be found in the cultural explosion that took place some 40,000 years ago and which Mithen explains as having resulted from the fact that humans for the first time became capable of integrating knowledge from the separate domains of the psychological, social, and technical intelligences. It is this new cognitive fluidity that made art possible as a way of representing reality in another than a purely mirror-like way (see also Pyysiäinen 1996a: 30-31). It is especially to be noted that the human capacity for art did not develop gradually, as it does in children. On the contrary, the first pieces of art were perfect from the outset, as the technical intelligence and skill was already in place. Human beings merely had to invent the possibility of using it in a novel way. In explaining both art and reli-

gion by this same theory, Mithen is unable to perceive or conceptualize any differences between these two domains. (Mithen 1998: 171-
202.) It is obvious, however, that such differences exist (as also recognized in Boyer and Walker 2000).

The domain of the counter-intuitive obviously includes, in addition
to religious representations, also scientific, disturbed, and fictional
ones. Furthermore, even an atheist can form counter-intuitive representations typical of religion; he or she merely does not consider them
to convey any information about external reality. As Saler (2001)
remarks, people do not just "have" representations; they also use
them. In this sense, the intuitive ontologies and their counter-intuitive
violations that form the necessary basis of religion, are not sufficient to
explain religious belief. We also have to explain why religious beliefs
are held to be unquestionably true in the absence of evidence, or even
when empirical evidence is exactly to the contrary.

It is thus tempting to think that it is religious belief that distinguishes religious representations from other kinds of counter-intuitive representations (Pyysiäinen 2001b). But then we should be able to explain
how we can distinguish between religion and science. Scientific representations too are taken to be literally true and to describe what is ultimately real. Or, to be more precise, scientific theories can be taken
either as directly describing an objective reality, as merely gradually
approximating an absolute truth which is never actually reached
("truthlikeness", Niiniluoto 1987: 156-289), or as having an instrumental value alone, i.e. making it possible to predict how things will
happen and to develop technologies (see Nagel 1961: 106-152; Hesse
1974.)

Whichever option we choose, scientific representations, unlike religious and other symbolic ones, are "truth preserving" in the sense that
scientists have the explicit intention of describing reality as accurately
as possible, of using empirical evidence, and of proposing coherent
theories. In science, there is no room for evocative symbolism of the
kind that typifies religious cognition based on abductive reasoning
(Sperber 1995; Boyer 1994b: 146-148). Although lay people may
accept scientific theories on authority alone, scientists have detailed
explanations of how their models, analogies, and theoretical concepts
refer to reality. (See the discussion of Carey and Atran in *Causal Cognition* (1996): 307-308; Sperber 1996: 91.)

Scientific representations also violate intuition in a different way
from religious ones. While religion tends to favor the concept of

agency even when it is intuitively not to be expected as an explanation (see Lawson 2001), scientific explanations are the exact opposite: they tend to reduce personalistic explanations to mechanistic ones. Here they may also violate Boyer's cognitive optimum, according to which a representation must be at once learnable and nonnatural in order to become widely distributed in a population (Boyer 1994b: 114, 118-124; 1999; Atran 1996: 234, 239-241.)

Scientific representations may violate Boyer's optimum in the sense that in them no intuitive elements are retained if evidence and logical coherence requires that they be abandoned. Limitations of learnability must play no role in science. They can be accepted because scientific representations usually do not become widely distributed except among small groups of specialists, who spend a great deal of time learning to understand scientific theories. There are institutional mechanisms, such as education, whose job it is to teach the necessary knowledge and skills required to become a scientist. (See also McCauley 2000; cf. Kuhn 1996.) It thus seems that a mere distinction between spontaneous and reflective beliefs à la Sperber is not enough: although both religion and science include reflective beliefs, religion is natural and science unnatural, as Lewis Wolpert (1994) and McCauley (2000) have argued. Religious representations are acquired without explicit tuition, whereas scientific representations need to be explicitly taught. In this sense, theological representations are closer to scientific than to religious ones, a view which Donald Wiebe (1991) has defended in detail (see also Pyysiäinen 1999a)[37].

Besides scientific truths, religious truths must also be differentiated from fiction. Although no one believes in the actual existence for example of such fictional characters as Joseph K. in Kafka's *The Trial*, or such objects as the picture of Dorian Gray, nevertheless good fiction is thought to express some deep truth about life. It is not *only* make-believe. We could thus try to say that religion is distinguished from fiction by the fact that religious representations are taken to be literally true, while fiction is only metaphorical.

This, however, is problematic; within the philosophy of religion and philosophical theology, there have been a number of attempts to explain religious representations in another way than the literal. They

---

37   It may be noted that one of the founders of Finnish comparative religion, Martti Haavio (1959: 6) wrote forty years ago that "higher religions," i.e. theological traditions, were not religions in the primary sense of the word, but "artificial forgeries."

may for example be considered as metaphorical expressions of certain basic existential questions, as expressions of commitment to a specific way of life, or as forming a peculiar "language game" expressive of a specific "form of life" (see Pyysiäinen 1996a: 57-63). Such views are not restricted to modern Christianity, but can also be found for instance in early Buddhism. According to some Mahāyāna philosophers, all the teachings of the Buddha are merely "skilful means" (Sanskrit *upāya*) by which the Buddha wanted to direct people to experience enlightenment. Their import does not follow from their intension or extension, but only from the way they are used to solicit a new insight. They are neither true or false in a literal sense. (See Pye 1979; Pyysiäinen 1993: 104-139.)

Two reservations, however, are called for here. First of all, such interpretations are usually made by religious experts who have been greatly influenced by a scientific way of thinking, and thus are not representative of thinking of the majority of believers. Second, even the experts do not usually consider that religion is merely a useful fiction (for an exception, see Kliever 1981). Although they consider religious utterances to be somehow "symbolic," they nevertheless tend to assume the existence of some specific level of reality which makes the use of these "symbols" meaningful. Thus it can be said for example that religious language *refers* to an objective god, even though it *describes* him only metaphorically (Soskice 1985: 109, 137-148). (See Wiebe 1991: 16-28.)

In this perspective, religious representations differ from fictional ones in that their truth and import is considered to be dependent on some mysterious, counter-intuitive dimension of reality, whereas fictional counter-intuitive representations convey truth only in so far as they metaphorically describe the ordinary reality of intuitive ontologies. Now, some would probably want to argue that even religious representations can be conceived of in this way. God for example can be interpreted as meaning nothing more nor less than life itself. But then one is hard pressed to explain in what sense religion thus conceived of differs from fiction. It is true that religion for example includes certain kinds of institutional forms and devotional practices, but the question is precisely why this is so. As the majority of believers do not understand their religion as only useful fiction, we can leave such explanations aside as mere academic curiosities.

Thus accepting the distinction that religious representations describe, from the point of view of the believer, a counter-intuitive reality, whereas fictional representations describe ordinary reality, albeit metaphorically, we are forced to admit that the religiosity of a representation is not its intrinsic property, but is based on the way it is *used*. Consider the following representations, both of which are counter-intuitive insofar as angels are agents without physical and biological properties:

1) On the mountain an angel appeared to him.
2) In the desert an angel appeared to him.

Obviously you cannot decide without further information which one of these is religious and which fictional. If for example you know that the first sentence is from a bestselling novel telling the story of a fictional hero of some imaginary tribe, you will hardly regard it as religious. You will know that the author does not mean that the event described actually happened. Furthermore, if you also know that the second sentence is from a Holy Book and describes the visions of a prophet, you will have no problem in identifying it as religious. It describes an event which people believe actually to have taken place.

What about disturbed beliefs, then? It is easy for instance to imagine a schizophrenic who believes that an angel occasionally appears to him or her at night. Here we have a counter-intuitive representation which expresses quite literally a belief about a counter-intuitive phenomenon taking place within ordinary reality. The only thing that distinguishes it from religious beliefs is that it is strictly idiosyncratic and therefore hinders communication between the person in question and other people. According to Frith's (1995) rather plausible theory, it is the result of a neuropsychological disorder that makes one incapable of metarepresentation: all kinds of beliefs are allowed a free access in the mind, without any metarepresentation. Thus, for example, "It is possible to imagine that 'there are lizards in my bedroom'" becomes "There are lizards in my bedroom," i.e. the metarepresentational context is dropped out. Such disorder may have its origin in abnormal brain structure. (See Cosmides and Tooby 2000.)

Consequently, the difference between religious and disturbed representations can also be approached both on the levels of thought and behavior on the one hand and on the level of neurophysiology on the other. Here I shall have to confine myself to the levels of thought and behavior only. On these levels only two types of difference between religion and mental disturbance can in principle be found. The first is the

difference between individual, idiosyncratic representations and cultural representations: religious representations are always part of some tradition and thus shared by a group of people. Therefore they can be used
effectively in life management, to find a basis for ethics, etc. (see also
Lawson and McCauley 1990: 155). It is especially important to emphasize that it is possible – in principle at least – to develop all kinds of ther-
apeutic techniques on the basis of religious counter-intuitive representations which thus can serve as means of gaining understanding of oneself
and of external reality. They are powerful tools that can be used both in
motivating oneself and to manipulate other people, in good and bad
alike, quite irrespective of whether religious counter-intuitive representations are true in a metaphysical sense.

Disturbed representations do not form such traditions as the religious ones even within a group of schizophrenics (although there
might be certain widely distributed motives); in thus being strictly
idiosyncratic, they merely hinder communication between people.
The second possible difference is that while such widely distributed
representations as religious ones must conform to Boyer's cognitive
optimum, disturbed might not. In not being widely diffused, they
might involve more extreme counter-intuitiveness, although this has
not as yet been empirically tested.

Thus we can draw the following conclusions concerning counter-
intuitive representations:

- Scientific representations that are actually understood are in principle not capable of becoming widely distributed because they are
  often extremely counter-intuitive and their acquisition thus takes a
  good deal of time and effort. They are highly reflective, not spontaneous. Yet they are not idiosyncratic but collective. It is another
  thing that some or even many scientific representations may
  become widely distributed in symbolic form, i.e. as not actually
  understood. They are then metarepresented, in such form for
  instance as '"$E = mc^2$" means something.'
- Ordinary religious representations (in contrast to theological ones)
  are capable of becoming widely distributed because they are optimally counter-intuitive and therefore attention-demanding, memorable, and evocative (i.e. they can be easily connected to a subject's
  other representations). Although reflective in Sperber's sense, they
  need not be explicitly taught, but can be acquired as an almost necessary byproduct of intuitive ontologies.

- Disturbed counter-intuitive representations are not widespread, but idiosyncratic. Their counter-intuitiveness may also be more radical than what is the case in religion. Yet they can hardly be characterized as reflective. Rather, they are the outcome of neurophysiological disorders, or otherwise more or less automatically produced. Were they consciously elaborated, the person in question should also be capable of controlling them, which is not the case.
- Fictional counter-intuitive representations can be either idiosyncratic or collective, spontaneous or reflective, because fiction is such a vague category. They are however distinguished from religious, disturbed and scientific representations in that they are never taken to be literally true. Or, if they are, then their nature has been mistaken for something else (or they are not counter-intuitive).

These various forms of counter-intuitive representations are illustrated in figure 4, in which the three dimensions of counter-intuitive – intuitive, (widely) distributed-idiosyncratic and spontaneous-reflective have been transformed from dichotomies into continuums. My idea in drawing this figure has to some extent been influenced by Littleton's (1965) way of placing folk narratives on a similar chart, the axes of which are formed by the continua factual-fabulous and secular-sacred. Thus a three-dimensional space, a "belief box," is provided in which various types of representations occupy a definite place according to their degree of counter-intuitiveness, spontaneity, and idiosyncracy. It might also be that being widespread is a function of spontaneity in the sense that the most widespread representations also are the most spontaneous ones (as was suggested to me in a conversation by Tom Sjöblom).

In all these cases of mixing knowledge from different domains – science, religion, fiction, and even mental disturbance – it is not the case that domain-specificity is being abandoned. From Mithen's (1998: 46-52) argumentation one may get the impression that he considers various kinds of violations of domain boundaries as counter-evidence for Cosmides and Tooby's theory of domain-specificity, although the subsequent chapters correct this interpretation. Yet the difference may not always be clear between violating the principles of domain-specificity and no domain-specificity at all. It should be stressed for example that the fact that children often behave toward their toys as though they were personal beings does not mean that their thinking does not contain distinct domains of naïve physics and social/psychological intelligence.

CI = counter-intuitive
I   = intuitive
WS = widespread
IS   = idiosyncratic
S   = spontaneous
R   = reflective

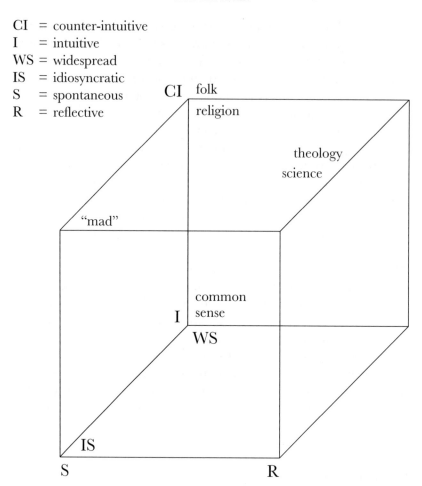

Fig. 4. "The belief box." This figure illustrates the mutual relationships between various types of mental representations using a spatial analogy. The three dimensions of the cubic are based on the continua counter-intuitive – intuitive, (widely) distributed – idiosyncratic, and spontaneous – reflective. The cubic can be thought of as a mental space in which various representations occupy a definite place according to their degree of counter-intuitiveness, spontaneity, and cultural diffusion.

Knowledge belonging to these domains is only *occasionally* mixed; children for instance do not *consistently* treat teddy-bears as living persons.

As Atran (1996: 241) puts it, were people not capable of recognizing counter-intuitive representations as exceptional, they would "suspect that someone eating a pork chop might be a cannibal, expect healthy houses to give birth to little houses, believe that animal(s) species can interbreed as indiscriminately as people can mate, turn on the radio to stop the wind from spreading fire, avoid provoking rocks that could fly up and strike you dead," etc. This, of course, is not the case, and most people all over the world, even children to a certain extent, are perfectly capable of finding their way in their daily lives. Counter-intuitive beliefs are exceptional and belong to special contexts (Atran 1996: 242).

Empirical evidence of counter-intuitiveness as a characteristic of religion

I have conducted empirical experiments to test the hypothesis that people consider counter-intuitive representations more likely to be religious than purely intuitive ones, by and large irrespective of the details of their content. In the first experiment the subjects (N = 85) were presented brief sentences expressing various kinds of beliefs and descriptions of events, both intuitive and counter-intuitive. They were then asked to rate on a scale form 1 to 5 how probably they considered each sentence to be religious. The result was that the counter-intuitive representations were considered significantly (p<.001) more likely to be religious than the intuitive ones. Typical examples of intuitive representations were "Old man Cluang wept while listening to John's sad story," "The Vezzi believe that the scepter of the king is made of fine gold," and "Boming is present on the hills." Counter-intuitive representations are exemplified by "The wooden statue of Bonong wept while listening to John's sad story," "The Vezzi believe that the scepter of the king can read people's thoughts," and "Boming is present everywhere at once." There were 26 intuitive and 13 counter-intuitive representations altogether, i.e. each counter-intuitive sentence had two intuitive alternatives. The subjects consisted of three groups of university students from Finland, Republic of Ireland, and Mid-West USA. (Pyysiäinen, Lindeman, and Honkela *forthcoming*.)

In another study I wanted to see whether such counter-intuitiveness that includes an agent, and especially an agent that has knowledge about the affairs of humans, is regarded as more likely religious. The subjects were recruited from among first year philosophy and anthropology students in Atlanta and in New York, USA (N = 71). Also in this study counter-intuitive representations scored higher than the intuitive ones. Those involving an agent scored higher (mean 3.39) than those without an agent (mean 2.47). Those involving an agent aware of and interested in the affairs of humans scored higher (mean 3.57) than those involving an agent without such interest and capacity (mean 3.12), but the reliability of the "ignorant agent" sentences was very low (4 items, Cronbach's α = .63). (Pyysiäinen, Lindeman, and Honkela *forthcoming*).

Thus counter-intuitiveness seems to be a statistically relevant phenomenon with regard to religiousness. When explicitly asked, people tend to connect the idea of counter-intuitiveness with religion. More precisely, when people have to evaluate different kinds of situations in terms of their possible religiousness, they consider situations that include a counter-intuitive element as more likely to be religious than others. It should be noted, however, that the alternatives offered allow different kinds of interpretations when they are considered in combinations. One could, for example reason that if Boming is present everywhere, he or she must be a god and the sentence "Boming is present everywhere at once" a religious one. But, from that it would also follow that the two other sentences about Boming are religious, provided that 'Boming' refers to the same being in all three sentences. Yet only a minority of subjects reasoned thus; the majority considered the sentence "Boming is present everywhere at once" more likely to be religious than the other two sentences about Boming. In other words, they have scored the sentences as separate items.

What probably happens is that the question "Is this religious?" activates in the subjects a tendency to attribute religiousness to those situations which call for some unnatural explanation. In other words, the question itself is taken as a cue that directs the inferences of the subjects. And, had the alternatives been a bit different, the subjects could even have been led to infer that some situations are very likely to be fictional, disturbed, or even scientific.

It is sometimes possible to tell from the content of a representation that is scientific, religious, fictional or crazy. But often this is not so. How, then, do people classify some representations and actions as being religious under certain conditions? We can begin to look for an answer by noting that very often the religious status of a given belief or practice is contested. This is especially apparent in the case of the so-called "new religious movements," which are often alleged either to be evidence for the mental disturbance of their members, or perceived merely as ways of making money, rather than forms of religion. It is in vain for various authorities to turn to scholars of religion for help in such questions; we cannot say what really is and what is not religion. (Cf. W.F. Sullivan 1996; L.E. Sullivan 1996). Even if counter-intuitive representations serve as an especially good defining characteristic of religion, the presence of counter-intuitiveness alone is not a sufficient criterion for something being an instance of religion. Nor is it possible to say what more is needed, as it seems that there are no jointly sufficient and singly necessary criteria according to which judge something as an instance of religion.

Returning to the idea of prototypes, discussed in the first chapter, we can only say that to some extent people tend to classify counter-intuitive beliefs and practices as religious guided by the tradition with which they are most familiar. If a new idea or practice appears to be close enough to the prototype, it may be classified as being religious. It is thus not only the specific content of the Christian (or other) tradition that forms the prototype, but also counter-intuitiveness as such can become an essential part of the prototype: it is part and parcel of religion that there is something counter-intuitive about it.

Other factors, such as morality, may also be relevant. Even if a practice were somehow reminiscent for instance of Christian practices, it would not be regarded as religious if it were considered immoral (for instance sacrificing young boys to a god). Thus, there is no one thing that decides whether something is or is not religious, the decision always being more or less a matter of opinion. This, in a way brings our deconstruction of the category of religion to a logical conclusion. 'Religion' is a concept that identifies the personalistic counter-intuitive representations and the related practices, institutions, etc. that are widely spread, literally believed, and actively used by a group of people in their attempts to understand, explain and control those aspects of life, and reality as a whole, that escape common sense and, more recently, scientific explanation.[38] The precise bound-

---

38   Elsewhere (Pyysiäinen 1997: 158) I have suggested that "[c]omparative religion studies how human thought, emotion, and behavior are affected by the fact that people feel that in reality there is always something they cannot, even in principle, fully understand, explain, and control."

aries of the class of such phenomena, however, are fuzzy (cf. Saler 2000).

The criterion of personalism distinguishes religion from science (as also noted by Robin Horton 1993: 348); counter-intuitiveness distinguishes it from practical common sense; in being widespread and used successfully in life management, religious representations differ from disturbed representations; and in being literally believed religious representations differ from fiction. Common sense, science, fiction, religion, and mental disturbance seem to form a fairly exhaustive inventory of the domains to which a representation can belong. Only jokes might be added as a specific mode or domain of thought. Jokes too manifest counter-intuitiveness, but now with the function of producing an element of amusing or entertaining surprise (See also Mithen 1998: 226). It may be that it is precisely because of this quite opposite kind of attitude toward counter-intuitiveness that explains why joking and piety have so often been considered mutually incompatible;[39] laughing at things sacred is a sacrilege, because laughter can be interpreted as a sign of the fact that one takes the real existence of something counter-intuitive as a sheer impossibility and therefore as an amusing idea.

I shall now move on to consider, in a considerably more speculative vein, the seriousness with which people relate to religious counter-intuitiveness. It seems, after all, to be this seriousness, i.e. religious belief, that makes it possible to use religious ideas in life management, although it could also be argued that it is the use(fulness) that creates the attitude of seriousness (Boyer in press Ch. 9). As we have seen, people often have a strong emotional attitude toward their somatically marked religious beliefs. The mere idea that a given religious belief might merely be a useful fiction may seem frightening or at least plain wrong to them. In the face of criticism, people often appeal to the religious authorities that for them guarantee the truth of such metarepresented beliefs as for example "'God loves the world' is true." "But it says so in the Bible!" is a common reply to a skeptic. People do not defend their religious beliefs as mere useful abstractions. Religious beliefs are more often than not intimately linked with people's other

---

39   In Umberto Eco's well-known historical novel *Il nome della rosa* (1980) for instance the old monk Jorge, living in 14th century Italy, wants to destroy the newly discovered manuscript of Aristotle's *Poetics* and eats it up, because he thinks that laughter destroys the sacred.

beliefs, and religious authorities thus occupy a central place in their lives. Suspecting that religious beliefs might not be true means suspecting that the authorities one has trusted are not worthy of their trust and that one's whole outlook on life should be reconsidered. The somatic markers binding people to their religion are rather similar to the emotional ties between a man and a woman in a long-standing marriage, which often makes divorce difficult and painful if not outright impossible. In addition to representations about love relationships, religious and perhaps also political ideals seem to have this special capacity for unifying people into a group of "believers," and thus also separating them from other people. This capacity is based on the somatic markers as we have seen.

These markers are established either gradually, through a repetitive exposure to the relevant beliefs, or in a sudden "religious experience" encoded in episodic memory. In both cases strong emotions are involved. For the problem of the mutual relationship between belief and use, this means that neither needs to have primacy over the other. In the doctrinal mode, belief both grows together with repeated use and also enhances use. It is a process of interaction. In the imagistic mode, belief may follow from a sudden experience, in which case it is not preceded by extensive use.

What is special about religious ideas is that they do not pertain to any particular natural domain, but form evocative symbolic knowledge with no fixed interpretation. They arise merely because they are possible, i.e. are a natural outcome of intuitive ontologies and of our capacity for cross-domain formations. Thus the way a certain kind of "transcendent" reference is attributed to religious representations is more or less arbitrary. It may be that, as people cannot be sure that all counter-intuitive representations are mere fictions, they have to have some means of dealing with the possibility that some of them may really be true. The status of such representations is that of an absolute truth, which distinguishes them from fictional, disturbed and scientific representations. Thus the ideas of counter-intuitiveness and of the domain-specificity of thought help us to provide a theoretical explanation of the fact, noted also by Geertz (p. 48 above), that religion involves an image of a genuine order of the world such that it can account for all kinds of ambiguities, puzzles and paradoxes, and that relates "man's sphere of existence to a wider sphere within which it is conceived to rest."

All this entails that religious knowledge cannot be considered representational or theoretical by believers. God for example is not considered to be merely a non-natural mental representation but a genuinely existing, although unperceived, agent (see Barrett 1998). Our knowledge about him (or her) does not depend on our capacities for knowing, but on god's own self-revelation. We do not say that our knowledge of god is derived from seeing, hearing, or touching, but from the fact that the supposed object of knowledge himself or herself reveals that knowledge to us. The same holds, *mutatis mutandis*, for other religions in which such notions as enlightenment, shamanic journeys, etc. fulfill roughly the same role as revelation in the Christian tradition (see Pyysiäinen 2001b). The point is that this special kind of knowledge presupposes a situation theory of representation: our knowledge of religious counter-intuitive things and processes is not our own construct but direct, unmediated knowledge about another level of reality.

Thus Perner's example (above) of how it is often useful to be situation theorist holds especially true in religion. It is not important that religious knowledge *can* sometimes be understood in a situationist manner – so can many other types of knowledge. As Kuhn (1996) observed, her subjects did not reflect on their theories as objects of cognition, but rather seemed to take them as direct reflections of how things are. What is important here, as I have tried to show in a number of instances, is that religious knowledge *cannot* be understood to be representational without serious paradoxes or an endless regress of arguments (Pyysiäinen 1996b; 1998; 1999a&b). Religious knowledge loses its specific nature when interpreted representationally, as shown by the critique often directed toward the scientific study of religion. One example of a paradox that results from taking religious knowledge as representational is offered by the idea of a Holy Book as the ultimate authority (Pyysiäinen 1999a&b):

1) The Bible is the word of god.
2) How do we know this?
3) Because it says so in the Bible.
4) How do we know that this is true?
5) Because the Bible is the word of god.

We have already seen that this logical problem is usually not encountered by ordinary believers, but only by the theologian who wants to see these steps as a deductive argument. However, it seems that an essential part of the ordinary believer's practical attitude is a situation theory: knowledge about god and the Bible is not in need of justification because it is somehow seen directly by those who are part of the relevant situation (the insiders). A logical problem arises only when knowledge about god is conceived of as a representation of the situation of "belief" and as such not itself part of the situation. The problems that follow force the theologian too finally to adopt a situation theory of religious knowledge.

My idea here parallels that of Lawson and McCauley (1990), who hold that a wide array of features in religious ritual structures can be explained by knowledge about the relevant CPS-agents. CPS-agents serve as the ultimate foundation of which religious rituals rest, and the place they occupy in any given ritual determines many features of the ritual in question. Substituting 'counter-intuitive agent' for 'CPS-agent,' we can say that counter-intuitive agents also act on other domains of religion than rituals to establish a closure to argumentation. It is not that such ideas have been invented to put a stop to an endless regression of arguments, but rather that they have been selected for this function because of their evocativeness. It is of course also possible merely to accept that human reasoning powers have certain insurmountable limits and that therefore we will never be capable of a complete and coherent explanation of reality; a fact that Kurt Gödel showed to hold for all formal systems (see Pyysiäinen 1996b;1999a&b; Kamppinen and Revonsuo 1993) in his famous mathematical proofs.[40] But the view that there is no ultimate foundation may itself assume the role of an ultimate foundation, as the deconstructionists have shown (see Hart 1989).

Thus for example the Buddhist author Nāgārjuna (first century AD?), whose real identity is still being discussed, argued in a short treatise that Vishnu could not be the creator of the world, because if the world needs an explanation for its existence then Vishnu (god) too needs such an explanation, leading to an infinite regression. Nor can Vishnu be eternal and the sole cause of his own existence, as, according to Nāgārjuna, only such entities can exist which are born (or have

---

40   Kurt Gödel showed in 1931 that a system sufficiently comprehensive to contain the whole of arithmetic can only be proved to be consistent if this proof employs rules of inference in certain essential respects different from the rules used within the system to be proved consistent. There thus arises the question of whether the system of these rules itself is consistent, and we are caught in a vicious circle. Secondly, Gödel demonstrated that all systems within which arithmetic can be developed are incomplete in the sense that "(g)iven any consistent set of arithmetical axioms, there are true arithmetical statements that cannot be derived from the set." (Nagel and Newman 1964. See Pyysiäinen 1996b: 202-203.)

arisen). And, if Vishnu was born, then there must have been a time when he did not exist. This, however, leads to a contradiction, because Vishnu is supposed to be the creator of everything. In Nāgārjuna's own view, all things arise in mutual co-dependence (the *pratītyasamutpāda*) and thus have no own essence (*svabhāva*); this, however, leads ultimately to the conclusion that there is no arising and passing away of phenomena, all phenomena being empty (*śūnya*). In this way, emptiness (*śūnyatā*) seems to become the ultimate foundation of everything. Nāgārjuna, however, may have wanted to launch 'emptiness' more as a critique of all ontology than as one more attempt at a positive ontology.[41] Yet this critique itself seems soon to have come to be understood as a foundational argument.

As we have seen, such counter-intuitive representations can serve as the ultimate basis for ethics, the question of the meaning of life, and for ultimate explanations regarding the universe, etc. because their counter-intuitiveness makes them transcendent to known reality. They can thus form a foundation which is itself not in need of a foundation, provided that one accepts them in a situation-theorist manner simply as given (like e.g. Swinburne 1996 (see note 5 on p. 16). Acknowledging that they are so accepted merely because *something* must be accepted simply as given (see Pihlström 1996: 393-394; Saariluoma 1997: 11-12), would deprive foundational religious representations of their absolute status. (See also Pyysiäinen 1999a&b.)

In saying that religious representations provide us with a sense of having some kind of control over things that would otherwise seem impossible to understand or control, I do not mean to suggest a functionalist interpretation of religion. All I mean is that once counter-intuitive representations are in existence, some of them become selected for such uses as we have seen. They make it possible to reason about the meaning of life, about good and bad, etc. in a foundational manner. An organized form of religion in a way restricts the amount and nature of acceptable counter-intuitive representations, and thus provides an order in counter-intuitive ideas that would not naturally come about. In this way, the chaos of all possible counter-intuitive

---

41   Nāgārjuna's critique of Vishnu as creator is presented in his *Īśvarakartrtvanirākrtih*, the Sanskrit original and Tibetan translation of which were published in 1904 by Th. Stcherbatsky. These, together with an English translation, have been reprinted in Stcherbatsky 1969: 1-16. Nāgārjuna's almost Humean criticism of causality and his ideas on emptiness can be found especially in his *Mulamadhyamakakārikā* (e.g. I:6, XXII: 10, XXIV:19, XVIII:7). (See Pyysiäinen 1993: 105-107, 111-113.)42.

ideas is restricted to an established tradition, which provides a more or less clear frame of reference in which to embed all half-understood, symbolic representations. In this way, such metarepresentations as "'Jesus is the son of god' is true" emerge, and religious authority is established. Likewise the idea that we cannot truly understand or control everything in reality now becomes easier to bear, as the unknown dimensions of existence can be taken to be ruled by god, *dharma* or whatever, who/which can be somehow manipulated by the right means. All this contributes to social and psychological cohesion by providing order in consciousness.

Although all of this is still highly speculative, I believe my speculations go a long way in the right direction. If Lawson and McCauley (1990) have established that religious rituals clearly have a structure in which CPS-agents play a central role, it is my ambitious suggestion that a similar structure could also be found in religion as a whole. Its description and empirical testing, however, is not an easy task. It requires the deducing of precise hypotheses from this general idea, and their subsequent empirical testing.

The general theory here outlined makes it possible to understand religion, not as a cognitive domain, but as "parasitic" to the various domains, a by-product of the intuitive ontologies, which has no clear boundaries. There are no inherently religious ideas, practices or "symbols," and no religious cognitive mechanisms, religious ideas being recognized as religious only by the uses to which they are put and by the attitude held towards them by believers. The most important characteristic of religion thus understood is a firm, emotional belief in the absolute truth of religious ideas, combined with the fact that those ideas are optimally counter-intuitive.

It is here that Durkheim's theory may have something to contribute: religion cannot be identified without paying attention to how counter-intuitive ideas are used in a society. Although religious counter-intuitive ideas cannot be said to be only "symbols" of the society, or of collective consciousness, they acquire their special status in collective social interaction. Although we need not postulate any mysterious "collective consciousness," the idea of the religiosity of an idea only makes sense in a community of individuals trying to go on living their lives together with each other. Religiosity cannot be the property of solitary ideas abstracted from all context (although people seem to be capable of recognizing religion without contextual information, with the help of stored prototypes).

As religion as a category thus is not in any sense a given, comparative religion deals with the processes whereby something becomes part of religion, rather than with religions as fixed givens. Throughout this book, I have tried to show the importance of taking into account the various cognitive factors that essentially shape the various dimensions of religion. This has proved to be an invaluable approach, that can shed light on issues that would otherwise remain incomprehensible. Quite importantly, I have been able to formulate testable hypotheses derived from a simple cognitive theory about religion.

From this theory, as we have seen, a number of empirical hypotheses for further testing can be derived. They all center around the idea that counter-intuitive representations provide structure in religion, in a like manner to the CPS-agents in Lawson and McCauley's (1990) theory of rituals. Methodologically, this offers a basis for studies that attempt to clarify the ways in which various kinds of counter-intuitive representations structure religious beliefs within various traditions. This form of comparative religion would rest on a sound theoretical basis, would allow the proposing and experimental testing of a diversity of empirical hypotheses, and would increase our knowledge of religion as a universal cognitive and social phenomenon as well as of various individual religious phenomena.

It might be useful theoretically to distinguish between theoretical and applied comparative religion, or the study of religions. Theoretical comparative religion would consist of theorizing about the general phenomenon of religion while applied comparative religion would focus on in-depth studies of individual religious phenomena. These two forms of comparative religion could not, however, in practice be kept apart as there can be no theorizing about religion without first hand knowledge of actual religious phenomena, and because such phenomena cannot be properly studied without a good theoretical basis. It should also be recognized that 'applied' does here not mean applying the results of scientific research in one's own religious life or the religious life of a given society. Practicing and studying religion should be kept clearly apart. Thus the distinction between theoretical and applied comparative religion is more an analytical tool than a real division between individual scholars or departments. Individual programs, however, could focus more on one side of the divide than the other, i.e. in them theory could either serve as mere tool, or its development could be the actual goal of the study.

Summary

In the present theory, the necessary but not sufficient characteristic of religion is counter-intuitiveness. Counter-intuitive representations are formed by violating the boundaries of intuitive ontological categories. These categories are understood as tacit knowledge structures characterizing a domain-specific mind. The human mind is not an all-purpose problem solver but a collection of separate content-specific cognitive mechanisms. To what extent these domains are innate and genetically determined cannot be decided within the present confines. I do not think, however, that nature and nurture are two exclusive factors; surely we are dealing with an interactive process in which both have a rightful place (as Elman et al. suggest). I also understand cognitive domains as not simply extensional but as domains of *phenomena*, i.e. as domains of what appears to us.

Religion is characterized by counter-intuitive representations in general, and by representations of counter-intuitive *agents* in particular. Preliminary empirical evidence suggests that counter-intuitiveness serves as the cue that activates a religious interpretation in subjects: people are more likely to connect counter-intuitive than merely natural events or beliefs in the context of religion. Although western subjects may here reason in the light of the Judeo-Christian tradition as the prototype of religion, it is the general idea of counter-intuitiveness that evokes the prototype. This suggests that counter-intuitiveness is an important part of a folk theory of religion.

By a folk theory I here mean an explicit commonsensical view that certain beliefs and practices are set apart from the ordinary because they relate to things that cannot be controlled by natural reasoning. It is an *explicit* theory about violations of *intuitive* (tacit) beliefs. It is a theory in the sense of a dynamic set of principles that makes it possible to systematize regularities and make predictions.

However, there presumably exists no specific domain of religious cognition. Religion is a category of thoughts and behaviors based on quite ordinary cognitive mechanisms. Processing counter-intuitive representations may require one or more special mechanisms, but not all counter-intuitiveness is religious and religion is much more than mere counter-intuitiveness. Religious counter-intuitive representations are distinguished from scientific, fictional and disturbed representations in that they make use of agency-explanations, do not aim at controlled and impersonal explanations, are not idiosyncratic but shared by a group of people, and are also believed, despite their counter-intuitiveness, to be literally true.

Studying religion scientifically thus means the study of how certain counter-intuitive representations come to be selected as objects of serious belief and are used in life management both individually and collectively. In other words, it is based on the fact that people are able to recognize certain beliefs and practices as being of special import, quite irrespective of whether they have an explicit *concept* of 'religion.' Durkheim's idea of collective authority is relevant in the sense that religious ideas acquire their aura of factuality and import in the process of being collectively employed in organizing social and personal life. This does not mean, however, that they are only "symbolic" representations of the society.

Theoretical comparative religion focuses on the development of theories about religious phenomena, whereas applied comparative religion studies religious phenomena in the light of these theories. This, however, is merely an analytical distinction; individual studies must always contain both aspects in varying degrees.

REFERENCES

Buddhist texts

Astadasasāhasrikāprajñāpāramitāsūtra (in a Gilgit Manuscript). Tr. in *The Large Sūtra on Perfect Wisdom* (ed. and tr. by E. Conze). Berkeley & Los Angeles & London: University of California Press, 1984 (1975).

Dīghanikāya, Vol. III. Ed. by J.E. Carpenter. London: The Pali Text Society & Luzac Company, 1960 (1911).

Hekiganroku. *The Blue Cliff Records*. Tr. and ed. with a commentary by R.D.M. Shaw. London: Michael Joseph, 1961.

Lankāvatārasūtra. *The Lankāvatārasūtra*. Tr. by D.T. Suzuki. London: George Routledge & Sons, 1932.

Mumonkan. *Zen Classics*, Vol. 4. Tr. and ed. by R.H. Blyth. Japan: The Hokuseido Press, 1966.

Nāgārjuna. *Īśvarakartrtvanirākrtih*. In Stcherbatsky 1969, pp. 1-16.

Nāgārjuna. *Mūlamadhyamakakārikā. Mūlamadhyamakakārikās (Mādhyamikasūtras) de Nāgārjuna avec la Prasannapadā de Candrakīrti*. Publié par Louis de la Vallée Poussin. (*Bibliotheca Buddhica*, IV.) St.-Petersbourg, 1903. [An English translation is to be found in F. Streng: *Emptiness*, pp. 183-220. Nashville: Abingdon Press, 1967.]

Pañcavimsatisahasrikāprajñāpāramitāsūtra. Partial translation in E. Conze (ed. & tr.) *The Large Sūtra on Perfect Wisdom*. Berkeley: University of California Press, 1984 (1975).

Papañcasudani of Buddhaghosa. An excerpt tr. in E. Conze: *Buddhist Scriptures*. Harmondsworth: Penguin, 1979 (1959).

Ratnagotravibhāgauttaratantra. Tr. by J. Takasaki. In *A Study on the Ratnagotravibhāga (Uttaratantra), Being a Treatise on the Tathāgatagarbha Theory of Mahāyāna Buddhism*. (*Serie orientale Roma*, 33.) Roma: Istituto Italiano per il Medio ed Estremo Oriente, 1966.

Udāna. Ed. by P. Steinthal. London: The Pali Text Society & Routledge and Kegan Paul, 1982 (1885).

Vinayapitakam. *The Vinaya Pitakam*. Ed. by H. Oldenberg. London & Edinburgh: Williams & Norgate, 1879-1883.

Western works

ABU-LUGHOD, Lila. 1991. 'Writing against Culture.' In *Recapturing Anthropology: Working in the Present* (ed. by R. Fox), pp. 137-162. Santa Fe: School of American Research Press.

AQUINAS, St. Thomas. *Summa Theologiæ* I-III. Ed. by Petri Caramello. Torino: Marietti 1962-63.

ALANEN, Lilli. 1980. 'Descartes's dualism and the philosophy of mind.' *Revue de Métaphysique et Morale* 3/1989: 391-413.

ALHO, Olli. 1976. *The Religion of the Slaves.* (*Folklore Fellows Communications*, 217.) Helsinki: Academia Scientiarum Fennica.

ALLEN, Douglas. 1978. *Structure and Creativity in Religion. Hermeneutics in Mircea Eliade's Phenomenology and New Directions.* (*Religion and Reason*, 14.) The Hague: Mouton.

AMES, Michael M. 1966. 'Ritual presentations and the structure of the Sinhalese Pantheon.' In *Anthropological Studies in Theravāda Buddhism* (ed. by M. Nash), pp. 27-50. *(Cultural Report Series*, 13.) New Haven: Yale University.

ANDRESEN, Jensine and Robert K.C. Forman (eds). 2000. *Cognitive Models and Spiritual Maps: Interdisciplinary Explorations of Religious Experience.* Thorverton: Imprint Academic.

ANTTONEN, Veikko. 1996. 'Rethinking the sacred: The notions of 'human body' and 'territory' in conceptualizing religion.' In *The Sacred and its Scholars* (ed. by T.A. Idinopulos and E.A. Yonan), pp. 36-64. (*Studies in the History of Religions (Numen Book Series)*, LXXIII.) Leiden: E.J. Brill.

ANTTONEN, Veikko. 2000. 'Sacred.' In *Guide to the Study of Religion* (ed. by W. Braun and R.T. McCutcheon), pp. 271-282. London & New York: Cassell.

ANTTONEN, Pertti J. 1992. 'The rites of passage revisited. A new look at Van Gennep's theory of the ritual process and its application in the study of Finnish-Karelian wedding rituals.' *Temenos* 28: 15-52.

ARMSTRONG, Karen. 1993. *A History of God.* London: Heinemann.

ARMSTRONG, Sharon Lee, Lila G. Gleitman, and Henry Gleitman. 1983. 'What some concepts might not be.' *Cognition* 12: 263-308.

ATRAN, Scott. 1990. *Cognitive Foundations of Natural History.* Cambridge, etc.: Cambridge University Press & Editions de la Maison des sciences de l'homme.

ATRAN, Scott. 1994. 'Core domains versus scientific theories: Evidence from systematics and Itza-Maya folkbiology.' In *Mapping the Mind* (ed. by L. Hirschfeld and S. Gelman), pp. 316-340. Cambridge: Cambridge University Press.

ATRAN, Scott. 1996. 'Modes of thinking about living kinds.' In *Modes of Thought* (ed. by D.R. Olson, and N. Torrance), pp. 216-260 New York: Cambridge University Press.

ATRAN, Scott. 1998. 'Folk biology and the anthropology of science: Cognitive universals and cultural particulars.' *Behavioral and Brain Sciences* 21: 547-609.

AVERILL, James R. 1980 (1976). 'Emotion and anxiety: Sociocultural, biological, and psychological determinants.' In *Explaining Emotions* (ed. by A. Oksenberg Rorty), pp. 37-72. Berkeley, and Los Angeles & London: University of California Press.

AYER, Alfred Jules. 1962 (1936). *Language, Truth and Logic*. London: Victor Gollancz.

BACON, Francis. 1963 (1605). *The Advancement of Learning*. Oxford: The Clarendon Press.

BANTON, Michael (ed.). 1968 (1966). *Anthropological Approaches to the Study of Religion*. London: Tavistock Publications.

BARKOW, Jerome H., Leda Cosmides, and John Tooby (ed.). 1995 (1992). *The Adapted Mind. Evolutionary Psychology and the Generation of Culture*. New York & Oxford: Oxford University Press.

BARNARD, G. William. 1997. *Exploring Unseen Worlds. William James and the Philosophy of Mysticism*. Albany: State University of New York Press.

BARNES, L. Philip. 1992. 'Walter Stace's philosophy of mysticism.' *Hermathena* 153: 5-20.

BARRETT, Justin L. 1998. 'Cognitive constraints on Hindu concepts of the divine.' *Journal for the Scientific Study of Religion* 37: 608-619.

BARRETT, Justin L. 1999. 'Theological correctness: Cognitive constraint and the study of religion.' *Method & Theory in the Study of Religion* 11: 325-339.

BARRETT, Justin L. 2000. 'Exploring the natural foundations of religion.' *Trends in Cognitive Sciences* 4: 29-34.

BARRETT, Justin L. 2001. 'Do children experience God as adults do? Retracing the development of God concepts.' In *Religion in Mind: Cognitive Perspectives on Religious Belief, Ritual and Experience* (ed. by J. Andresen), pp. 173-190. Cambridge: Cambridge University Press.

BARRETT, Justin L., and Frank Keil. 1996. 'Conceptualizing a nonnatural entity: Anthropomorphism in God concepts.' *Cognitive Psychology* 31: 219-247.

BARRETT, Justin L., and Melanie A. Nyhof. 2001. 'Spreading non-natural concepts: The role of intuitive conceptual structures in memory and transmission of cultural materials.' *The Journal of Cognition and Culture* 1: 69-100.

BARRETT, Stanley R. 1988 (1984). *The Rebirth of Anthropological Theory.* Toronto & Buffalo & London: University of Toronto Press.

BARTHES, Roland. *Mythologies.* 1986 (1957). Selected and translated by A. Lavers. London: Paladin.

BATESON, Gregory. 1994 (1936). *Naven : A Survey of the Problems Suggested by a Composite Picture of the Culture of a New Guinea Tribe Drawn from Three Points of View.* Stanford, CA: Stanford University Press.

BAYLES, Michael D., and Kenneth Henley. 1989 (1983). *Right Conduct. Theories and Applications.* New York: Random House.

BECHTEL, William. 1994. 'Levels of description and explanation in cognitive science.' *Minds and Machines* 4: 1-25.

BELIER, Wouter W. 1999. 'Durkheim, Mauss, classical evolutionism and the origin of religion.' *Method & Theory in the Study of Religion* 11: 24-46.

BELL, Catherine. 1997. *Ritual. Perspectives and Dimensions.* New York & Oxford: Oxford University Press.

BERGER, Peter L., and Thomas Luckmann. 1966. *The Social Construction of Reality.* New York: Anchor Books/ Doubleday.

BERGER, Peter, and Hansfried Kellner. 1978. 'On the conceptualization of the supernatural and the sacred.' *Dialog* 17: 36-42.

BERNER, Ursula 1979. *Die Bergpredigt: Rezeption und Auslegung im 20. Jahrhundert. (Göttinger Theologische Arbeiten,* 12.) Göttingen: Vandenhoeck & Ruprecht.

BEYER, Peter. 1984 (1977). 'Introduction.' In Niklas Luhmann: *Religious Dogmatics and the Evolution of Societies,* pp. v-xlvii. Tr. by P. Beyer. New York & Toronto: Edwin Mellen Press.

BEYER, Peter. 1994. *Religion and Globalization.* London etc.: Sage.

BLOCH, Maurice. 1989 (1985). 'From cognition to ideology.' In Bloch: *Ritual, History and Power,* 106-136. London & Atlantic Highlands, NJ: The Athlone Press.

BLOOMFIELD, Morton W. 1952. *The Seven Deadly Sins: An introduction to the History of Religious Concept, with Special Reference to Medieval English Literature. (Studies in Language and Literature.)* Michigan: State College Press.

BOND, George D. 1988. *The Buddhist Revival in Sri Lanka.* Columbia: South Carolina University Press

BOYER, Pascal. 1987. 'The stuff "traditions" are made of: On the implicit ontology of an ethnographic category.' *Philosophy of the Social Sciences* 17: 49-65.

BOYER, Pascal. 1993a. 'Cognitive aspects of religious symbolism.' In *Cognitive Aspects of Religious Symbolism* (ed. by P. Boyer), pp. 4-47. Cambridge: Cambridge University Press.

BOYER, Pascal. 1993b. 'Pseudo-natural kinds.' In *Cognitive Aspects of Religious Symbolism* (ed. by P. Boyer), pp. 121-141. Cambridge: Cambridge University Press.

BOYER, Pascal. 1994a. 'Cognitive constraints on cultural representations: Natural ontologies and religious ideas.' In *Mapping the Mind* (ed. by L. Hirschfeld, and S. Gelman), pp. 39-67. Cambridge: Cambridge University Press.

BOYER, Pascal. 1994b. *The Naturalness of Religious Ideas. A Cognitive Theory of Religion*. Berkeley & Los Angeles & London: University of California Press.

BOYER, Pascal. 1996a (1995). 'Causal understandings in cultural representations: Cognitive constraints on inferences from cultural input.' In *Causal Cognition* (ed. by D. Sperber, D. Premack and A.J. Premack), pp. 615-644. Oxford: Clarendon Press.

BOYER, Pascal. 1996b. 'Religion as impure subject: A note on cognitive order in religious representation in response to Brian Malley.' *Method & Theory in the Study of Religion* 8: 201-213.

BOYER, Pascal. 1996c. 'What makes anthropomorphism natural: Intuitive ontology and cultural representations.' *The Journal of the Royal Anthropological Institute* (N.S.) 2: 83-97.

BOYER, Pascal. 1998. 'Cognitive tracks of cultural inheritance: How evolved intuitive ontology governs cultural transmission.' *American Anthropologist* 100: 876-889.

BOYER, Pascal. 1999. 'Cognitive aspects of religious ontologies: How brain processes constrain religious concepts.' In *Approaching Religion*, part I (ed. by T. Ahlbäck), pp. 53-72. (*Scripta Instituti Donneriani*, 17:1.) Åbo: The Donner Institute.

BOYER, Pascal. 2000. 'Evolution of the modern mind and the origins of culture: religious concepts as a limiting case.' In *Evolution and the Human Mind* (ed. by P. Carruthers and A. Chamberlain), pp. 93-112. Cambridge: Cambridge University Press.

BOYER, Pascal. 2001. 'Cognitive inheritance tracks for cultural representations.' In *The Debated Mind: Evolutionary Psychology Versus Ethnography* (ed. by H. Whitehouse, pp. 57-89). Oxford: Berg.

BOYER, Pascal. In press. *Religion Explained*. New York: Basic Books.

BOYER, Pascal, and Sheila Walker. 2000. 'Intuitive ontology and cultural input in the acquisition of religious concepts.' In *Imagining the Impossible. Magical, Scientific, and Religious Thinking in Children* (ed. by K.S. Rosengren, C.N. Johnson, and P.L. Harris), pp. 130-156. Cambridge: Cambridge University Press.

BOYER, Pascal, and C. Ramble. In press. 'Cognitive templates for religious concepts: Cross-cultural evidence for recall of counterintuitive representations.' *Cognitive Science.*

BREWER, William F., Clark A. Chinn, and Ala Samarapungavan. 2000. 'Explanation in scientists and children.' In *Explanation and Cognition* (ed. by F.C. Keil and R. Wilson), pp. 279-298. Cambridge, MA: The MIT Press.

BRINGSJORD, Selmer, and Michael Zenzen. 1997. 'Cognition is not computation: The argument from irreversibility.' *Synthese* 113: 285-320.

BRÜMMER, Vincent. 1984. *What Are We Doing when We Pray? A Philosophical Inquiry.* London: SCM Press.

BUCK, C.D. 1949. *A Dictionary of Selected Synonyms in the Principal Indo-European Languages: A Contribution to the History of Ideas.* Chicago: The University of Chicago Press.

BUNNAG, Jane. 1973. *Buddhist Monk, Buddhist Layman.* Cambridge: Cambridge University Press.

BURKERT, Walter. 1996. *Creation of the Sacred: Tracks of Biology in Early Religions.* Cambridge, MA: Harvard University Press.

BYRNE, Peter. 1998. *The Moral Interpretation of Religion.* Edinburgh: Edinburgh University Press.

CAREY, Susan. 1996a (1995). 'On the origin of causal understanding.' In *Causal Cognition* (ed. by D. Sperber, D. Premack, and A.J. Premack), pp. 268-302. Oxford: Clarendon Press.

CAREY, Susan. 1996b. 'Cognitive domains as modes of thought.' In *Modes of Thought* (ed. by D.R. Olson and N. Torrance), pp. 187-215. New York: Cambridge University Press.

CAREY, Susan, and Elizabeth Spelke. 1994. 'Domain-specific knowledge and conceptual change.' In *Mapping the Mind* (ed. by L. Hirschfeld and S. Gelman), pp. 169-200. Cambridge: Cambridge University Press.

Causal Cognition. 1996 (1995). Ed. by Dan Sperber, D. Premack, and A.J. Premack. Oxford: Clarendon Press.

CHADWICK, Henry. 1966. *Early Christian Thought and the Classical Tradition.* Oxford: Clarendon Press.

CHALMERS, David J. 1997 (1996). *The Conscious Mind*. New York & Oxford: Oxford University Press.

CHANTRAÎNE, Pierre. 1968. *Dictionnaire étymologique de la langue Grecque*. Paris: Éditions Klincksieck.

CHURCHLAND, Paul M. 1989. *A Neurocomputational Perspective*. Cambridge, MA & London: The MIT Press.

CHURCHLAND, Paul M. 1995. *The Engine of Reason, the Seat of the Soul. A Philosophical Journey into the Brain*. Cambridge, MA & London: The MIT Press.

CHURCHLAND, Paul M. 1996a. 'Flanagan on moral knowledge.' In *The Churchlands and their Critics* (ed. by R.N. McCauley), pp. 302-306. Oxford: Blackwell 1996.

CHURCHLAND, Paul M. 1996b. 'Learning and conceptual change: The view from the neurons.' In *Connectionism, concepts, and folk psychology* (ed. by A. Clark and P. Millican), pp. 7-43. Oxford: Clarendon Press.

CLARK, Andy. 1997. *Being There. Putting Brain, Body, and World Together Again*. Cambridge, MA: MIT Press.

CLARK, Andy. 1998. 'Connectionism, moral cognition, and collaborative problem solving.' In *Mind and Morals. Essays on Ethics and Cognitive Science* (ed. by L. May, M. Friedman, and A. Clark), pp. 109-127. Cambridge & London: The MIT Press.

COLLINS, Steven. 1982. *Selfless Persons*. Cambridge: Cambridge University Press.

COLLINS, Steven. 1993. 'The discourse on what is primary (Aggañña Sutta). An annotated translation.' *Journal of Indian Philosophy* 21: 301-393.

COLLINS, Steven. 1996. 'The Lion's roar of the wheel-turning king: A response to Andrew Huxley's "The Buddha and the Social contract".' *Journal of Indian Philosophy* 24: 421-446.

COMSTOCK, W. Richard. 1984. 'Toward open definitions of religion.' *Journal of the American Academy of Religion* 52: 499-517.

Confessio Augustana. 1807. Accuratius edita a D. Michaele Webero. Vitebergae: Friderici Immanuelis.

CONZE, Edward. 1960. *The Prajñāpāramitā Literature*. (*Indo-Iranian Monographs*, VI.) 'S-Gravenhage: Mouton & Co.

COPLESTON, Frederick. 1950. *A History of Philosophy*, Vol. II. London: Burns Oates & Washbourne.

CORLESS, Roger J. 1978. 'Sacred text, context, and proof-text.' In *The Critical Study of Sacred Texts*, Vol. 2 (ed. by W.D. O'Flaherty), pp. 257-270. (*Berkeley Religious Studies Series*, 2.) Berkeley: Graduate Theological Union.

COSMIDES, Leda, and John Tooby. 1994. 'Origins of domain specificity: The evolution of functional organization.' In *Mapping the Mind* (ed. by L. Hirschfeld and S. Gelman), pp. 85-116. Cambridge: Cambridge University Press.

COSMIDES, Leda, and John Tooby. 2000. 'Consider the source: The evolution of adaptations for decoupling and metarepresentation.' In *Metarepresentations* (ed. by D. Sperber), pp. 53-115. Oxford: Oxford University Press.

COSMIDES, Leda, John Tooby, and Jerome H. Barkow. 1995 (1992). 'Introduction: Evolutionary psychology and conceptual integration.' In *The Adapted Mind. Evolutionary Psychology and the Generation of Culture* (ed. by J.H. Barkow, L. Cosmides, and J. Tooby), pp. 1-15. New York & Oxford: Oxford University Press.

DAMASIO, Antonio R. 1996 (1994). *Descartes' Error. Emotion, Reason and the Human Brain*. London: Papermac.

DAMASIO, Antonio R. 1999. *The Feeling of What Happens. Body and Emotion in the Making of Consciousness*. New York & San Diego & London: Harcourt.

D'ANDRADE, Roy. 1995. *The Development of Cognitive Anthropology*. Cambridge, MA: Cambridge University Press.

DE BONO, Edward. 1990 (1969). *The Mechanism of Mind*. Harmondsworth: Penguin.

DE SILVA, Padmasiri. *Environmental Philosophy and Ethics in Buddhism*. London & New York: Macmillan Press & St. Martin's Press.

DE SOUSA, Ronald. 1980. 'The rationality of emotions.' In *Explaining Emotions* (ed. by A. Oksenberg Rorty), pp. 127-151. Berkeley & Los Angeles & London: University of California Press.

DENNETT, Daniel C. 1987. *The Intentional Stance*. Cambridge, MA & London: The MIT Press.

DENNET, Daniel C. 1993 (1991). *Consciousness Explained*. Harmondsworth: Penguin.

DENNET, Daniel C. 1997a (1996). *Kinds of Minds*. New York: Phoenix.

DENNETT, Daniel C. 1997b. 'Qualia' (in conversation with M. Gazzaniga). In M. Gazzaniga: *Conversations in the Cognitive Neurosciences*, pp. 175-193. Cambridge, MA & London: MIT Press.

DIAMOND, Jared. 1999 (1997). *Guns, Germs, and Steel*. New York & London: W.W. Norton & Company.

DICKIE, Jane R., Amy K. Eshleman, Dawn M. Merasco, Amy Shepard, Michael Vander Wilt, and Melissa Johnson. 1997. 'Parent – child relationships and children's images of God.' *Journal for the Scientific Study of Religion* 36: 25-43.

DOUGLAS, Mary. 1970. *Natural Symbols*. London: Barrie & Rockliff: The Cresset Press.

DOUGLAS, Mary. 1984 (1966). *Purity and Danger*. London etc.: Ark Paper Backs.

DULANEY, S., and A.P. Fiske. 1994. 'Cultural rituals and obsessive-compulsive disorder: Is there a common psychological mechanism?' *Ethos* 22: 243-283.

DURKHEIM, Émile. 1926 (1893). *De la division du travail social*. Paris: Felix Alcan.

DURKHEIM, Émile. 1966 (1895). *The Rules of Sociological Method*. Tr. by S.A. Solovay, and J.H. Mueller, ed. by George E.G. Catlin. New York & London: The Free Press & Collier Macmillan.

DURKHEIM, Émile. 1937 (1912). *Les formes élémentaires de la vie religieuse*. Paris: Félix Alcan.

ECO, Umberto. 1980. *Il nome della rosa*. Milano: Bompiani.

EHRENBERG, Margaret. 1995 (1989). *Women in Prehistory*. London: British Museum Press.

EKMAN, Paul. 1980 (1977). 'Biological and cultural contributions to body and facial movement in the expression of emotions.' In *Explaining Emotions* (ed. by A. Oksenberg Rorty), pp. 73-101. Berkeley & Los Angeles & London: University of California Press.

ELIADE, Mircea. 1974 (1949). *The Myth of the Eternal Return, or Cosmos and History*. Tr. by W.R. Trask. (*Bollingen Series* XLVI.) New York: Routledge and Kegan Paul.

ELIADE, Mircea. 1951. *Le chamanisme et les techniques archaïques de l'extase*. Paris: Payot.

ELIADE, Mircea.1976 (1958). *Patterns in Comparative Religion*. London: Sheed and Ward.

ELIADE, Mircea. 1959 (1957). *The Sacred and the Profane*. Tr. by Willard Trask. New York: A Harvest Book.

ELIADE, Mircea. 1961. 'Götter und Bilder.' *Antaios* II (hrsg. von Eliade and E. Junger), pp. 485-501.

ELKSNIS Andra, and Myra Szachara. 1996. 'Children's magical beliefs: A report on recent studies in developmental psychology.' *Method & Theory in the Study of Religion* 8: 191-200.

ELLIS, Albert. 1975 (1962). *Reason and Emotion in Psychotherapy*. Secaucus, NJ: Lyle Stuart.

ELMAN, Jeffrey L., Elizabeth A. Bates, Mark H. Johnson, Annette Karmiloff-Smith, Domenico Parisi, and Kim Plunkett. 1998 (1996). *Rethinking Innateness. A Connectionist Perspective on Development.* Cambridge, MA & London: The MIT Press.

EPSTEIN, Seymour. 1990. 'Cognitive – experiential self-theory.' In *Handbook of Personality. Theory and Research* (ed. by L.A. Pervin), pp. 165-192. New York & London: The Guilford Press.

ERDOSY, George. 1985. 'The origin of cities in the Ganges Valley.' *Journal of the Economic and Social History of the Orient* 28: 81-109.

ERIKSON, Erik H. 1958. *Young Man Luther.* London: Faber and Faber.

EVANS-PRITCHARD, E.E. 1937. *Witchcraft, Oracles and Magic Among the Azande.* Oxford: Clarendon Press.

EVERS, Hans-Dieter. 1977. 'The social complexity of South-East Asian Religion: The current debate on Buddhism.' *Journal of Asian Studies* 37: 183-185.

FERM, Deane William. 1986. *Third World Liberation Theologies. An Introductory Survey.* Maryknoll: Orbis Books

FISCHER, Roland. 1971. 'A cartography of the ecstatic and meditative states.' *Science* 174: 897-904.

FISCHER, Roland. 1986. 'Toward a neuroscience of self-experience and states of self-awareness and interpreting interpretations.' In *Handbook of States of Consciousness* (ed. by B.B. Wolman and M. Ullman), pp. 3-30. New York: Van Nostrand Reinhold Company.

FITZGERALD, Timothy. 1996. 'Religion, Philosophy and Family Resemblances.' *Religion* 26: 215-236.

FITZGERALD, Timothy. 1997. 'A critique of "religion" as a cross-cultural category.' *Method & Theory in the Study of Religion* 9: 91-110.

FLACK, Jessica C., and Frans B.M. de Waal. 2000a. '"Any animal whatever:" Darwinian Building Blocks of Morality in Monkeys and Apes.' In *Evolutionary Origins of Morality. Cross-Disciplinary Perspectives* (ed. by L.D. Katz), pp. 1-29. Thorverton: Imprint Academic.

FLACK, Jessica C., and Frans B.M. de Waal. 2000b. 'Being nice is not a building block of morality. Response to commentary discussion.' In *Evolutionary Origins of Morality. Cross-Disciplinary Perspectives* (ed. by L.D. Katz), pp. 67-77. Thorverton: Imprint Academic.

FLANAGAN, Owen. 1998. 'Ethics naturalized: Ethics as human ecology.' In *Mind and Morals. Essays on Ethics and Cognitive Science* (ed. by L. May, M. Friedman, and A. Clark), pp. 19-43. Cambridge & London: MIT Press.

FLEW, Antony. 1972 (1955). 'Theology and Falsification A & B.' In *New Essays in Philosophical Theology* (ed. by A. Flew and A. MacIntyre), pp. 96-99, 106-108. London: SCM Press.

FODOR, Jerry A. 1975. *The Language of Thought.* Cambridge, MA: Harvard University Press.

FODOR. Jerry. 1983. *Modularity of Mind.* Cambridge, MA: MIT Press.

FODOR, Jerry A. 1998. *Concepts: Where Cognitive Science Went Wrong.* Oxford: Clarendon Press.

FORMAN, Robert K.C. 1990. 'Introduction: Mysticism, constructivism, and forgetting.' In *The Problem of Pure Consciousness. Mysticism and Philosophy* (ed. by R.K.C. Forman), pp. 3-49. New York & Oxford: Oxford University Press.

FORMAN, Robert K.C. 1993. 'Mystical knowledge. Knowledge by identity.' *Journal of the American Academy of Religion* 61: 705-738.

FORMAN, Robert K.C. 1994. '"Of Capsules and Carts:" Mysticism, language and the *via negativa.*' *Journal of Consciousness Studies* 1: 38-49.

FRANKENA, William K. 1973 (1963). *Ethics.* Englewood Cliffs, N.J.: Prentice-Hall.

FRITH, Christopher D. 1995 (1992). *The Cognitive Neuropsychology of Schizophrenia.* Hove: Erlbaum (UK) Taylor & Francis.

GALLAGHER, Shaun, and Andrew N. Meltzoff. 1996. 'The earliest sense of self and others: Merleau-Ponty and recent developmental studies.' *Philosophical Psychology* 9: 211-233.

GARDNER, Howard. 1983. *Frames of Mind: The Theory of Multiple Intelligences.* New York: Basic Books.

GARDNER, Howard. 1987 (1985). *The Mind's New Science.* USA: BasicBooks.

GAZZANIGA, Michael S. (ed.) 1997. *Conversations in the Cognitive Neurosciences.* Cambridge, MA & London: MIT Press.

GEERTZ, Armin W. 1997. 'Theory, definition, and typology: Reflections on generalities and unrepresentative realism.' *Temenos* 33: 29-47.

GEERTZ, Clifford. 1960. *The Religion of Java.* Glencoe: The Free Press.

GEERTZ, Clifford. 1973. *The Interpretation of Cultures.* New York: Basic Books.

GEERTZ, Clifford. 1980. *Negara. The Theatre State in Nineteenth-Century Bali.* Princeton: Princeton University Press.

GELMAN, Susan A., and Lawrence A. Hirschfeld. 1999. 'How biological is essentialism?' In *Folkbiology* (ed. by D. Medin and S. Atran), pp. 403-446. Cambridge, MA: The MIT Press.

GELLNER, Ernest. 1990 (1988). *Plough, Sword and Book. The Structure of Human History*. Chicago: The University of Chicago Press.

GETTY, Alice. 1962. *The Gods of Northern Buddhism*. Rutland, VT: C. E. Tuttle Co.

GIDDENS, Anthony. 1978. *Durkheim*. Glasgow: Fontana/Collins.

GIMBUTAS, Marija. 1982 (1974). *The Goddesses and Gods of Old Europe, 6500-3500 B.C.* [original edition: The Gods and Goddesses of Old Europe, 7000 to 3500 BC. Myths, Legends and Cult Images.] London: Thames & Hudson.

GIMELLO, Robert M. 1983. 'Mysticism in its contexts.' In *Mysticism and Religious Traditions* (ed. by S. Katz), pp. 61-88. Oxford etc.: Oxford University Press.

GOMBRICH, Richard. 1988. *Theravāda Buddhism. A Social History from Ancient Benares to Modern Colombo*. London & New York: Routledge & Kegan Paul.

GOODE, W.J. 1949. 'Magic and religion. A continuum.' *Ethnos* 14: 172-182.

GOODY, Jack. 2000. *The Power of the Written Tradition*. Washington and London: Smithsonian Institution Press.

GOPNIK, Alison, and Henry M. Wellman. 1996. 'The theory theory.' In *Modes of Thought* (ed. by D.R. Olson and N. Torrance), pp. 257-293. New York: Cambridge University Press.

GOPNIK, Alison, Andrew N. Meltzoff, and Patricia K. Kuhl. 2001 (1999). *The Scientist in the Crib. What early Learning Tells us about The Mind*. New York: Perennial.

GREEN, Miranda Jane. 1997 (1986). *The Gods of the Celts*. Gloucester: A. Sutton.

GREENFIELD, Patricia M. 1991. 'Language, tools and brain. The ontogeny and phylogeny of hierarchically organized sequential behavior.' *Behavioral and Brain Sciences* 14: 531-595.

GRIFFITHS, Paul E. 1997. *What Emotions Really Are*. Chicago & London: University of Chicago Press.

GRIFFITHS, Paul J. 1994. *On Being Buddha. The Classical Doctrine of Buddhahood. (SUNY Series, Toward a Comparative Philosophy of Religions.)* Albany: State University of New York Press.

GUDEMAN, Stephen. 1986. *Economics as Culture*. London & Boston & Henley: Routledge and Kegan Paul.

GUSTAFSON, James M. 1982 (1978). *Protestant and Roman Catholic Ethics*. Chicago & London: The University of Chicago Press.

GUTHRIE, Stewart. 1980. 'A cognitive theory of religion.' *Current Anthropology* 21: 181-203.

GUTHRIE, Stewart. 1993. *Faces in the Clouds.* New York: Oxford University Press.

GUTHRIE, Stewart. 1996. 'Religion: What is it?' *Journal for the Scientific Study of Religion* 35: 412-419.

GUTIERREZ, Gustavo. 1972. *Theología de la liberación.* Lima: Perspectivas.

HAAVIO, Martti. 1951. *Karjalan jumalat* [Carelian Gods]. Helsinki: WSOY.

HAMAYON, Roberte. 1990. *La chasse à l'âme. Esquisse d'une théorie du chamanisme sibérien.* Nanterre: Société d'ethnologie.

HAMMOND, Phillip E. 1986. 'Religion in the modern world.' In *Making Sense of Modern Times: Peter L. Berger and the Vision Interpretive Sociology* (ed. by James D. Hunter and Stephen C. Ainlay), pp. 156-158. London: Routledge & Kegan Paul.

HARE, R.M. 1963. *Faith and Reason.* Oxford: Oxford University Press.

HARMAN, Gilbert. 1986. *Change in View. Principles of Reasoning.* Cambridge, MA & London: The MIT Press.

HARRÉ, Rom (ed.). 1986. *The Physical Sciences Since Antiquity.* London & Sydney: Croom Helm.

HARRIS, Paul L. 'Thinking by children and scientists: False analogies and neglected similarities.' In *Mapping the Mind* (ed. by L. Hirschfeld and S. Gelman), pp. 294-315. Cambridge: Cambridge University Press.

HART, Kevin. 1989. *The Trespass of the Sign. Deconstruction, Theology and Philosophy.* Cambridge, etc.: Cambridge University Press.

HEIDEGGER, Martin. 1987 (1927). *Being and Time.* Tr. by J. Macquarrie & E. Robinson. Oxford: Basil Blackwell.

HEMPEL, C. G. 1965. *Aspects of Scientific Explanation and Other Essays in the Philosophy of Science.* New York: The Free Press.

HESSE, Mary. 1974. *The Structure of Scientific Inference.* London & Basingstoke: Macmillan.

HINDE, Robert A. 1999. *Why Gods Persist. A Scientific Approach to Religion.* London & New York: Routledge.

HIRAKAWA, Akira. 1990. *A History of Indian Buddhism.* Tr. by P. Groner. (*Asian Studies at Hawaii*, 36.) University of Hawaii Press.

HIRSCHFELD, Lawrence A., and Susan A. Gelman. 1994. 'Toward a topography of mind: An introduction to domain specificity.' In *Mapping the Mind* (ed. by L. Hirschfeld and S. Gelman), pp. 3-35. Cambridge: Cambridge University Press.

HOBBES, Thomas. 1985 (1651). *Leviathan*. London: Penguin Classics.

HOLT, John Clifford. 1981. *Discipline: The Canonical Buddhism of the Vinayapitaka*. Delhi: Motilal Banarsidass.

HONKELA, Timo. 2000. 'Self-organizing maps in symbol processing.' In *Hybrid Neural Systems* (ed. by S. Wermter and R. Sun), pp. 348-362. Berlin and Heidelberg: Springer.

HONKO, Lauri. 1979. 'Theories concerning the ritual process.' In *Science of Religion. Studies in Methodology* (ed. by L. Honko), pp. 369-390. (*Religion and Reason*, 13.) The Hague & Paris & New York: Mouton.

HONKO, Lauri. 2000. 'Text as process and practice: The textualization of oral epics.' In *Textualization of Oral Epics* (ed. by L. Honko), pp. 3-54. (*Trends in Linguistics, Studies and Monographs*, 128.) Berlin and New York: Mouton de Gruyter.

HORTON, Robin. 1993 *Patterns of Thought in Africa and the West. Essays on Magic, Religion, and Science*. Cambridge: Cambridge University Press.

HOUSEMAN, Michael, and Carlo Severi. 1998. *Naven or the Other Self. A Relational Approach to Ritual Action*. (*Studies in the History of Religions (Numen Book Series)*, LXXIX.) Leiden & Boston & Köln: Brill.

HULTKRANTZ, Åke. 1980 (1967). *The Religions of the American Indians*. Tr. by M. Setterwall. Berkeley & Los Angeles & London: University of California Press.

HUSSERL, Edmund. 1958 (1950). *Die Idee der Phänomenologie*. Hrsg. von W. Biemel. (*Husserliana*, II.) Haag: Martinus Nijhoff.

HUSSEY, Edward. 1986. 'Matter theory in ancient Greece.' In *The Physical Sciences Since Antiquity* (ed. by R. Harré), pp. 10-28. London & Sydney: Croom Helm.

HUXLEY, Andrew. 1996. 'The Buddha and the Social Contract.' *Journal of Indian Philosophy* 24: 407-420.

JACKSON, Anthony. 1979. 'Commentary' [on Honko and Peacock]. In *Science of Religion. Studies in Methodology* (ed. by L. Honko), pp. 414-420. (*Religion and Reason*, 13.) The Hague & Paris & New York: Mouton.

JACKSON, Frank, and Philip Pettit. 1996. 'Causation in the philosophy of mind.' In *Connectionism, Concepts, and Folk Psychology* (ed. by A. Clark and P. Millican), pp. 75-99. Oxford: Clarendon Press.

JACOBSEN, Thorkild. 1976. *The Treasures of Darkness. A History of Mesopotamian Religion*. New Haven & London: Yale University Press.

JAMES, William. 1884. 'What is an emotion?' *Mind* 9: 188-205.

JAMES, William. 1971 (1901-1902). *The Varieties of Religious Experience*. London & Glasgow: Collins, Fontana.

JAMGÖN Kongtrul Lodrö Tayé. 1998. *Buddhist Ethics*. Tr. & ed. by The International Translation Committee founded by V.V. Kalu Rinpoché. Ithaca, NY: Snow Lion.

JANTZEN, Grace M. 1989. 'Mysticism and experience.' *Religious Studies* 25: 295-315.

JENSEN, Jeppe Sinding. 1993. 'Is a phenomenology of religion possible? On the ideas of a human and social science of religion.' *Method & Theory in the Study of Religion* 5: 109-133.

JENSEN, Jeppe Sinding. 2001. 'Phenomenology of religion as a project in cultural analysis and the "problem of universals".' *Temenos* 35.

JOHANSSON, Rune E.A. 1985 (1979). *The Dynamic Psychology of Early Buddhism.* (*Scandinavian Institut of Asian Studies Monograph Series*, 37.) London & Malmö: Curzon Press.

JOHNSON, Mark. 1987. *The Body in the Mind*. Chicago & London: The University of Chicago Press.

JOHNSON, Mark. 1997 (1993). *Moral Imagination. Implications of Cognitive Science for Ethics.* Chicago & London: The University of Chicago Press.

JOHNSON, Mark L. 1998 (1996). 'How moral psychology changes moral theory.' In *Mind and Morals. Essays on Ethics and Cognitive Science* (ed. by L. May, M. Friedman, and A. Clark), pp. 44-68. Cambridge & London: MIT Press.

KAMPPINEN, Matti, and Antti Revonsuo. 1993. 'Ultimate Relativism.' In *Consciousness, Cognitive Schemata, and Relativism* (ed. by M. Kamppinen), pp. 229-242. Dordrecht & Boston & London: Kluwer Academic Publishers.

KARMILOFF-SMITH, Annette. 1992. *Beyond Modularity. A Developmental Perspective on Cognitive Science*. Cambridge, MA & London: The MIT Press.

KARMILOFF-SMITH, Annette. 1994. 'Précis of *Beyond modularity: A developmental perspective on cognitive science.*' *Behavioral and Brain Sciences* 17: 693-745.

KATZ, Leonard D. (ed.). 2000. *Evolutionary Origins of Morality. Cross-Disciplinary Perspectives*. Thorverton: Imprint Academic.

KATZ, Steven. 1978. 'Language, epistemology and mysticism.' In *Mysticism and Philosophical Analysis* (ed. by S. Katz), pp. 22-74. New York: Oxford University Press.

KATZ, Steven. 1983. 'The "conservative" character of mysticism.' In *Mysticism and Religious traditions* (ed. by S. Katz), pp. 3-60. New York: Oxford University Press.

KATZ, Steven. 1985. 'Recent work on mysticism.' *History of Religions* 25: 76-86.

KAUFFMAN, Stuart A. 1993. *The Origins of Order. Self-Organization in Evolution.* New York & Oxford: Oxford University Press.

KEARNEY, Michael. 1975. 'World view theory and study.' *Annual Review of Anthropology* 4: 247-270.

KEESING, Roger M. 1974. 'Theories of Culture.' *Annual Review of Anthropology* 3: 73-97.

KENNEY, John Peter. 1991. *Mystical Monotheism. A Study in Ancient Platonic Theology.* Hanover & London: Brown University Press.

KEOWN, Damien. 1995. *Buddhism & Bioethics.* New York: St. Martin's Press.

KLIEVER, Lonnie D. 1981. 'Fictive religion: Rhetoric and play.' *Journal of the American Academy of Religion* 49: 657-669.

KRYMKOWSKI, Daniel H., and Luther H. Martin. 1998. 'Religion as an independent variable: Revisiting the Weberian hypothesis.' *Method & Theory in the Study of Religion* 10: 187-198.

KUHN, Deanna. 1996. 'Is good thinking scientific thinking?' In *Modes of Thought* (ed. by D.R. Olson, and N. Torrance), pp. 261-281. New York: Cambridge University Press.

LANGER, Susanne. 1942. *Philosophy in a New Key.* Cambridge, MA: Harvard University Press.

LANGER, Susanne. 1953. *Feeling and Form.* New York: Charles Scribner's Sons.

LASZLO, Ervin. 1975. *The Systems View of the World: The Natural Philosophy of the New Developments in the Sciences.* Oxford: Blackwell.

LAWSON, E. Thomas. 1996. 'Theory and the new comparativism, old and new.' *Method & Theory in the Study of Religion* 8: 31-35.

LAWSON, E. Thomas. 1999. 'Keeping religion in mind.' In *Approaching Religion,* part I (ed. by T. Ahlbäck), pp. 139-149. (*Scripta Instituti Donneriani,* 17:1.) Åbo: The Donner Institute.

LAWSON, E. Thomas. 2001. 'Psychological perspectives on agency.' In *Religion in Mind: Cognitive Perspectives on Religious Belief, Ritual and Experience* (ed. by J. Andresen), pp. 141-172. Cambridge: Cambridge University Press.

LAWSON, E. Thomas, and Robert N. McCauley. 1990. *Rethinking Religion. Connecting Cognition and Culture.* Cambridge: Cambridge University Press.

LEACH, Edmund. 1979 (1976). *Culture and Communication.* Cambridge: Cambridge University Press.

LEDOUX, Joseph. 1998 (1996). *The Emotional Brain.* New York: Simon & Schuster.

LESLIE, Alan. 1994. 'ToMM, ToBy, and Agency: Core architecture and domain specificity.' In *Mapping the Mind* (ed. by L. Hirschfeld and S. Gelman), pp. 119-148. Cambridge: Cambridge University Press.

LESLIE, Alan. 1996 (1995). 'A theory of agency.' In *Causal Cognition* (ed. by D. Sperber, D. Premack, and A.J. Premack), pp. 121-141. Oxford: Clarendon Press.

LEVINE, Michael P. 1998. 'A cognitive approach to ritual: New method or no method at all?' *Method & Theory in the Study of Religion* 10: 30-60.

LÉVI-STRAUSS, Claude. 1979 (1958). *Structural Anthropology*. Tr. by C. Jacobson, and G. Schoepf. Harmondsworth: Penguin.

LEWIS, Gilbert. 1988 (1980). *Day of Shining Red. An Essay on Understanding Ritual.* (*Cambridge Studies in Social Anthropology*, 27.) Cambridge, etc.: Cambridge University Press.

LITTLETON, C. Scott. 1965. 'A two-dimensional scheme for the classification of narratives.' *Journal of American Folklore* 78: 21-27.

LLOYD, Geoffrey. 1996. 'Science in antiquity.' In *Modes of Thought* (ed. by D.R. Olson, and N. Torrance), pp. 15-33. New York: Cambridge University Press.

LOPEZ, Donald Jr. 1995. 'Introduction.' In *Buddhism in Practice* (ed. by D. Lopez Jr.), pp. 3-36. Princeton: Princeton University Press.

LOUTH, Andrew. 1985 (1981). *The Origins of the Christian Mystical Tradition*. Oxford: Clarendon Press.

LOVEJOY, Arthur O. 1964 (1936). *The Great Chain of Being*. Cambridge, MA & London: Harvard University Press.

LUHMANN, Niklas. 1984 (1977). *Religious Dogmatics and the Evolution of Societies.* Tr. by P. Beyer. New York & Toronto: The Edwin Mellen Press.

LUHMANN, Niklas. 1982a. (1977). 'Durkheim on morality and the division of labor.' In Luhmann: *The Differentiation of Society*, pp. 3-19. Tr. by S. Holmes, and C. Larmore. New York: Columbia University Press.

LUHMANN, Niklas. 1982b. 'The economy as a social system.' In Luhmann: *The Differentiation of Society*, pp. 190-225. Tr. by S. Holmes, and C. Larmore. New York: Columbia University Press.

LUHMANN, Niklas. 1982c. 'The differentiation of society.' In Luhmann: *The Differentiation of Society*, pp. 229-254. Tr. by S. Holmes, and C. Larmore. New York: Columbia University Press.

LUKES, Steven. 1977 (1973). *Émile Durkheim*. Harmondsworth: Penguin.

LUTHER, Martin. *D. Martin Luther's Werke, kritische Gesamtausgabe* (= WA). Weimar: Hermann Böhlaus Nachfolger. T. 2 (1931), 11 (1900) 56 (1938), 57 (1939).

MacIntyre, Alasdair. 1982 (1981). *After Virtue*. London: Duckworth.

Macquarrie, John. 1988 (1963). *Twentieth-Century Religious Thought*. London: SCM Press.

Malley, Brian. 1995. 'Explaining order in religious systems.' *Method & Theory in the Study of Religion* 7: 5-22.

Malley, Brian. 1997. 'Causal holism in the evolution of religious ideas: A reply to Pascal Boyer.' *Method & Theory in the Study of Religion* 9: 389-399.

Mannermaa, Tuomo. 1998. 'Justification and *theosis* in Lutheran-Orthodox perspective.' In *Union with Christ. The New Finnish Interpretation of Luther* (ed. by C.E. Braaten, and R.W. Jenson), pp. 25-41. Grand Rapids & Cambridge: William B. Eerdmans Publishing Company.

Mausbach, Joseph. 1936-1938. *Katolische Moraltheologie I-III*. Neu bearbeitet und hrsg. von P. Tischleder. Münster: Aschendorffsche Verlagsbuchhandlung.

May, Larry, Marilyn Friedman, and Andy Clark. 1998 (1996). 'Introduction.' In *Mind and Morals. Essays on Ethics and Cognitive Science* (ed. by L. May, M. Friedman, and A. Clark), pp. 1-15. Cambridge & London: MIT Press.

McCauley, Robert N. (ed.). 1996. *The Churchlands and their Critics*. Oxford: Blackwell 1996.

McCauley, Robert N. 2000. 'The naturalness of religion and the unnaturalness of science.' In *Explanation and Cognition* (ed. by F.C. Keil and R. Wilson), pp. 61-85. Cambridge, MA: The MIT Press.

McCauley, Robert N. 2001. 'Ritual, memory, and emotion: Comparing two cognitive hypotheses.' In *Religion in Mind: Cognitive Perspectives on Religious Belief, Ritual and Experience* (ed. by J. Andresen), pp. 115-140. Cambridge: Cambridge University Press.

McCauley, Robert N., and E. Thomas Lawson. 1996. 'Who owns "culture"?' *Method & Theory in the Study of Religion* 8: 171-190.

McCutcheon, Russell T. 1997a. *Manufacturing Religion. The Discourse on Sui Generis Religion and the Politics of Nostalgia*. Oxford: Oxford University Press.

McCutcheon, Russell T. 1997b. '"My theory of the brontosaurus:" Postmodernism and "theory" of religion.' *Studies in Religion / Sciences Religieuses* 26: 3-23.

McLeod, Peter, Kim Plunkett, and Edmund T. Rolls. 1998. *Introduction to Connectionist Modeling of Cognitive Processes*. Oxford & New York & Tokyo: Oxford University Press.

McNamara Patrick. 2001. 'The frontal lobes and religion.' In *Religion in Mind:*

Cognitive Perspectives on Religious Belief, Ritual and Experience (ed. by J. Andresen), pp. 237-256. Cambridge: Cambridge University Press.

MEDIN, Douglas, and Scott Atran (eds.). 1999. *Folkbiology.* Cambridge, MA & london: The MIT Press.

MERLEAU-PONTY, Maurice. 1992 (1945). *Phenomenology of Perception.* Tr. by Colin Smith. London & New Jersey: Routledge & The Humanities Press.

MITHEN, Steven. 1998 (1996). *The Prehistory of the Mind.* London: Phoenix.

MOORE, G.E. 1922 (1903). *Principia Ethica.* Cambridge: Cambridge University Press.

MUNZ, Peter. 1959. *Problems of Religious Knowledge.* London & Southampton: SCM Press.

MUNZ, Peter. 1964. *Relationship and Solitude.* London: Eyre & Spottiswoode.

MUNZ, Peter. 1973. *When the Golden Bough Breaks. Structuralism or Typology?* London & Boston: Routledge & Kegan Paul.

MURPHY, Gregory, and Douglas Medin. 1985. 'The role of theories in conceptual coherence.' *Psychological Review* 92: 289-316.

NAGEL, Ernest, and James R. Newman. 1964 (1959). *Gödel's Proof.* London: Routledge & Kegan Paul.

NAGEL, Ernest. 1961. *The Structure of Science.* London: Routledge & Kegan Paul.

NEWBERG, Andrew B., and Eugene D. d'Aquili. 2000. 'Neuropsychology of religious & spiritual experience.' In *Cognitive Models and Spiritual Maps: Interdisciplinary Explorations of Religious Experience* (ed. by J. Andresen and R.K.C. Forman), pp. 251-266. Thorverton: Imprint Academic.

NIELSEN, Kai. 1997. 'Naturalistic explanations of religion.' *Studies in Religion/Sciences Religieuses* 26: 441-466.

NIINILUOTO, Ilkka. 1987. *Truthlikeness.* (*Synthese Library*, 185.) Dordrecht etc.: Reidel.

NYGREN, Anders. 1966. *Eros och Agape.* Stockholm: Aldus/Bonniers. [English translation *Eros and Agape*, tr. by P.S. Watson, The University of Chicago Press 1982.]

OATLEY, Keith. 1996. 'Inference in narrative and science.' In *Modes of Thought* (ed. by D.R. Olson, and N. Torrance), pp. 123-140. New York: Cambridge University Press.

ORTONY, Andrew, and Terence J. Turner. 1990. 'What's basic about basic emotions?' *Psychological Review* 97: 315-331.

OSHERSON, Daniel N., and Edward E. Smith. 1981. 'On the adequacy of prototype theory as a theory of concepts.' *Cognition* 9: 35-58.

OTTO, Rudolph. 1969 (1917). *The Idea of the Holy*. Tr. J.W. Harvey. London & Oxford & New York: Oxford University Press.

Oxford Latin Dictionary. 1968. Oxford: Clarendon Press.

PADEN, William E. 1994 (1988). *Religious Worlds*. Boston: Beacon Press.

PADEN, William E. 1992. *Interpreting the Sacred*. Boston: Beacon Press.

PADEN, William E. 1996a. 'Sacrality as integrity: "Sacred order" as a model for describing religious worlds.' In *The Sacred and its Scholars* (ed. by T.A. Idinopulos and E.A. Yonan), pp. 36-64. (*Studies in the History of Religions (Numen Book Series)*, LXXIII.) Leiden: E.J. Brill.

PADEN, William E. 1996b. 'Elements of a new comparativism.' *Method & Theory in the Study of Religion* 8: 5-14.

PADEN, William E. 1999. 'Sacrality and worldmaking: New categorial perspectives.' In *Approaching Religion*, part I (ed. by T. Ahlbäck), pp. 165-180. (*Scripta Instituti Donneriani*, 17:1.) Åbo: The Donner Institute.

PADEN, William E. 2000. 'World.' In *Guide to the Study of Religion* (ed. by W. Braun, and R.T. McCutcheon), pp. 334-347. London & New York: Cassell.

Pāli-English Dictionary. 1972 (1921-1925). Ed. by T.W. Rhys Davids, and W. Stede. London: The Pāli Text Society & Routledge and Kegan Paul.

PALS, Daniel L. 1996. *Seven Theories of Religion*. New York & Oxford: Oxford University Press.

PARPOLA, Asko. 1988. 'The coming of the Aryans to Iran and India and the cultural and ethnic identity of the Dāsas.' *Studia Orientalia* 64: 195-302.

PARPOLA, Asko. 1993. 'Bronze age Bactria and Indian religion.' In *L'ancien Proche-orient et les indes / Ancient Near East and India*, pp. 81-87. (*Studia Orientalia*, 70.) Helsinki: The Finnish Oriental Society.

PARPOLA, Simo. 1993. 'Cultural parallels between India and Mesopotamia: Preliminary considerations.' In *L'ancien Proche-orient et les indes / Ancient Near East and India*, pp. 57-64. (*Studia Orientalia*, 70.) Helsinki: The Finnish Oriental Society.

PATAI, Raphael. 1954. 'Religion in Middle Eastern, Far Eastern, and Western culture.' *Southwestern Journal of Anthropology* 10: 233-254.

PENNER, Hans. 1983. 'The mystical illusion.' In *Mysticism and Religious Traditions* (ed. by S. Katz), pp. 89-116. Oxford etc.: Oxford University Press.

PENTIKÄINEN, Juha. 1968. *The Nordic Dead-Child Tradition*. (*Folklore Fellows Communications*, 202.) Helsinki: Academia Scientiarum Fennica.

PENTIKÄINEN, Juha. 1987 (1978). *Oral Repertoire and World View*. (*Folklore Fellows Communications*, 219.) Helsinki: Academia Scientiarum Fennica.

PERNER, Josef. 1993 (1991). *Understanding the Representational Mind*. Cambridge, MA & London: The MIT Press.

PERSINGER, Michael A. 1983. 'Religious and mystical experiences as artifacts of temporal lobe function: A general hypothesis.' *Perceptual and Motor Skills* 57: 1255-1262.

PERSINGER, Michael A. 1984a. 'Striking EEG profiles from single episodes of glossolalia and transcendental meditation.' *Perceptual and Motor Skills* 58: 12-133.

PERSINGER, Michael A. 1984b. 'Propensity to report paranormal experiences is correlated with temporal lobe signs' *Perceptual and Motor Skills* 59: 583-586.

PERSINGER, Michael A. 1984c. 'People who report religious experiences may also display enhanced temporal-lobe signs.' *Perceptual and Motor Skills* 58: 963-975.

PERSINGER, Michael A. 1985. 'Death anxiety as a semantic conditioned suppression paradigm.' *Perceptual and Motor Skills* 60: 827-830.

PERSINGER, Michael A. 1987. *Neuropsychological Bases of God Beliefs*. New York & Westport & London: Praeger.

PEURA, Simo. 1998. 'Christ as favor and gift: The challenge of Luther's understanding of justification.' In *Union with Christ. The New Finnish Interpretation of Luther* (ed. by C.E. Braaten, and R.W. Jenson), pp. 42-69. Grand Rapids & Cambridge: William B. Eerdmans Publishing Company.

PIKE, Kenneth. 1967 (1954-55). *Language in Relation to a Unified Theory of the Structure of Human Behavior*. The Hague & Paris: Mouton.

PINKER, Steven. 1994. *The Language Instinct*. New York: HarperCollins.

PLUTCHIK, Robert. 1980. 'A general psychoevolutionary theory of emotion.' In *Emotion. Theory, Research, and Experience*, Vol. I (ed. by R. Plutchik, and H. Kellerman), pp. 3-33. San Diego etc.: Academic Press.

PÖHLMANN, Horst Georg. 1973. *Abriss der Dogmatik*. Gütersloh: Gütersloher Verlagshaus Gerd Mohn.

POLOMA, Margaret. 1997. 'The "Toronto Blessing:" Charisma, institutionalization, and revival.' *Journal for the Scientific Study of Religion* 36: 257-271.

PROUDFOOT, Wayne. 1985. *Religious Experience*. Berkeley: University of California Press.

PUTNAM, Hilary. 1981. *Reason Truth and History*. Cambridge: Cambridge University Press.

PYE, Michael. 1978. *Skilful Means*. London: Duckworth.

PYYSIÄINEN, Ilkka. 1987. 'The Buddha. A biographical image in relation to cosmic order.' In *Mythology and Cosmic Order* (ed. by R. Gothóni, and J. Pentikäinen), pp. 115-123. (*Studia Fennica* 32.) Helsinki. The Finnish Literature Society.

PYYSIÄINEN, Ilkka. 1988. Perimmäiset kuvat. Buddhan elämäkerran merkitys theravadan kaanonissa. With a summary in English. [The Ultimate Images. The Meaning of the Buddha's Biography in the Theravada Canon.] (*Annals of the Finnish Society for Missiology and Ecumenics*, 53.) Helsinki: The Finnish Society for Missiology and Ecumenics.

PYYSIÄINEN, Ilkka. 1992. 'Paradise regained. The religious features of primal therapy.' *Temenos* 28: 161-176.

PYYSIÄINEN, Ilkka. 1993. *Beyond Language and Reason. Mysticism in Indian Buddhism.* (*Annales Academiae Scientiarum Fennicae, Dissertationes Humanarum Litterarum*, 66.) Helsinki: Academia Scientiarum Fennica.

PYYSIÄINEN, Ilkka. 1996a. *Belief and Beyond. Religious Categorization of Reality.* (*Religionsvetenskapliga skrifter*, 33). Åbo: Åbo Akademi.

PYYSIÄINEN, Ilkka. 1996b. 'Jñanagarbha and the God's-Eye view.' *Asian Philosophy* 6: 197-206.

PYYSIÄINEN, Ilkka. 1997. *Jumalan selitys* [God Explained]. Helsinki: Otava.

PYYSIÄINEN, Ilkka. 1998. 'Somewhere over the rainbow? Cosmogony and mystical decreation.' *Method & Theory in the Study of Religion* 10: 157-186.

PYYSIÄINEN, Ilkka. 1999a. 'Holy Book – A treasury of the incomprehensible. The invention of writing and religious cognition.' *Numen* 46: 269-290.

PYYSIÄINEN, Ilkka. 1999b. 'God as ultimate reality in religion and in science.' *Ultimate Reality and Meaning* 22(2): 106-123.

PYYSIÄINEN, Ilkka. 2000. 'Variation from a cognitive perspective.' In *Thick Corpus, Organic Variation and Textuality in Oral Tradition* (ed. by L. Honko), pp. 181-195. (*Studia Fennica Folkloristica*, 7.) Helsinki: Finnish Literature Society.

PYYSIÄINEN, Ilkka. 2001a. 'Phenomenology of religion and cognitive science. The case of religious experience.' *Temenos* 35.

PYYSIÄINEN, Ilkka. 2001b. 'Cognition, emotion, and religious experience.' In *Religion in Mind: Cognitive Perspectives on Religious Belief, Ritual and Experience* (ed. by J. Andresen), pp. 70-93. Cambridge: Cambridge University Press.

PYYSIÄINEN, Ilkka, and Kimmo Ketola. 1999. 'Rethinking "God". The Concept of "God" as a category in Comparative Religion.' In *Approaching Religion, part I* (ed. by T. Ahlbäck), pp. 207-214. (*Scripta Instituti Donneriani*, 17:1.) Åbo: The Donner Institute.

Pyysiäinen, Ilkka, Marjaana Lindeman, and Timo Honkela. *Forthcoming.* 'Religion and counter-intuitive representations.'.

Quinn, Philip L. 1978. *Divine Commands and Moral Requirements.* Oxford: Clarendon Press.

Räisänen, Heikki. 1990. *Beyond New Testament Theology.* London: SCM Press.

Raiskila, Vesa. 1995. 'Secularization and religious change.' *Temenos* 31: 145-161.

Rājavaramuni, Phra. 1990. 'Foundations of Buddhist social ethics.' In *Ethics, Wealth, and Salvation* (ed. by R.F. Sizemore, and D.K. Swearer), pp. 29-53. Columbia: University of South Carolina Press.

Ramachandran, V. S., W. S. Hirstein, K. C. Armel, E. Tecoma, and V. Iragui. 1997. 'The neural basis of religious experience.' 27th Annual Meeting, New Orleans, LA, October 25-30, 1997. *Society for Neuroscience Abstracts* 23(2): 519.1.

Ramachandran, V(ilayanur) S., and Sandra Blakeslee. 1999 (1998). *Phantoms in the Brain.* New York: Quill, William Morrow.

Rappaport, Roy A. 1999. *Ritual and Religion in the Making of Humanity.* (*Cambridge Studies in Social and Cultural Anthropology*, 110.) Cambridge: Cambridge University Press.

Raunio, Antti. 1998. 'Natural law and faith: The forgotten foundations of ethics in Luther's theology.' In *Union with Christ. The New Finnish Interpretation of Luther* (ed. by C.E. Braaten, and R.W. Jenson), pp. 96-124. Grand Rapids & Cambridge: William B. Eerdmans Publishing Company.

Revonsuo, Antti. 1994. 'In search of the science of consciousness.' In *Consciousness in Philosophy and Cognitive Neuroscience* (ed. by A. Revonsuo, and M. Kamppinen). Hillsdale, NJ: Lawrence Erlbaum.

Revonsuo, Antti. 1995. *On the Nature of Consciousness. Theoretical and Empirical Explorations.* (*Annales Universitatis Turkuensis B 209.*) Turku: The University of Turku.

Reynolds, Frank E. 1990. 'Ethics and wealth in Theravāda Buddhism. A study in comparative religious ethics.' In *Ethics, Wealth, and Salvation* (ed. by R.F. Sizemore, and D.K. Swearer), pp. 59-76. Columbia: University of South Carolina Press.

Rips, Lance J. 1995. 'The current status of research on concept combination.' *Mind & Language* 10: 72-104.

Rosch, Eleanor. 1975. 'Cognitive representations of semantic categories.' *Journal of Experimental Psychology* 104: 192-233.

Rosch, Eleanor. 1978. 'Principles of categorization.' In *Cognition and Catego-*

rization (ed. by E. Rosch, and B.B. Lloyd), pp. 27-48. Hillsdale: Lawrence Erlbaum Associates.

Rosch, Eleanor, and Carolyn B. Mervis, 1975. 'Family resemblances: Studies in the internal structure of categories.' *Cognitive Psychology.* 7: 573-605.

Rousseau, Jean-Jacques. 1980 (1762). *The Social Contract.* Tr. by M. Cranston. London: Penguin Classics.

Rubin, David C. 1997 (1995). *Memory in Oral Traditions.* New York & Oxford: Oxford University Press.

Ryba, Thomas. 1991. *The Essence of Phenomenology and Its Meaning for the Scientific Study of Religion.* (*Toronto Studies in Religion,* 7.) New York etc.: Peter Lang.

Ryle, Gilbert. 1990 (1949). *The Concept of Mind.* Harmondsworth: Penguin.

Saariluoma, Pertti. 1995. *Chess Players' Thinking. A Cognitive Psychological Approach.* London & New York: Routledge.

Saariluoma, Pertti. 1997. *Foundational Analysis. Presuppositions in Experimental Psychology.* London: Routledge.

Sahlins, Marshal. 1968. *Tribesmen.* (*Prentice-Hall Foundations of Modern Anthropology Series.*) Englewood Cliffs: Prentice-Hall.

Sahlins, Marshall. 1972. *Stone Age Economics.* Chicago: Aldine.

Saler, Benson. 2000 (1993). *Conceptualizing Religion. Immanent Anthropologists, Transcendent Natives, and Unbound Categories.* With a new preface. New York & Oxford: Berghahn Books.

Saler, Benson. 2001. 'On what we may believe about beliefs.' In *Religion in Mind: Cognitive Perspectives on Religious Belief, Ritual and Experience* (ed. by J. Andresen), pp. 47-69. Cambridge: Cambridge University Press.

Salmon, Wesley C. 1984. *Scientific Explanation and the Causal Structure of the World.* Princeton: Princeton University Press.

Salmon, Wesley C. 1989. *Four Decades of Scientific Explanation.* Minneapolis: University of Minnesota Press.

Sandbacka, Carola. 1987. *Understanding other Cultures.* (*Acta Philosophica Fennica,* 42.) Helsinki: Societas Philosophica Fennica.

Schachter, Stanley, and Jerome Singer. 1962. 'Cognitive, social and physiological determinants of emotional state.' *Psychological Review* 69: 379-399.

Scott, Alwyn. 1995. *Stairway to the Mind.* New York: Springer/Copernicus.

Searle, John R. 1980. 'Minds, brains, and programs.' *Behavioral and Brain Sciences* 3: 417-457.

SEARLE, John R. 1995 (1992). *The Rediscovery of the Mind.* Cambridge, MA: The MIT Press

SELLARS, Wilfried. 1963. *Science, Perception and Reality.* London: Routledge & Kegan Paul.

SHARF, Robert H. 1995. 'Buddhist modernism and the rhetoric of meditative experience.' *Numen* 42: 228-283.

SHARF, Robert. 2000. 'The rhetoric of experience and the study of religion.' In *Cognitive Models and Spiritual Maps* (ed. by J. Andresen and R.K.C. Forman), pp. 267-287. Thorverton: Imprint Academic.

SIIKALA, Anna-Leena. 1978. *The Rite Technique of the Siberian Shaman.* (*Folklore Fellows Communications*, 220.) Helsinki: Academia Scientiarum Fennica.

SILVERMAN, Sydel. 1981. *Totems and Teachers. Perspectives on the History of Anthropology.* New York: Columbia University Press.

SMART, Ninian. 1973a. *The Phenomenon of Religion.* London: Macmillan.

SMART, Ninian. 1973b. *The Science of Religion, and the Sociology of Knowledge.* Princeton: Princeton University Press.

SMART, Ninian. 1983. *Worldviews. Crosscultural Explorations of Human Beliefs.* New York: Charles Scribner's Sons.

SMART, Ninian. 1985 (1983). 'Religion, myth, and nationalism.' In *Religion and Politics in the Modern World* (ed. by P.H. Merkl, and N. Smart), pp. 15-28. New York & London: New York University Press.

SMITH, Adam. 1952 (1776). *An Inquiry Into the Nature and Causes of the Wealth of Nations.* (*Great Books of the Western World*, 39.) Chicago & London & Toronto: Encyclopædia Britannica, Inc.

SMITH, B.L. (Ed.) 1978. *Religion and Legitimation of Power in Sri Lanka.* Chambersburg: South and Southeast Asia Studies.

SMITH, Jonathan, Z. 1978. *Map Is Not Territory. Studies in the History of Religions.* (*Studies in Judaism in Late Antiquity*, 23.) Leiden: E.J. Brill.

SMITH, Jonathan, Z. 1982. *Imagining Religion.* Chicago: University of Chicago Press.

SOLOMON, Robert C. (Ed.) 1999. *Wicked Pleasures. Meditations on the Seven "Deadly" Sins.* Lanham: Rowman & Littlefield.

SOSKICE, Janet Martin. 1985. *Metaphor and Religious Language.* Oxford: Clarendon Press.

SPERBER, Dan. 1995 (1974). *Rethinking Symbolism.* Cambridge: Cambridge University Press.

SPERBER, Dan. 1994. 'The modularity of thought and the epidemiology of representations.' In *Mapping the Mind* (ed. by L. Hirschfeld and S. Gelman), pp. 39-67. Cambridge: Cambridge University Press.

SPERBER, Dan. 1996a. *Explaining Culture. A Naturalistic Approach.* Oxford: Blackwell.

SPERBER, Dan. 1996b. 'Why are perfect animals, hybrids, and monsters food for symbolic thought?' *Method & Theory in the Study of Religion* 8: 143-169.

SPERBER, Dan, and Deirdre Wilson. 1988 (1986). *Relevance. Communication and Cognition.* Cambridge, MA: Harvard University Press.

SPIRO, Melford E. 1968 (1966). 'Religion: Problems of definition and explanation.' In *Anthropological Approaches to the Study of Religion* (ed. by M. Banton), pp. 85-126. London: Tavistock Publications.

SPIRO, Melford E. 1972 (1970). *Buddhism and Society.* New York: Harper & Row.

STAAL, Frits. 1989. *Rules without Meaning.* (*Toronto Studies in Religion*, 4.) New York: Peter Lang.

STACE, W.T. 1961 (1960). *Mysticism and Philosophy.* London: Macmillan.

STANOVICH, Keith E., and Richard F. West. 2000. 'Individual differences in reasoning: Implications for the rationality debate?' *Behavioral and Brain Sciences* 23: 645726.

STCHERBATSKY, Th(eodor). 1969. *Papers of Th. Stcherbatsky.* Tr. by H.C. Gupta, ed. by D. Chattopadhyaya. (*Soviet Indology Series*, No. 2.) Calcutta: Indian Studies Past and Present.

STCHERBATSKY, Th(eodor). 1930-32. *Buddhist Logic* I-II. (*Bibliotheca Buddhica*, XXVI.) Leningrad: Izdatel'stvo Akadmii Nauk CCCP.

STERN, Daniel N. 1985. *The Interpersonal World of the Infant.* USA: Basic Books.

STRONG, John. 1983. *The Legend of King Aśoka.* Princeton: Princeton University Press.

SULLIVAN, Winnifred Fallers. 1996. 'Competing theories of religion and law in the supreme court of the United States: An Hasidic case.' *Numen* 43: 184-212.

SULLIVAN, Lawrence E. 1996. '"No longer the Messiah": US Federal Law Enforcement view of religion in connection with the 1993 siege of Mount Carmel near Waco, Texas.' *Numen* 43: 213-234.

SUNDÉN, Hjalmar. 1966. 'Koān [*sic*] Übung und Nervensystem.' *Kairos* 8: 193-196.

SUNDÉN, Hjalmar. 1990. 'Saint John of the Cross in the light of Satori.' *Temenos* 26: 115-128.

SWINBURNE, Richard. 1996. *Is there a God?* Oxford & New York: Oxford University Press.

SYREENI, Kari. 1987. *The Making of the Sermon on the Mount: A Procedural Analysis of Matthew's Redactorial Activity.* Pt. 1: Methodology & Compositional Analysis. (*Annales Academiae Scientiarum Fennicae. Dissertationes Humanarum Litterarum*, 44.) Helsinki: Academia Scientiarum Fennica.

TAMBIAH, S(tanley) J. 1970. *Buddhism and the Spirit Cults in North-East Thailand.* Cambridge: Cambridge University Press.

TAMBIAH, S(tanley) J. 1986. *Sri Lanka. Ethnic Fratricide and the Dismantling of Democracy.* Chicago & London: The University of Chicago Press.

TART, Charles T. (ed.). 1969. *Altered States of Consciousness.* New York, etc.: John Wiley & Sons.

TAVES, Ann. 1999. *Fits, Trances, & Visions. Experiencing Religion and Explaining Experience from Wesley to James.* Princeton, NJ: Princeton University Press.

THOMAS, Eward J. 1975 (*1927). The Life of Buddha as Legend and History.* London: Routledge and Kegan Paul.

TOMKINS, Silvan. 1980. 'Affect as amplification: Some modifications in theory.' In *Emotion. Theory, Research, and Experience*, Vol. I (ed. by R. Plutchik, and H. Kellerman), pp. 141-164. San Diego etc.: Academic Press.

TOOBY, John, and Leda Cosmides. 1995 (1992). 'The psychological foundations of culture.' In *The Adapted Mind. Evolutionary Psychology and the Generation of Culture* (ed. by J.H. Barkow, L. Cosmides, and J. Tooby), pp. 19-136. Oxford: Oxford University Press.

TUOMELA, Raimo. 1985. *Science, Action, and Reality.* (*Episteme*, 12.) Dordrecht & Boston & Lancaster: D. Reidel.

TURIEL, Eliot. 1983. *The Development of Social Knowledge.* Cambridge: Cambridge University Press.

TURIEL, Eliot, Carolyn Hildebrandt, and Cecilia Wainryb. 1991. *Judging Social Issues.* (*Monographs of the Society for Research in Child Development*, Vol. 56, No. 2.) Chicago: The University of Chicago Press.

TURNER, Victor. 1981 (1967). *The Forest of Symbols.* Ithaca & London: Cornell Paperbacks.

TURNER, Victor. 1969. *The Ritual Process.* London: Routledge & Kegan Paul.

TYLOR, Edward Burnett. 1994 (1871). *Primitive Culture I-II.* Collected Works, Vols. 3 – 4. London: Routledge/Thoemmes Press.

UTRIAINEN, Terhi. 2001. 'Bodies and others making religion. Phenomenology of the body and the study of religion.' *Temenos* 35.

VAN DER LEEUW, G(erardus). 1986 (1933). *Religion in Essence and Manifestation.* Tr. by J.E. Turner. Princeton, New Jersey: Princeton University Press.

VAN GENNEP, A(rnold). 1977 (1909). *The Rites of Passage.* Tr. by M.B. Vizedom, and G.L. Caffee. London & Henley: Routledge & Kegan Paul.

VARELA, Francesco. 1996. 'Neurophenomenology. A methodological remedy for the Hard Problem.' *Journal of Consciousness Studies* 3: 330-349.

VARELA, Francisco, Eleanor Rosch, and Evan Thompson. 1996 (1991). *The Embodied Mind. Cognitive Science and Human Experience.* Cambridge, MA & London: The MIT Press.

VERSNEL, H.S. 1991. 'Some reflections on the relationship magic – religion.' *Numen* 38: 175-197.

VESALA, Kari Mikko. 1995. *Bateson's Theory of Learning and the Context of Small Business Entrepreneurship. (Working Papers 1/1995.)* Helsinki: Department of Social Psychology, University of Helsinki.

VETTER, Tilmann. 1988. *The Ideas and Meditative Practices of Early Buddhism.* Leiden: E.J. Brill.

VIAL, Theodore M. 1999. 'Opposites attract: The body and cognition in a debate over baptism.' *Numen* 46: 121-145.

VOGET, Fred W. 1975. *A History of Ethnology.* New York, etc.: Holt, Rinehart and Winston.

WAARDENBURG, Jacques. 1978. *Reflections on the Study of Religion. (Religion and Reason,* 15.) The Hague & Paris & New York: Mouton.

WAARDENBURG, Jacques. 1986. *Religion und Religionen (Sammlung Göschen,* 2228.) Berlin & New York: Walter de Gruyter.

WACH, Joachim. 1946 (1944). *Sociology of Religion.* Chicago: Chicago University Press.

WACH, Joachim. 1951. *Types of Religious Experience.* London: Routledge and Kegan Paul.

WACH, Joachim. 1958. *The Comparative Study of Religions.* Ed. with an introduction by J. M. Kitagawa. New York: Columbia University Press.

WALPOLA, Rahula. 1982 (1959). *What the Buddha Taught.* London: Gordon Fraser.

WEBER, Max. 1966 (1922). *The Sociology of Religion.* Tr. by E. Fischoff. London: Methuen & Co.

WESTERMARCK, Edward. 1921 (1891). *The History of Human Marriage* I-III. London: Macmillan.

WESTERMARCK, Edward. 1906/1926 (1906-1908). *The Origin and Development of the Moral Ideas I-II* (vol. II in second ed.). London: Macmillan.

WHITEHOUSE, Harvey. 1992. 'Memorable religions: Transmission, codification and change in divergent Melanesian contexts.' *Man* n.s. 27: 777-797.

WHITEHOUSE, Harvey. 1995. *Inside the Cult. Religious Innovation and Transmission in Papua New Guinea.* Oxford: Clarendon Press.

WHITEHOUSE, Harvey. 2000. *Arguments and Icons. Divergent Modes of Religiosity.* Oxford: Oxford University Press.

WIEBE, Donald. 1991. *The Irony of Theology and the Nature of Religious Thought.* (*McGill-Queen's Studies in the History of Ideas*, 15.) Montreal: McGill-Queen's University Press.

WIEBE, Donald. 1994. 'From religious to social reality: the transformation of "religion" in the academy.' In *The Notion of 'Religion' in Comparative Research.* Selected Proceedings of the XVI IAHR Congress (ed. by U. Bianchi), pp. 837-845. Roma: "L'erma" di Bretschneider.

WIEBE, Donald. 1999a. *The Politics of Religious Studies.* New York: St. Martin's Press.

WIEBE, Donald. 1999b. 'Appropriating religion. Understanding religion as an object of science.' In *Approaching Religion*, part I (ed. by T. Ahlbäck), pp. 253-272. (*Scripta Instituti Donneriani*, 17:1.) Åbo The Donner Institute.

WILLIAMSON, W. Paul, and Howard H. Pollio. 1999. 'The phenomenology of religious serpent handling: A rationale and thematic study of extemporaneous sermons.' *Journal for the Scientific Study of Religion* 38: 203-218.

WILSON, Bryan R. (Ed.). 1970. *Rationality.* Oxford: Basil Blackwell.

WILSON, Edward O. 1998. *Consilience. The Unity of Knowledge.* New York: Alfred A. Knopf.

WINCH, Peter. 1970. 'Understanding a primitive society.' In *Rationality* (ed. by B.R. Wilson), pp. 78-111. Oxford: Basil Blackwell.

WITTGENSTEIN, Ludwig. 1966 (1938, 1942-46). *Lectures and Conversations on Aesthetics, Psychology and Religious Belief.* Compiled from notes taken by Yorick Smythies, Rush Rhees and James Taylor. Ed. by C. Barrett. Oxford: Basil Blackwell.

WOLFSON, Harry A. 1965 (1947). *Religious Philosophy.* New York: Atheneum.

WOLPERT, Lewis. 1994 (1992). *The Unnatural Nature of Science.* Cambridge, MA: Harvard University Press.

VON WRIGHT, Georg Henrik. 1963. *The Varieties of Goodness.* London & New York: Routledge and Kegan Paul & The Humanities Press.

VON WRIGHT, Georg Henrik. 1975 (1971). *Explanation and Understanding.* London: Routledge and Kegan Paul.

ZAJONC, Robert. 1980. 'Feeling and thinking: Preferences need no inferences.' *American Psychologist* 35: 151-175.

ZUESSE, Evan. 1987. 'Ritual.' In *Encyclopedia of Religion* (ed. by M. Eliade et al.), Vol. 12: 405-422. New York: Macmillan.

INDEX OF NAMES

INDEX OF SUBJECTS